AFTER

THE

DEATH

OF

POETRY

AFTER THE DEATH OF POETRY

Poet and Audience in Contemporary America

VERNON SHETLEY

Duke University Press   Durham & London 1993

© 1993 Duke University Press

All rights reserved

Printed in the United States of America on acid-free paper ∞

Typeset in Sabon by Tseng Information Systems.

Permissions appear on page v of this book.

Library of Congress Cataloging-in-Publication Data

appear on the last printed page of this book.

Grateful acknowledgment is made to the following:

Excerpts from *Self-Portrait in a Convex Mirror* by John Ashbery. Copyright © 1972, 1973, 1974, 1975 by John Ashbery. Used by permission of Viking Penguin, a division of Penguin Books USA Inc.

"Some Trees" by John Ashbery from *Some Trees* (New York: Ecco Press, 1977). Copyright © 1956 by John Ashbery. Reprinted by permission of Georges Borchardt, Inc., for the author.

"These Lacustrine Cities" and "The Skaters" by John Ashbery from *Rivers and Mountains* (New York: Ecco Press, 1977). Copyright © 1962, 1963, 1964, 1966 by John Ashbery. Reprinted by permission of Georges Borchardt, Inc., for the author.

"Loving Mad Tom," "Daffy Duck in Hollywood," and "The Serious Doll" by John Ashbery from *Houseboat Days* (New York: Viking, 1977). Copyright © 1975, 1976, 1977 by John Ashbery. Reprinted by permission of Georges Borchardt, Inc., for the author.

"Soonest Mended," "Summer," and "Definition of Blue" by John Ashbery from *The Double Dream of Spring* (New York: Ecco Press, 1975). Copyright © 1966, 1967, 1968, 1969, 1970 by John Ashbery. Reprinted by permission of Georges Borchardt, Inc., for the author.

Excerpts from *Selected Poems* and *Self-Portrait in a Convex Mirror* by John Ashbery (Manchester: Carcanet, 1986). Copyright © 1986 by John Ashbery. Reprinted by permission of Carcanet Press Limited.

"The Kiwi Bird in the Kiwi Tree" by Charles Bernstein. Copyright © 1988 by *Rethinking Marxism*. Reprinted by permission of *Rethinking Marxism*.

Excerpts from *The Complete Poems: 1927–1979* by Elizabeth Bishop. Copyright © 1979, 1983 by Alice Helen Methfessel. Reprinted by permission of Farrar, Straus, Giroux, Inc.

Excerpts from the unpublished writings of Elizabeth Bishop are used with permission from her Estate. Copyright © 1993 by Alice Helen Methfessel.

to my mother

and to my father

CONTENTS

ACKNOWLEDGMENTS

My greatest debt is to Ellen Levy, whose intel-
lectual companionship has been an invaluable
resource to me for many years. She read every
chapter of this study but the last, made many
suggestions that strengthened the manuscript,
and many more that would have improved it further had I been
better able to follow them.

I have profited from the critical sense and fine ear of David Ferry,
who also read every chapter except the last and who has corrected
many infelicities of both prose and argument. Among my colleagues
of the last eight years, upon whose help and support I have relied
many times, I wish especially to thank Philip Finkelpearl. Jonathan
Arac and David Bromwich have encouraged this project in many
ways. And I am particularly grateful for Helen Vendler's many acts
of generosity and kindness.

I began working on this study while a Rockefeller Scholar in Resi-
dence at the Poetry Center of the 92nd Street Y, and completed
much of it while a Mellon Junior Faculty Fellow at Harvard Univer-

sity; my thanks to both the Rockefeller and Mellon Foundations. I wish to express my gratitude as well to Karl Kirchwey of the Poetry Center, and Rick Hunt of Harvard University, for having made my tenure as Scholar and Fellow, respectively, pleasant and rewarding. Nancy MacKechnie of the Vassar College Library's Special Collections graciously handled my queries. My thanks to Alice Methfessel for permission to quote from unpublished material by Elizabeth Bishop.

Acknowledg-

ments

AW John Ashbery, *A Wave* (New York: Viking P, 1984).

AWK John Ashbery, *As We Know* (New York: Viking P, 1979).

BTE James Merrill, *Braving the Elements* (New York: Atheneum, 1972).

CLS James Merrill, *The Changing Light at Sandover* (New York: Atheneum, 1982).

CP Elizabeth Bishop, *Complete Poems: 1927–1979* (New York: Farrar, Straus, Giroux, 1983).

CPAR Jerome McGann, "Contemporary Poetry, Alternate Routes." *Critical Inquiry* 13 (Spring 1987): 624–647.

DC James Merrill, *Divine Comedies* (New York: Atheneum, 1985).

DDS John Ashbery, *The Double Dream of Spring* (1970; reprint, New York: Ecco P, 1976).

EBDH David Bromwich, "Elizabeth Bishop's Dream Houses." *Raritan* 4.1 (Summer 1984): 77–94.

HD	John Ashbery, *Houseboat Days* (New York: Viking P, 1977).
MRP	Jerome McGann [Anne Mack and J.J. Rome, pseud.], "Marxism, Romanticism, and Postmodernism: An American Case History." *South Atlantic Quarterly* 88:3 (Summer 1989): 605–32.
ND	James Merrill, *Nights and Days* (New York: Atheneum, 1966).
NS	Ron Silliman, *The New Sentence* (New York: Roof Books, 1987).
NYQ	John Ashbery, "Craft Interview with John Ashbery." *New York Quarterly* 9 (Winter 1972): 10–33.
PECF	Jerome McGann [Anne Mack, J.J. Rome, Georg Mannejc, pseud.], "Private Enigmas and Critical Functions, with Particular Reference to the Writing of Charles Bernstein." *New Literary History* 22 (1991): 441–64.
RM	John Ashbery, *Rivers and Mountains* (New York: Ecco P, 1977).
RNF	Robert McPhillips, "Reading the New Formalism." *Sewanee Review* 97:4 (October–December 1989): 73–96.
SP	John Ashbery, *Self-Portrait in a Convex Mirror* (New York: Viking P, 1975).
TCO	John Ashbery, *The Tennis Court Oath* (Middletown, Conn.: Wesleyan UP, 1962).
WNANF	Robert McPhillips, "What's New About the New Formalism?" In *Expansive Poetry: Essays on the New Narrative and the New Formalism*, ed. Frederick Feirstein (Santa Cruz: Story Line P, 1989), 195–298.
WS	James Merrill, *Water Street* (New York: Atheneum, 1962).

T. S. Eliot stated in 1921 that "poets, in our civilization . . . must be *difficult*" ("Metaphysical Poets" 248). While Eliot hedges this dictum with the qualification "it appears likely," his growing authority, wielded through both precept and example, soon made what were likelihoods to his eye into the guiding principles of a generation of poets. However far short modernism may have fallen of fulfilling its other ambitions, the reception of modernist poetry demonstrates that the goal of creating a difficult writing had been achieved with a thoroughness that may have surprised even some of the poets who strove toward it. Eliot explains the necessity of difficulty in terms of the nature of the world inhabited by the modern poet: "Our civilization comprehends great variety and complexity, and this variety and complexity, playing upon a refined sensibility, must produce various and complex results" (248). Eliot's language here, resembling as it does the famous image of catalysis put forward in "Tradition and the Individual Talent," makes difficulty a passive effect of circumstances rather than a deliberate choice on the part of the poet. Poetic difficulty arises, on this account, from the almost automatic interaction of modern civilization and the poet's mind; Eliot thus shields modernist poetry from the charge of deliberate obscurantism, converting what might have been perceived as a flaw into an index of cultural value. Poetry that fails to be difficult, Eliot implies, either must be the product of an insufficiently "refined" sensibility or must be failing in its job of giving comprehensive expression to contemporary life.

Not every reader was persuaded by Eliot's magisterial assumptions, however, and hostility to modernist difficulty persisted for decades. When Delmore Schwartz observed in 1941 that "the characteristic of modern poetry which is most discussed is of course its difficulty, its famous obscurity" (3), he was lamenting the way in which one aspect of modernist practice had achieved a notoriety, and become a sticking point for readers, far out of proportion to what he felt was its real significance. Even some sophisticated and highly trained readers of poetry deplored the consequences of modernism's program of difficulty. Eliot posits that "the poet must become more and more comprehensive, more allusive, more indirect, in order to force, to dislocate if necessary, language into his meaning" (248). Graham Hough seems almost to be answering Eliot point for point when he seeks the reasons for modern poetry's "narrow appeal": "The wilful Alexandrianism, the allusiveness and multiplicity of reference, above all, the deliberate cultivation of modes of organisation that are utterly at variance with those of ordinary discourse—these are the main reasons for the disappearance of Johnson's common reader" (26). Hough was by no means entirely unsympathetic to modernism, but for him, having done in the "common reader" was a serious charge that called for a stern judgment on the guilty parties.

Some seven decades after Eliot's pronouncement, difficulty remains, if not quite the preoccupation it was in the years between the wars, a vexed issue in contemporary poetry. Poetry is still thought of as difficult; indeed, it is still possible for a poet to create something of a scandal of difficulty, as a survey of John Ashbery's reception would demonstrate. More importantly, common readers, of poetry at least, seem to have been driven ever closer to extinction. The last time they were sighted in large numbers was in the 1960s, refreshing themselves in the New England landscapes of Robert Frost. Since then, their numbers seem to have steadily dwindled, and even the occasional report of their return, as, for instance, in the brief vogue enjoyed by Vikram Seth's yuppie verse-novel *The Golden Gate*, seems more an index of their general dearth than a sign of a rebound in the population. Yet, for the most part, poetry today is less Alexandrian, less allusive, and cultivates modes of organization closer to ordinary discourse than was the case in the high modernist moment; Joseph Epstein justly observes that "contemporary poetry has not grown more but less difficult, and the audience still isn't there" (16). A change in poetry, it appears, has failed to change a general perception that poetry is somehow hard of access, and that its rewards are not commensurate with its demands. More than ever it seems that Walter Benjamin's rueful remark holds true: "Only in rare instances is lyric poetry in rapport with the experience of its readers" (110). Today poetry itself, any poetry, has become difficult for even the more ambitious general reader as the habits of thought and communication inculcated by contemporary life have grown to be increasingly at variance with those demanded for the reading of poetry.

Most probably nothing can bring back the hour when a poet attracted the notice of a broad range of the reading public in the way that Frost, and before him Tennyson, did. What is disturbing and novel about the situation of poetry today is that it has lost the attention not merely of common readers but of intellectuals, even of many intellectuals whose chief interests are literary. Charles Altieri observed in 1984 that "speculative criticism and literary theory now engage the interests and wield the authority that poetry did within modernism" (204), but poetry's slide from intellectual respectability began a good decade before Altieri's remark; Robert Lowell may have been the last poet who was felt to be required reading for people with a serious interest in literature. While one can only sympathize with the impulse behind efforts to restore a broad general readership to poetry, now and for the foreseeable future such efforts are likely to remain in the realm of utopian fantasy. It doesn't seem entirely unrealistic, however, to imagine that poetry might regain the allegiance of intellectuals, might win back some of those readers who have abandoned it for speculative criticism and literary theory. Such readers, clearly, are not being kept away from poetry by any perception of its difficulty; they are more than willing to tackle difficult texts. Whatever program I propose in the course of this volume involves making poetry more difficult rather than less; I hope to persuade the reader that only by increasing the level of intellectual challenge it offers can current poetry once again make itself a vital part of intellectual culture.

Although the term *difficulty* appears frequently in the critical writing of the twentieth century, it has received surprisingly little theoretical attention. Hazard Adams, in his useful survey, proposes that "the notion of literature's difficulty must have begun with the first interpreter" (23), and one can certainly find sporadic considerations of the question from the beginnings of critical literature. Obscurity, as Manfred Fuhrmann demonstrates in his excellent overview, was a subject of discussion for the classical rhetoricians and critics, and the tradition of allegorical interpretation of Homeric and biblical texts did much, as Adams notes, to focus attention on opaque or occult aspects of the meanings of texts in subsequent critical traditions. Still, it seems clear that difficulty becomes an urgent problem in thinking about literature only in relatively recent times. Marc Friedlander remarks that "in the literature or in the other arts in Europe there is no evidence from a period more remote than the last hundred and fifty years that would justify a theory that creative works have always seemed obscure or difficult at the time they were created. Nor does it appear that obscurity was, before that time, a consequential problem in criticism" (362). The relative belatedness of critical concern with difficulty is an important clue about the nature of literary difficulty itself.

I begin from the premise that difficulty is not an inherent quality of texts but rather a particular kind of relation between author and reader. I share this view with the contributors to a recent volume edited by Alan Purves, *The Idea of Difficulty in Literature*, who, whatever their differences, seem to agree that difficulty should be located *between* text and reader rather than within the text itself:

> Difficulty is less a property of texts themselves than of the ways in which institutions train us to read. [Touponce 53]

> "Difficulty" is not a feature of particular texts, but the result of the similarity or disparity between dimensions of the text and the socially embedded and motivated interpretive processes of particular readers. [Hynds 117]

> No text is easy or difficult outside the norms and standards of the community that determines: 1) what is necessary and sufficient knowledge; 2) what is an adequately framed discussion of

that text . . . ; and 3) what is an appropriate aesthetic disposition toward the text. [Purves 166]

Many traditions of poetry, of course, have particularly prized the esoteric and recondite; one thinks of *trobar clus* in Provençal, of Gongorism in Spanish, or of the metaphysical style in English. Yet, as Friedlander remarks, these traditions did not provoke the outraged response that greeted modernist difficulty, nor did they make difficulty or obscurity a central category of critical response. Metaphysical poetry has often been taken, in twentieth-century criticism, to be the chief example of a consciously difficult style. It's no accident that Eliot announces his conclusion regarding the necessary difficulty of modern poetry in an essay on "The Metaphysical Poets." But as Stephen Orgel points out, there is no evidence that Donne, exemplar of the metaphysical style for the modernists, was writing in a deliberately obscure fashion, nor that his contemporaries would have blamed him for it had he done so (244–45); Ben Jonson's objections to Donne focused on questions involving poetic decorum rather than literal meaning. The difference between the reception of "metaphysical" strategies in Donne's time and in the later moment when "the revival of Donne . . . was accomplished, amid bitter charges of obscurity, by T. S. Eliot and the New Criticism" (Adams 35) may be ascribed to the vastly different circumstances of poetry's circulation in the two eras. During his lifetime, Donne's poems were distributed in manuscript, an arrangement that obviously engenders a far greater closeness between poet and reader than does the printed page. Donne was well positioned to disseminate to his readers, whether directly or indirectly, a set of ideas about poetry that would help them to understand the peculiarities of his own technique and provide them with ways of making sense of his works. Drummond of Hawthornden records Jonson's objections to Donne's *Anniversarie*, but he records as well Jonson's report of Donne's explanation (Jonson, *Discoveries* 4). If poets must create their audiences, those who circulate their works in manuscript have a decided advantage.

Perhaps it will be useful here to propose a distinction between *obscurity* and *difficulty,* using the former term to refer to those elements of language that resist easy semantic processing,[1] and the latter for the reader's response to those elements. Obscurity, then, refers to features within a text, such as allusion, syntactical dislocations, and figurative substitutions, while difficulty refers to something that occurs between reader and text, one kind of possible response to textual obscurity. Because obscure texts demand that readers supply information not available in the work itself, the degree to which readers can negotiate such texts depends on the knowledge, skills, and presuppositions they bring with them to the poem. The difficulty of *The Waste Land* hinges not simply on its extensive use of allusion—Thomas Gray and Matthew Arnold are highly allusive poets without being, to most readers of poetry, difficult—but on the poem's unusually wide and out-of-the-way range of reference, and on the way that Eliot's allusions in turn invoke a particular notion of poetic and cultural history, an understanding of which depends in significant measure on Eliot's prose. Readers of modernist poetry have become adept at negotiating elaborately involuted or fragmentary syntax, and this skill has undoubtedly led to a diminution in the perceived difficulty of certain premodernist work. Emily Dickinson's poems once had to be regularized for public consumption; now readers pride themselves on their ability to navigate the staccato syntax and disjunctive dashes of the poems as Dickinson wrote them. And certain types of figurative substitutions may be opaque or transparent depending on the reader's familiarity. To use the figurative construction "whale-road" (*hronrád*) without any indication of the more literal term for which it substitutes ("sea") might baffle a reader unfamiliar with the convention, but surely anyone in the community for whom Old English poetry was originally composed would have been familiar with the term, or at least with the kind of wordplay it represents, and thus would have little trouble comprehending it.

In practice, then, readers' training, expectations, and knowledge have everything to do with whether particular forms of language are experienced as difficult. The problems readers had with poems like Ezra Pound's "In a Station of the Metro" can hardly be ascribed to the tactics present in recognizably obscure poetry:

> The apparition of these faces in the crowd;
> Petals on a wet, black bough.

There is a piece of ellipsed syntax here, of course. Adding "is like" between the first and second lines would clarify their relation, at the price of destroying the poem completely; it's the very essence of the poem that the relation between the two be presented by juxtaposition rather than as metaphor. But it can scarcely have been this use of asyndeton that made this poem, and others like it, off-putting to many early-twentieth-century readers; what troubled them was more likely the poem's absence of point (in several senses), its refusal to be recognizably epigrammatic, as English tradition would dictate of a poem this brief. The question that the poem raises is not so much What does it mean? but rather What makes it a poem? What *kind* of poem is it? The difficulty of a work like "In a Station of the Metro" lies not in parsing the sentences (or sentence fragments) but in determining the nature of the genre to which the poem belongs. If Donne was the first poet to be chided for obscurity, surely Wordsworth was the first poet to have asked, and tried to answer, this question about his own work. Jonson's difficulty with Donne's *Anniversarie* seems to have been of this generic kind; Drummond of Hawthornden reports Jonson's remarks as follows: "That Dones Anniversarie was profane and full of Blasphemies that he told Mr. Donne, if it had been written of ye Virgin Marie it had been something to which he answered that he described / the Idea of a Woman and not as she was" (4). Donne was able to explain himself directly to an influential critic; faced with a similar problem, poets since Wordsworth have been compelled to write essays and manifestos.

The form of difficulty Jonson experienced with Donne's *Anniversarie* is perhaps a subset of what George Steiner, in his essay "On Difficulty," refers to as "modal difficulty" (27–33). Going through Steiner's typology of difficulty in detail may help shed some light on the questions under consideration here. Steiner posits four kinds of difficulty in poetry: *contingent, modal, tactical,* and *ontological*. Contingent difficulty involves all those problems of understanding that may be remedied by the acquisition of knowledge and encompasses allusion, bodies of doctrine and ideas that have passed from common knowledge, and lexical shifts that leave words or meanings behind. What Steiner calls modal difficulty "lie[s] with the beholder" (33); it occurs when the reader, though having an "'understanding' . . . of the rough and ready sort represented by paraphrase" (28), nevertheless fails to respond to the work. Modal difficulty, Steiner writes, occurs when "we fail to see a justification for poetic form, [when] the root-occasion of the poem's composition eludes or repels our internalized sense of what poetry should or should not be about" (28). Intellectually, such gaps between reader and poem can be bridged by a fuller awareness of the conventions and standards within which the poem was composed. But as Steiner warns, the reader's intellectual grasp of a set of alien conventions does not necessarily ensure aesthetic response; a reader may have a comprehensive understanding of the principles that underlie a work and still remain untouched by it.

Steiner's categories of tactical and ontological difficulty are more difficult to grasp and more difficult to distinguish from one another. Steiner's discussion of contingent and modal difficulties locates them as phenomena of response rather than effects intentionally produced by the poet; tactical and ontological difficulty are products of the poet's intention. Tactical difficulty, in Steiner's account, arises from "the intermediate status of all language between the individual and the general"; poets must use an impersonal and debased material—language—to express their unique perceptions. This "insoluble . . . contradiction" drives poets to linguistic violence; they employ neologism, archaism, elision, distortion, and displacement to shape the common idiom into an instrument of individual expression. It is perhaps a difference of degree, then, rather than of kind that separates tactical from ontological difficulty, for what Steiner terms ontological difficulty has its roots in the "inauthentic situation of man in an environment of eroded speech" (44). But if contingent, modal, and tactical difficulties are "part of the contract of ultimate or preponderant intelligibility between poet and reader" (40), ontological difficulties aim at subverting rather than conditioning or qualifying communication between poet and reader. They are the product of "a drastic mutual disenchantment of artist and society" (41). And thus ontological difficulties, as Steiner puts it, "seem to have their history" (41); they first appeared in the wake of romanticism and became epidemic in the era of modernism.

Steiner's discussion is an instance of the way in which even a synchronic typology of difficulty is inevitably drawn into historical considerations. If poets in every era have faced the problem of the exhaustion of linguistic resources (the arrival of Petrarchan language and imagery in English seems to predate by only a brief period the production of parodies of it), only in the last hundred or so years have poets begun to experience a radical disaffection from language itself, to feel that the social realm is so thoroughly inauthentic that a socially mediated tool such as language must be all but irredeemably compromised. Tactical difficulty arises from the problem at the very root of the project of lyric, that of embodying subjectivity in the impersonal and resistant medium of language. Steiner implies that this problem is intensified to the point where quantity becomes quality as the poet's alienation from the social world and its publicly available languages grows. Some apologists for modernism, such as Allen Tate and Ernst Curtius, deny any real distinction between modern poetry and earlier poetry, insisting that the poetic strategies that produced modernist obscurity had ample precedent in poetic tradition (Tate 123, Curtius 360). While he agrees with Tate and Curtius that many of the features that make for difficulty (what I would term "obscurity") are present throughout the history of poetry, Steiner nevertheless argues that modernist difficulty is different in degree and in kind from its predecessors.

Steiner describes his first two categories of difficulty, contingent and modal, as originating in temporal distance. The common knowledge of one day fades into the recondite learning of another, or gets lost altogether, while changes in the form of life render the social forms, including the aesthetic forms, of one era indifferent or repellent to its successors. What Steiner sees as the results of temporal change, however, we might recode in terms of interpretive communities; contingent and modal difficulties occur when works travel across the boundaries of interpretive communities, and such passages can take place spatially as well as temporally. Different groups of readers have different skills and expectations; allusions familiar to one segment of an audience may be mysterious to another, and received conventions that structure the sense of what makes an utterance a poem may vary widely. Even granting Tate's contention that the techniques of modernism have ample historical precedent, the reception of modern poetry makes plain that many readers didn't have the equipment to decipher it, and if the work of poets like Eliot no longer strikes us as particularly difficult, it is because critics like Tate have provided us with that equipment.

What the outcry over modernist difficulty indicates, then, is that a gulf had opened between poets and readers: difficulty was an effect, and not a cause, of the disappearance of the common reader. Earlier instances of extreme poetic obscurity occurred within interpretive communities sufficiently close-knit to transmit, along with the poems, ways of reading adequate to them. In an earlier age Eliot might have circulated his poems, as Donne did, in manuscript, with the far greater opportunity to control and shape the terms of reading that such a means of distribution entails. But with the disappearance of the institution of patronage, a coterie audience, though necessary for the experimental poet, was hardly sufficient, and the modernist poets had to publish, even if Yeats fantasized at times about creating "an audience like a secret society" (212–13). In 1934 C. Day Lewis directly ascribed modern poetry's difficulty to the amorphous and fragmented state of the audience it found itself addressing:

> Where the community is swollen, spiritually disorganized and heterogeneous; where there is no widely accepted system of morals and no clearly defined circumference of imagination . . . the sensitive individual feels compelled to retire upon himself. . . . The poet now . . . is bound to be obscure, for he is talking to himself and to his friends—to that tiny, temporarily isolated unit with which communication is possible, with whom he can take a certain number of things for granted. [37]

While Lewis's limitation of interpretive insiders to the poet and "his friends" is obviously melodramatic, it represents a powerful desire for the ability to shape the reader's response to and understanding of the poem, a desire that the conditions of literary life in the modern era had frustrated.

So the modern poets wrote manifestos and critical prose in unprecedented quantities to try to communicate to readers the principles at work in their poems. Wordsworth, of course, was a pioneer in this, as in so many other regards. Though disclaiming the "foolish hope of *reasoning* [the reader] into an approbation" of his poems, Wordsworth's "Preface" clearly means to provide its readers with an alternative set of conventions for evaluating poetry, and so it's appropriate that Wordsworth speaks the language of contract, that he uses terms like "formal engagement," "promise," and "an engagement . . . voluntarily contracted" (242–44).[2] Wordsworth is confronting a "modal" difficulty with his readers, one caused not by temporal distance but by an increase in the size and heterogeneity, as well as the social and political polarization, of the reading public; he finds himself confronting an audience who, he imagines, will be inclined to "inquire by what species of courtesy these attempts may be permitted to assume that title [of poetry]" (244). The difficulty of his work, Wordsworth surmises, will lie in considerations not of semantics but of genre; his poems will seem to fall outside the internalized bodies of convention and expectation that govern readers' sense of what counts as poetry, even though their "prose sense" is accessible (perhaps too accessible). For all that modern poetry deploys a formidable apparatus of obscurity, it would not have been difficult for readers unless there had existed the sort of disparity Wordsworth points to in his own situation, between the poet's and the reader's ideas of what constitutes a poem.

So far I have discussed difficulty in negative terms, as a feature of writing that points to, or is symptomatic of, an estrangement between poet and audience. But just as conflict, in Georg Simmel's terms, is a form of sociation (80–83), so difficulty—the absence or failure of communication—is itself a form of communication; it communicates, if nothing else, itself. The opacities of Allen Tate's "Ode to the Confederate Dead" put the reader on notice that the poem demands "all his intellectual resources . . . all the persistence and alertness that he now thinks only of giving to scientific studies" (123). Through the elements that make it difficult, Tate's poem communicates an idea about the nature of poetry, tells us that for this poet, poetry is not simple, sensuous, and passionate, but complex, intellectual, and ambivalent. Difficulty, as David Trotter argues, was a tool for selecting, out of an amorphous reading public, the audience with whom the poet had something in common (15). But beyond selecting readers, difficulty also functioned to educate readers, to tutor them in the kinds of demands that the poet's work made.

Modernist poets had to undertake the education of their readers themselves because their culture was no longer producing the readers they needed. On one hand, the knowledge and skills demanded by daily life in the modern world had become increasingly distant from those required by poetry, and poetry itself, as a form of cultural capital,[3] was losing its value, leading to what Walter Benjamin describes as a "greater coolness of the public even towards the lyric poetry that had been handed down as part of its own cultural heritage" (110). On the other hand, the deliberately comprehensive, allusive, and indirect poetry Eliot and other modernists felt was necessary to represent modern life no longer responded to the reading strategies that had served in preceding generations. Pope and Tennyson could assume, in a way Eliot and Pound could not, that the interpretive equipment their readers brought to their poems was more or less adequate. In an *American Scholar* forum on "Obscurity in Modern Literature" in 1945, W. Y. Tindall linked the "separation of poet from audience" to the forms of pedagogy: "The blame for this separation falls more perhaps upon society than upon the poet; for society exiled the poet before he exiled himself. And popular education, confirming his exile, continues to prepare the reader for Tennyson" (353). In a situation in which "popular education" was producing readers unequipped for modern poetry, the poets had no choice but to propose their own program of education for readers; it's hard to imagine a poet of an earlier generation titling an essay, as Pound did, "How to Read." One reason modern poetry was so difficult was that it undertook to perform itself a pedagogical function that earlier poets had safely left to institutions: it proposed to put forward, in the very act of creating them, new paradigms for poetry.

Nineteen forty-five may well have been among the last years in which Tindall might have accused the institutions of education of leaving readers unprepared for modernism. A body of criticism devoted to championing and explaining modern poetry had been growing for some two decades by then and was poised to take over the universities. The movement into teaching positions of poet-critics identified with New Criticism, and thus with the modernist revolution, like Tate, Yvor Winters, and R. P. Blackmur, confirmed the triumph of modernism—its movement from the margins to the center of literary culture—and coincided with a more general absorption of cultural life into the academy. The enormous weight of the university thus was placed behind modernism, and techniques of reading closely adapted to modern poetry were taught to a new generation of readers. The academy was now making modernist readers and was rapidly becoming the only arena in which readers were made, as the belletrist and bohemian social spaces where the art of modernism had been nurtured were gradually absorbed into the academic orbit. The poets of the postwar years found a new audience, one accustomed to making sense of modernist "difficulty" and fitted with habits of reading and standards for judgment that enabled them to grasp and respond to the witty, paradoxical, erudite, and fragmented constructions typical of high modernism.

A large segment of the poets who emerged in the postwar years availed themselves of this new, institutionally produced audience, creating a style both institutionally sanctioned and "modern," what W. D. Snodgrass once referred to as "academic experiment" (47). Richard Wilbur, Anthony Hecht, John Hollander, Adrienne Rich, W. S. Merwin, Donald Hall, and James Wright are only a few of the poets whose work, at least early in their careers, recognizably aimed itself toward the audience produced by the institutional dissemination of New Critical reading strategies. Robert Lowell, the poet who most successfully engaged this audience, made no secret of the influence that New Critical writings had had on his creative work: "When I was twenty and learning to write, Allen Tate, Eliot, Blackmur, and Winters, and all those people were very much news.

You waited for their essays, and when a good critical essay came out it had the excitement of a new imaginative work" (237). James Breslin notes that "every stylistic feature of [Lowell's] poems marks them as obscure, difficult—hard to write and hard to read" (18); but he goes on to observe as well that Lowell's reward for his difficulty, in contrast to the outrage that greeted T. S. Eliot's early work, was prizes and fellowships: "Eliot had to create his own audience, Lowell received one ready-made—the one created (in the main) by Eliot" (20). The local difficulty of Lowell's work was indeed formidable, but it was a difficulty of interpretation rather than the more fundamental kind of modal difficulty that points to disagreements about the very nature of poetry; few readers questioned the propriety of Lowell's writing a symbol-ridden, highly allusive poetry whose coherence was achieved through imagery rather than through logical argument or narrative.

This comfortable relation between poet and audience threatened to eradicate the element of risk and dissonance that had been such an important component of modernist identity. The academic modernists strove to keep alive their quarrel with the world, writing essays with titles like "The Isolation of Modern Poetry" and "The Obscurity of the Poet" in which they blamed their society for the marginal status of poetry and poets in it. But as poets and critics became increasingly established within the academy, postures of revolt became increasingly difficult to maintain. For a generation of poets raised on a myth of aesthetic vanguardism in which the extent of readers' resistance to a work was an index of its value, the passing of an age of antagonism between poetry and its readers was no unmixed blessing.

Of course, a substantial contingent of poets resisted the academic capture of modernism. A few eccentrics like Robert Bly rejected the whole of Anglo-American poetic modernism. Most of his contemporaries were not so thoroughgoing, though, preferring to emphasize neglected aspects of the modernist heritage or to champion romantic and prophetic traditions that modernism had devalued. Allen Ginsberg and fellow Beats found inspiration in Blake and Whitman, poets who had been specific objects of Eliotic suspicion, while Charles Olson and the "Projectivists" chose William Carlos Williams, a minor figure in the New Critical canon, as a central influence. By 1960, the "war of the anthologies" had broken out; the academic modernists gathered in *New Poets of England and America* were joined on the bookshelves that year by Donald Allen's antiacademic anthology *The New American Poetry*, which quickly brought to prominence alternatives to the verse that had shaped itself to fit New Critical reading practices.

The opposition between academic formalists and avant-garde experimentalists in the 1950s and 1960s has been adequately described elsewhere, for the most part in terms that follow the self-understanding of the insurgents, who saw themselves fighting for spontaneity as opposed to calculation, immediacy as opposed to reflection, innovation as opposed to tradition, freedom as opposed to constraint (J. Breslin 1–22). Stepping back from the terms of the debate as it occurred, however, one can see a ground of shared assumptions between the two camps. With the exception of a few eccentrics like Bly, this contest played itself out as a debate over different ways of embodying the values represented by modernism, or over which set of values present in modernism was properly to be appealed to by its inheritors. Lowell may have favored Eliot (as filtered through Tate), and Ginsberg may have favored Pound and Williams, but both located their most immediate and important sources of inspiration in the high modernist generation. The two sides shared a sense of the enormous consequences of the decision to write in "closed" or "open" forms; both exhibited what one might call an attitude of technological determinism, an assumption that formal choices were the central, defining distinctions in poetry. Both were at times given to apocalyptic rhetoric regarding the unholy alliance of consumerism and the military-industrial complex; the political visions of Lowell's "Where the Rainbow Ends" and Ginsberg's "Howl" manifest, at least in tone, some striking similarities. Indeed, one might see the two camps as having split between them the audience bequeathed by modernism, an audience that had been defined by its estrangement from bourgeois values and cultural forms, with the academic formalists having inherited the elite intellectuals and the New American Poets having inherited that segment of the modernist audience whose antibourgeois energies were channeled into bohemian life-styles and utopian politics.

Poets who began their careers in the period after World War II, then, faced a set of options that presented itself with a certain clarity. They could write according to New Critical prescription and avail themselves of the substantial audience that had been created by the installation of modernism within the academy. Or they could join an antiacademic opposition that had shaped itself as a mirror image of the academic formalism it was rejecting and so stage an appeal

After

the Death

of Poetry

to the alienated urbanites who had traditionally populated Bohemia and formed the audience of the avant-garde. Spokesmen for the New American Poets tended to represent their movement in the terms of heroic rebellion, a liberation from academic constraints into a new poetic of spontaneity and freedom. Not every observer, even among those outside the formalist camp, agreed; surely John Ashbery had Ginsberg and the Beats in mind in 1968 when he remarked that

> protests against the mediocre values of our society such as the hippie movement seem to imply that one's only way out is to join a parallel society whose stereotyped manners, language, speech and dress are only reverse images of the one it is trying to reject. . . . Is there nothing, then, between the extremes of Levittown and Haight-Ashbury, between an avant-garde which has become a tradition and a tradition which is no longer one? [393]

In my chapter on John Ashbery I try to discuss more fully the way he places himself between the poles of an institutionalized modernism and a reflexive avant-gardism. For the moment, I want to propose that both alternatives lacked the dynamic quality that had characterized the relations of the high modernist poets with their audience. Modernist rhetoric had acted to select, and in some measure to produce, its readers from a diffuse reading public; the poets of the postwar period found their audiences for the most part already selected and trained. David Trotter remarks that "the audience for poetry today is no longer diffuse, having been to a large extent preselected and trained by academic study. Whether or not a contemporary poet is read for the right reason may well depend less on his rhetorical exertions than on the way that audience has been taught" (148–49). The New American Poets aligned themselves less directly with the reading strategies through which modernism had entered and conquered the university, so they wrote manifestos, founded magazines and presses, and engaged in the sort of audience-building measures typical of the early days of modernism. But they were using modernist values to appeal to an audience already imbued with an appreciation and understanding of those values; the Beats and Projectivists, in their polemical writings and in their poems, were trying to claim for themselves the values of experimentation and formal innovation that modernism had privileged, rather than proposing new measures of value. The New American Poets put forward an idea about modernism and its consequences different from that of the poets shaped by the New Criticism, but they depended on their audience's identification and sympathy with modernism, and so, no less than the academic formalists, addressed themselves to a readership that had been created by the triumph of modernism in the university. This is perhaps what Richard Poirier has in mind when he remarks of writers like Ginsberg and Jack Kerouac (and William Carlos Williams) that "such writers are simply not difficult enough to persuade anyone not already given over to their ideologies" (41). Poirier makes this remark, by the way, in a volume that contains a sustained polemic against modernist "difficulty." I suspect that behind it is a sense that the writers he mentions (to whom we might add such figures as Robert Creeley, Robert Duncan, and Olson) remain too much within what he describes as "the idea that innovation in the arts is a form of cultural heroism" (112), an idea whose propagation was dependent on the institutionalization of modernism that the counterculturalists professed to oppose.

I can hardly do justice here to Poirier's rich and sinuous argument against modernist difficulty, which is itself in part directed against the notion that books have arguments that are available to summary. But I want to consider for a moment his account of the sort of relation between reader and writer established by modernist difficulty as a way of introducing the three poets at the center of this book. Poirier complains that the difficult modernist text places us in a kind of double bind as readers; we are encouraged by many elements of the text "to locate principles of order and structure beneath a fragmentary surface . . . only to have it then suggested by other elements in the text that we have been acting in a rather fussy and heavy-handed fashion, embarrassingly without aristocratic ease" (102–3). Poirier protests that "no one *can* be the right kind of reader for books of this sort," which demand that the reader be "at the same time casual and encyclopedic" (106). The allusiveness of modern literature, he implies, is a form of bad faith; it demands study from the reader at the same time that it suggests that the fit audience is confined to those who can understand without study, who wield a depth and breadth of knowledge and expertise similar to the poet's.

Poirier, then, is compelled to imagine a middle way between insufficiently difficult writers such as Ginsberg and others like T. S. Eliot, the ostentatious difficulty of whose work masks, in Poirier's view, an "extreme procedural hesitancy" (107), a profoundly uneasy relation between the poet and the forms he creates. It's my view that the most interesting and successful poets who have emerged since 1945 have tried to find some kind of middle way between the alternatives of a poetry descended from Eliot, which had become all too well accommodated to its readers' habits and strategies, and the oppositional poetics of a figure like Ginsberg, which seemed too much a negative image of the academic mode, and which was predicated on a no longer plausible notion of cultural heroism inherited uncritically from the modernist generation. In their different ways, Elizabeth Bishop, James Merrill, and John Ashbery sought to place themselves outside the opposition described by the war of the anthologies, to find audiences that could be addressed in terms outside those that defined the conflict between the academics and the antiacademics.

In the succeeding chapters of this volume I discuss in detail the forms of difficulty devised by these poets. Here, I wish briefly to formulate some of the issues surrounding each poet's strategy of resistance to institutionalized modernism and to consider the potential of each poet's inventions in the context of the present. A great deal has happened in American poetry since the 1950s, of course, and the polarization I described above no longer prevails. The battle of the anthologies ended long ago, with the result not so much a victory by one side or the other as a blurring of the divisions, as many of the erstwhile formalists—Merwin, Hall, Wright, and Rich, among others—switched sides to adopt "open" forms. By the end of the decade an anthology dedicated to the proposition that "the strongest and most alive poetry in America had abandoned or at least broken the grip of traditional meters and had set out, once again, into 'the wilderness of unopened life'" (Berg and Mezey xi) could include almost equal numbers of alumni of each of the combatants in the sectarian battle that began the 1960s. In our own moment it surely remains the case that, in David Trotter's rueful words, "there can be little poetry published today on which the shadow of an institutional readership does not fall" (146); but at the same time, the institutions that "make" readers operate more heterogeneously now than they did in the heyday of the New Criticism's influence. One can identify at least one significant division: in the past twenty years creative writing programs, granting MFA (Master of Fine Arts) degrees, have multiplied to the point where they can offer a counterweight to literature departments and offer their own standards, strategies, and paradigms of reading. Reading and thinking about poetry are now divided between two institutional structures with vastly different cultures and outlooks.

of subjectivity toward which Language poetry often seems to aspire and the unexamined belief in the power of subjectivity to shape meaningful poetic forms often seen among the MFA mainstream or the New Formalist faith in the power of traditional poetic forms to give valid shapes to subjectivity. These three approaches seem to me to mark out the chief avenues of possibility for American poetry at the moment. Each imagines a different resolution of the fundamental problem, or, if one prefers, the fundamental contradiction, of lyric, that of embodying subjectivity in public language, a problem whose urgency has been tremendously heightened in our time by the radical skepticism about the nature and claims of subjectivity characteristic of contemporary thought. Language poetry proposes to overcome this problem by exposing subjectivity as an effect of language, reducing the self to a trope or figure that is more properly unmasked than expressed. The mainstream poetry of personal lyric privileges the values of accurate observation and direct statement, shielding itself from intellectual skepticism by the apparent limitations of its claims. The New Formalism offers a reversion to traditional forms, positing that those forms can themselves provide a sufficient mediation between private feeling and public expression. One might ask, though, whether all three of these strategies are not too exclusively given to "lyricism" or to the attractions of "lucidity"; perhaps the most promising modes of development for poetry lie in finding ways to acknowledge at once the competing claims of lyricism and lucidity. In so doing, one might be able to place oneself at something of a distance from both of poetry's institutional audiences, with a hope of finding an audience sufficiently flexible in its responses that it can look beyond institutional alignments.

In the three chapters that follow, I try to evaluate the current situation of American poetry, and suggest some conclusions about its prospects, by examining the work of three poets who came to prominence in the years after the Second World War: Elizabeth Bishop, James Merrill, and John Ashbery. They are among the first generation of American poets to confront the problem of the institutionalization of modernism. All three attempt to formulate a space outside, or at least at an angle to, the modernist assumptions that animated both the academics and their countercultural rivals. They are united as well in their disavowal of the heroic attitudes inherited from modernism by poets as different as Lowell and Ginsberg, and in their skeptical self-consciousness about the strategies they employ in translating subjectivity into form. Self-consciousness has become a reflex of art after modernism and in itself no longer bears any particular value; but I hope to persuade the reader that each of the three submits his or her imaginative stances to a genuine questioning by the skeptical consciousness. Each stands in a kind of double relation to one of the prominent contemporary modes I've identified. Each has influenced a significant number of younger poets; beyond direct influence, each exemplifies a set of strategies currently in widespread use. At the same time, I feel that these three poets more richly explore the rhetorical and imaginative possibilities of the particular stances they embody than do most of their inheritors, and so it is for the most part to their work, rather than to that of the generation that has followed them, that one must turn to imagine possible futures for poetry.

Bishop's combination of reticence and craft have made her an attractive model, both to poets of her own generation seeking an alternative to the symbolist-metaphysical style and to a younger generation of poets for whom the vatic and confessional modes that replaced formalism as the poetic mainstream began to pale. The mummy truths of "deep image" and neosurrealist styles had rather quickly turned into rhetoric, and the idea of an unmediated expression of subjectivity that had informed the confessional mode was revealed as simply one more literary convention by the immediate proliferation of confessional poems. Under these circumstances, the modesty of the apparent claims in Bishop's work seemed a promising alternative. That modesty would shield the poetry from skeptical deflation, while the use of familiar descriptive and narrative strategies would provide an attachment to a world shared with the reader, overcoming the too often solipsistic self-enclosure of the confessional mode. Wyatt Prunty describes a transformation in poetic strategies from organization by symbol to organization by similitude, taking the mid-to-late-1950s change in Robert Lowell's style as representative. But the shift in Lowell's work was preceded by, and influenced by, a shift in Bishop's, in which she left behind "metaphysical" structures of extended metaphor to adopt the descriptive and anecdotal strategies that were to prove so influential. What has been insufficiently recognized until now, I think, is the extent to which Bishop's uses of similitude differ from those of most of the poetry of direct observation that has descended from her work or operates through apparently similar strategies. Rather than serving the descriptive and decorative functions usual in the poetry of observation, Bishop's similitudes point to gaps and differences and encourage the reader to focus on elements of unlikeness as much as on elements of sameness; metaphor itself becomes an instrument of skepticism as the poet uses it to question the mind's appetite for analogy. If Bishop's poetry seems at first to offer a "lyrical" focus on transcriptions of individual experience, on closer examination one can see at work in it a more troubled examination of the relation between experience and the patterns of language that are called on to express it.

James Merrill has clearly influenced a number of the poets allied with the movement known as New Formalism, which itself harks back, and not merely in name, to the academic formalism of which Merrill was, in the 1950s, a junior member. Many of the 1950s formalists, such as W. S. Merwin, James Wright, Donald Hall, and Adrienne Rich, abandoned traditional prosodic and stanzaic structuring and evolved in directions of greater apparent spontaneity, directness, and colloquialism as the 1950s turned into the 1960s; whether confessional, surrealist, or "scenic,"[6] the styles they developed proposed a greater immediacy of contact with experience and forms of expression closer to speech. Others, like Anthony Hecht, John Hollander, and Richard Wilbur, for the most part declined to join this move away from erudition and paradox toward less evidently calculated rhetorics. Merrill has in some sense split this difference. He has continued to produce sonnets and quatrains throughout his career; at the same time, he has also written in free verse, and his range has expanded to encompass at one end an almost Mallarméan opacity and at another a Byronic chattiness. What is noteworthy about Merrill's stylistic development is that he has never been tempted to imagine that a more colloquial diction or a freer prosody is any less arbitrary or artificial than any other stylistic choice. This has led Merrill to install as one of the chief themes of his poetry a reflection on the arbitrary nature of language and literary form, and thus on the arbitrary nature of the subjectivity constituted by language and represented in literary form. While the New Formalists, as I argue below, seem to believe subjectivity need only be decanted into the objectifying container of traditional form to be valid for an audience, Merrill, though he frequently employs traditional forms, does so with a full awareness that they no longer in themselves provide a viable contract between poet and reader. The fourth section of "The Thousand and Second Night," in which the poet offers a comic ventriloquism of a New Critical reading of the poem's opening, aims its irony toward both the routinization of response encouraged by "close reading" and the humane faith in the affirmations of form that accompanied it:

> Now if the class will turn back to this, er,
> Poem's first section—Istanbul—I shall take
> What little time is left today to make
> Some brief points. So. The rough pentameter
>
> Quatrains give way, you will observe, to three
> Interpolations, prose as well as verse.
> Does it come through how each in turn refers
> To mind, body, and soul (or memory)?
>
> . . . . .
>
>   Yes, what now? Ah. How and when
> Did he "affirm"? Why, constantly. And how else
> But in the form. Form's what affirms. That's well
> Said, if I do—[*Bells ring.*] Go, gentlemen.
> [ND 14–15]

Merrill stands at a mocking distance from the instructor's self-satisfied apothegm, yet he knows that he has little besides the affirmations of form to offer. Merrill's achievement, I contend, rests in the way his work acknowledges the attraction of contemporary skepticisms regarding subjectivity and language at the same time that he invokes the power of at least the ghost of the "metrical contract" that once bound reader and poet through the agency of shared experience in poetic form.

John Ashbery, however equivocally, is acknowledged as a leading influence on the movement that has come to be known as Language poetry, even as he has come under attack from some of that movement's academic champions. Ashbery shapes his style through a systematic negation of the conventions that New Criticism established; his work takes for granted the prevalence of New Critical reading habits and treats those habits much as the modernists treated the Tennysonian habits of the readers of their day. Ashbery thus attempts to make reading difficult again, and judging from the reception of his work, one has to grant him success at least on that score. But Ashbery's most radical assault on institutionalized reading strategies is embodied in his second book, *The Tennis Court Oath*, and since then he has worked in less radically unaccommodating styles. While his writing remains inimical to New Critical reading practices, it strives not so much to erase the traces of subjectivity as to shelter them from the pressure of modes of thought associated with "lucidity." Ashbery's compromise aligns itself against the reflexes of an institutionally produced audience for poetry at the same time that it refuses the myth of heroic experimentalism that fueled the Beat and Projectivist movements (from the latter of which Language poetry traces its lineage).

The three poets I discuss at length in the next three chapters are united not merely by particular poetic strategies but also by their sexual orientation; though I have chosen not to explore this commonality in detail, it may well have had an effect in shaping their forms of relation to the audiences they imagined. David Trotter refers to the "secret complement" of modernist poetry—those readers with whom the poet shared a set of values, a culture, that would enable them to supply much that was left inexplicit in the poems. Trotter remarks, "These poets could expect that the true reader would demonstrate his or her competence by supplying the information which their poems gestured at but finally withheld" (15). Certainly the works of the three poets I examine are rich in both gestures and withholding, and all three may well have imagined a "secret complement" for whom homosexual identity provided a framework for understanding that had no need for explicit articulation. While I remain not entirely persuaded by Lee Edelman's tracing of a gay cryptology in Bishop's work, surely Bishop's lesbianism had everything to do with the kind of poet she became. Reticence and silence seem to have come naturally to her, but that innate bias must have been powerfully reinforced by the need for certain kinds of secrecy in her emotional life. Judging by the few poems and fragments in her oeuvre that treat the erotic, the climate of hostility to homosexuality that prevailed through most of Bishop's lifetime thwarted the development of what might have been a remarkable love poet. And a deconstructive reading might afford rich material for an analysis that would link the thematic of likeness and unlikeness I attempt to trace in the poems to the dynamics of likeness and unlikeness involved in homosexuality.

The progressively greater openness regarding his sexuality that develops in the course of Merrill's career seems roughly correlated with a greater openness of form and colloquiality of diction, suggesting a connection between the symbolist opacity of the early poems and a sexuality that dared speak only in hints and implications. Certainly, poems like "Childlessness" and "The Broken Home" take

on new meaning when read with knowledge of the poet's homo-
sexuality; some readers at the time of publication may well have
understood a set of gestures or oblique suggestions other readers
could recognize only in the light of the greater explicitness of Mer-
rill's later work. Indeed, my reading of the fourth sonnet of "The
Broken Home" as a scene of sexual instruction, whose occult im-
port involves the etiology of the poet's homosexuality, depends on
the reader's following a series of buried puns whose badness verges
on, or falls over into, camp. While the camp sensibility is hardly
limited to the gay world, it surely finds itself most at home there;
understanding the sonnet's reference to the poet's sexuality demands
a kind of "gay" reading, demands both that the reader be alert to
a certain kind of innuendo and that he or she accept the propriety
of communicating this serious burden through a set of decidedly
bad puns.[7]

The sources in biography for the poet's work are more cryptic
in John Ashbery's case than in those of Bishop or Merrill, and the
poet's sexuality may have much to do with that. Ashbery seems to
have been destined to be a love poet, but he found the way blocked
by the imperative of secrecy surrounding the love he would have
taken as his subject. "Some Trees," the title poem of his first volume,
is plainly a love poem, and Ashbery insisted in a 1986 interview that
the poem was written for and about a particular person: " 'Some
Trees' . . . was definitely written about somebody I was in love with"
(Tranter 102). And yet the dance of hesitations it enacts seems any-
thing but plain, and much in the poem is available, from our current
vantage, to a reading that sees the poem's reticence as generated by
a need for concealment. The poet depicts himself and the lover

> Arranging by chance
>
> To meet as far this morning
> From the world as agreeing
> With it . . .
> [*Some Trees* 51]

While these lines may be taken to express no more than the distance
from "the world" that any love enforces upon those who share it, the
passage might also be read with specific reference to gay sexuality.
Lovers meeting surreptitiously might indeed arrange a meeting that
appears to be "by chance," and the odd syntax of the sentence, in
which the lovers themselves are made the measure of their distance

from the world, perhaps hints at a more profound disagreement with the way of "the world" than can be easily or directly expressed. The closing of the poem posits a self-protective enclosure of private speech:

> Placed in a puzzling light, and moving,
> Our days put on such reticence
> These accents seem their own defense.

Again, the reticence of these lines defeats any attempt to attach their need for "defense" to any specific threat, yet one can certainly imagine that in 1956, at least for the poet and his lover, and perhaps for a certain range of readers as well, these lines may have been read with a more specific form of self-protective silence in mind.

I discuss the New Formalist and Language poetry movements in terms of the forms of relation to their readers that they propose. Different as their diagnoses and prescriptions for American poetry are, the two movements share a sense that poetic form is the crucial element in poetry's relations to subjectivity and audience. They share as well a polemical distance from the poetic mainstream of the MFA programs, in which the free-verse personal lyric holds sway. Being, at least until recently, positioned outside the university, both have employed many of the audience-building measures devised by the early-twentieth-century avant-gardes: starting magazines (or taking over existing ones), organizing readings, compiling anthologies, and publishing manifestos. Both, in their very different ways, see their prescriptions as a way for American poetry to break free of a debilitatingly narrow focus on the private self, and so engage readers on a broader and more stable ground than that provided by spontaneous and immediate expression of individual states of consciousness.[8]

The New Formalists assume the continuing viability of the metrical contract proposed by traditional verse form. In their view, the inherited body of metrical and stanzaic conventions offers a means of connection between poet and reader whose authority is rooted in nature, or is at least immune to the corrosive effects which our intellectual skepticisms have had on other bodies of poetic convention. Indeed, today's New Formalists often distinguish themselves from the 1950s poets who went under the same name by pointing to the greater colloquiality of diction and syntax in the contemporary poets (Allen, "Transcending the Self" 8); apparently, the conventions that underlie "literary" and "artificial" diction and syntax are transitory, while those underlying metrical form are not.[9] For the New Formalists, subjectivity becomes valid for the reader through the process of being submitted to the impersonal discipline of traditional metrical form. Though many of the spokespersons for this movement regard T. S. Eliot ambivalently, their notion of the objectifying function of traditional prosody bears a noteworthy resemblance to Eliot's account of the poetic process as an escape from personality through submission to the impersonal order of language.

The Language poets carry on a much more radical assault on the forms of subjectivity that structure mainstream poetics. If the New Formalists repeat, with a difference, the strategies of the academic formalists of the 1950s, the Language poets trace their lineage back to Charles Olson and the movement, Projectivism, that he founded. They share Olson's disdain for what he termed "the lyrical interference of the individual as ego" (156) and endeavor, by a comprehensive program of stylistic violence, to eradicate any vestiges of subjectivity in their work. For the Language poets, the problem is not so much how to find valid forms to embody subjectivity as how to find forms that will reveal the arbitrary and constructed nature of subjectivity itself. In this way, Language poetry shares its project with the antifoundational skepticisms that dominate academic literary theory. In one sense the more radical Language poets seem to have reached a sort of outer limit of iconoclasm as they reject not merely the conventions peculiar to the contemporary personal lyric but those that have governed the presentation of subjectivity in poetry since at least the Renaissance.[10] At the same time, the Language poets plainly invest themselves in the modernist equation of formal innovation with cultural heroism. Evaluating their work demands, on the one hand, that we judge whether this persistent modernist myth remains viable in our time, and whether the Language poets' rejection of inherited forms of coherence and structure in the name of a postmodernity figured in terms of an absolute rupture from the past gives up too much in its denial of any contemporary validity to the historical experience sedimented in those forms.

I close with a consideration of what might be termed the "Is poetry dead?" controversy, a long-simmering question brought to the boil in 1988 by Joseph Epstein's article "Who Killed Poetry?" As Epstein points out, the notion that prose has definitively bested poetry in their competition goes back at least to Edmund Wilson's 1934 essay "Is Verse a Dying Technique?" Epstein's article, reprinted in the *Associated Writing Programs Bulletin*, provoked a predictably outraged set of responses from the poets invited to reply. Most of the respondents asserted the health and quality of the contemporary poetic product, and like Allen Tate (with whom they otherwise have little in common) in an earlier era, blamed the audience for its failure to give contemporary poetry the serious attention it deserves. Since the publication of Epstein's article, a number of discussions of the issues it raised have appeared in general-interest journals like *Atlantic* and *New Republic*, most proposing various strategies for restoring a broad general readership to poetry. Probably this is an ambition, or a fantasy, shared by a sizable majority of poets, and one to which only the Language poets, with their alternative notion of a Leninist vanguardism, seem immune.

Most of the proposals for accomplishing this restoration revolve around retaking ground formerly yielded to prose. Jonathan Holden, whose book *The Fate of American Poetry* presents perhaps the most deeply considered advocacy of this position in recent criticism,[11] urges poetry to expand the range of experience it treats as a means of addressing a broader audience: "It is in its subject matter, its 'content,' that American poetry can further enlarge its capability" (137). Noble as Holden's ambitions are, I feel the program they lead him to propose is at best utopian and at worst potentially harmful to poetry's chances of actually making a difference in contemporary literary culture. The conditions that Walter Benjamin in the 1930s identified as leading to the reading public's indifference to poetry have only intensified in the succeeding decades, and it's hard to imagine that the process of change will be slowed, much less reversed. Attempts to revive the fortunes of poetry by abandoning lyrical for narrative modes in order to compete with prose fiction seem highly unrealistic; the first step to restoring poetry's respectability among thinking people would be to admit frankly that prose has taken over many of the jobs once performed by poetry and that poetry must give up any idea of retaking that lost turf. Instead, poetry must concentrate on winning back the community of intellectuals, the most recent defectors from the ranks of its readers; I hasten to remind my readers that *intellectual* and *academic* are by no means synonymous. What can poetry offer to do for intellectuals that other kinds of writing cannot? To answer with crude brevity, I think poetry can still propose to do what lyric has always proposed to do: to embody subjectivity in shared, public forms; to record the form and pressure of the time upon consciousness. But given that our era is one dominated, intellectually, by various radical skepticisms, that recording must itself show the mark of those skepticisms, must itself demonstrate the poet's awareness of the corrosive doubt about the nature of subjectivity itself that thinking people now inhabit. Speculative criticism can articulate the doubt, but only poetry can tell us how living with and in that doubt affects the nature of our feelings; poetry can represent for us the ways in which the quality of our experience has been transformed by the developments that speculative criticism presents discursively. But poetry can do so only if poets are willing to brave the element of skeptical consciousness, only if they submit their own poetic assumptions to a rigorous and fundamental inquiry. In the analyses that follow, I hope to suggest some ways that poets might rise to that challenge, might make things difficult not only for their readers but for themselves.

Knowledge withheld is a recurrent motif in Elizabeth Bishop's poems. "I know what I know," says her almanac (*CP* 123); her loon "kept his own counsel" (*CP* 125); and in the scenes she describes, "whatever the landscape had of meaning" appears to be held back, "in the interior" (*CP* 67). Something is secreted within "The Monument" about which the poet can only speculate, while Crusoe's island remains unnameable and so unknowable. The biographical sources for this recurrent theme are not hard to find; her father's death and her mother's subsequent breakdown thrust the five-year-old Bishop into a puzzling and opaque world, rich in urgent and dangerous secrets. The ensuing period of being shuttled between various relatives surely helped to shape the powerful personal reticence often remarked upon by those who knew her. Reticence is a quality often posited of Bishop's poetry as well, and many commentators have noted and praised both the concern for craft highlighted by the poet's self-effacing manner and her reluctance to moralize her scenes and narratives.[1] John Ashbery, for instance, remarks that "I find her [Bishop's] poetry terribly exciting because she can describe something perfectly and not draw any moral from it, and she doesn't have to at that point" (Koethe 180). I want to examine the way in which the silences of the poems shape Bishop's relation to her readers, and particularly to explore the way in which a strategy of withholding both moral statement and personal information enabled Bishop to be at once a "writer's writer's writer," in Ashbery's words, and also perhaps the favorite poet of the *New Yorker* audience.

David Kalstone remarks about Bishop that "her work is admired by many poets who do not admire one another" (*Five Temperaments* 12), and among the younger generation of poets today this remains the case; Bishop is claimed as an influence both by New Formalists and by many in the MFA mainstream. In the broad range of her admirers she resembles Robert Frost, who was, however equivocally, a modernist (whose critical supporters included Ezra Pound) while also appealing to a class of reader otherwise alienated from the modernist movement—the "general reader who buys books in their thousands" (Frost, *Selected Letters* 98). The growth of Frost's reputation among partisans of the modernist revolution proceeded through a determined excavation of the "Other Frost," to invoke Randall Jarrell's essay by that title, a Frost whose darknesses and ambiguities are those of a modernist poet, a figure far more "hard," "odd," and "gloomy" (in Jarrell's terms) than the "sensible, tender, humorous poet" beloved by the public. This revaluation has been accelerated in the last fifteen or so years by biographical revelations that have paradoxically made Frost more interesting as a poet as they have made him less likable as a person; the replacement of the "neighborly" Frost by a more complicated, if less attractive, figure has had a favorable effect so far as critical attention to his poetry is concerned.[2]

The course of Bishop's reception bears a good deal of resemblance to Frost's (Parker 21–22). A number of the early poems of both poets quickly became anthology pieces (in Bishop's case, notably "The Map," "The Man-Moth," and "The Fish") at the same time that both had to endure a certain condescension from "advanced" critics. Frost was often weighed at the value of his public persona, as a plain-spoken, unintellectual embodiment of Yankee toughness and wisdom; and praise of Bishop's "charm" usually carried with it an implicit or explicit reminder of the limitations of that quality. If Frost was a regionalist, Bishop was a miniaturist, the circumscription of whose work was often seen in terms of gender rather than geography (Alvarez 324–26). Facts of Bishop's life that have only recently become available to open discussion—her lesbianism and the profound unhappiness of her childhood—have helped to erase the image of effortless charm and lightness and replace it with a sense of the emotional burdens hidden beneath the apparently casual surfaces. While biographical revelations in Bishop's case, unlike Frost's, have made her a more rather than a less attractive character, in both cases greater knowledge of the life has made the poetry seem richer, stranger, and more complex.

So the critic John Unterecker, in his account of Bishop's "Poem," darkens its seemingly untroubled description by cross-referencing a detail to the story "In the Village," behind which stands the biographical fact of Bishop's mother's breakdown. Encountering "the hint of steeple" (176), Unterecker remarks, "We have no choice but to remember the Presbyterian church steeple that in the story 'In the Village' threatens to echo an insane mother's scream" (77). Anne Stevenson, who knew Bishop and knew the facts of her painful childhood long before they became widely disseminated, warns her readers that Bishop's poetry, "for all its whimsicality, comes from the heart of despair itself" (121). Only after Bishop's death, however, have critics been free to reread the poetry in ways that highlight its experience of "deformity," "existential loneliness," and "epistemological murk or vacancy," to use the terms of Helen Vendler's shrewd essay (*Music* 298–99), which occupies in Bishop's reception a position similar to Jarrell's essays in Frost's. Charles Tomlinson, in his review of *Questions of Travel*, contrasts Bishop's poetry of wandering rather unfavorably with "the more radical homelessness of Rilke or Lawrence" (89); since 1966, what we know of Bishop has helped reveal in her work a sense of homelessness deeper and more disturbing than Tomlinson allowed. Similarly, our knowledge of Bishop's lesbianism provides a subtext that complicates and enriches our understanding of the poetry, as in Lee Edelman's ingenious detection of possible double meanings in "In the Waiting Room."[3] If, as David Bromwich remarks, "to the reader who returns to these poems for their own sake, the question likeliest to recur is: what are they concealing?" (EBDH 84), criticism now has some ready answers that until recently were either unknown or, for those who knew, unsayable. But biographical knowledge can only encourage, rather than create, new readings, and surely both Bishops—the "miniaturist" and the poet of "existential loneliness"—are there in the poems.

One might see Bishop's mature work as a prime instance of what Richard Poirier terms, in polemical opposition to modernist difficulty, "density": "By 'density' I mean to describe a kind of writing which gives, so it likes to pretend, a fairly direct access to pleasure, but which becomes, on longer acquaintance, rather strange and imponderable" (130). Poirier lists Frost prominently among the exemplars of this quality of density, and Robert Mazzocco seems to have something similar to Poirier's "density" in mind when he remarks of one of Bishop's poems that "you'd have to go back to Frost for another poem as slyly unaccommodating" (5). Markedly "unaccommodating" poets were to be found aplenty among Bishop's contemporaries, most notably her friend and rival Robert Lowell; Mazzocco points here to the skill with which Bishop's work, unlike the more evidently difficult poetry of many of her peers, conceals its recalcitrance and strangeness behind an appearance of openness.

Though Bishop's work never approaches the levels of opacity attained by the early Lowell, this apparent openness is much more evident in her later works. Thomas Travisano, referring to the first half of *North and South*, notes that "many readers have found these early poems difficult" (19), and by this he means difficult in something of a modernist, or at least a New Critical, sense. Adrienne Rich remarks that, reading *North and South* at the time of its publication, she found some of the poems "impenetrable: intellectualized to the point of obliquity . . . or using extended metaphor to create a mask" (15). The landscapes and situations of Bishop's early poems are recognizably within the reigning neometaphysical paradigm, even if she made the less usual choice of Herbert rather than Donne and Marvell as her chief metaphysical influence. The highly wrought, deliberately artificial worlds of the first part of *North and South* link the poems to prevailing 1950s formalist models: the poem about an object, real ("Cirque d'Hiver") or imagined ("The Imaginary Iceberg," "The Monument"), the Audenesque ballad ("Love Lies Sleeping"), or the fairy-tale parable ("The Man-Moth," "The Weed"). Many of these early poems turn on the kind of extended metaphor that was one of the chief stylistic progeny of the modernist marriage of metaphysical and symbolist modes, a fundamental analogy that governs the entire poem: the soul is like an imaginary iceberg, the poet is like a man-moth or the man who sleeps on the top of a mast, dreams are like armored cars, the city is like a body. These analogies share at once the unlikeliness of the metaphysical conceit and the self-enclosure of the symbolist mode.[4]

With the transformation in Bishop's style inaugurated by "Florida," the creation of aesthetic worlds is replaced in her poetry by catalogs of observations, and a new relationship to metaphor is established.[5] Where the earlier poems posit arbitrary and far-fetched analogies as starting points, then work out their consequences, Bishop's metaphors in her subsequent work persuade us not so much to focus on unsuspected similarities but rather to measure skeptically degrees of likeness and difference.[6] The late poem "Crusoe in England," for instance, implicitly urges the reader to attend to the metaphoricity of metaphor, to keep the literal firmly in mind along with the symbolic. Crusoe's snail shells merely resemble "beds of irises," so when he takes the figure for the fact—"I tried / reciting [poetry] to my iris-beds"—we're hardly surprised that the recital is a failure. In "Crusoe," metaphor may indeed become treacherous:

> I'd dream of things
> like slitting a baby's throat, mistaking it
> for a baby goat.
> [CP 165]

That a rhyming pair's similarity in sound points to an occult coincidence of meaning is a persistent myth or dream of poetry; here that dream becomes a nightmare as phonic similarity betrays the imagination. "Brazil, January 1, 1502" establishes an unsettling set of linkages between "our eyes" and those of the conquistadores, and between these invaders' vision of the New World and the "familiar" myths and assumptions they brought with them; the construction of similarity leads directly to a savage violence. In the bulk of Bishop's work, negative simile, notations of what a thing is *not* like, is an important tool of investigation, while positive expressions of likeness are frequently meant to direct our attention as much to difference as to similarity.

Bishop's work might be said, then, to exhibit to some extent the transition from a "closed" to a more "open" poetic that is the commonplace account of the progress of American poetry in the decades after the Second World War. At the same time Bishop, from the very beginning of her career, refrained from many of the strategies adopted by her more deliberately difficult and more self-consciously ambitious contemporaries. Her poems contain little learned allusion, rarely invoke historical events, and are little given to the violent wrenchings of syntax that were the stock in trade of poets like Berryman. Ekphrastic poems by her contemporaries confront well-known monuments of Western pictorial tradition; Bishop writes about the "Large Bad Picture" painted by a great-uncle. So, when Robert Lowell, in the late 1950s, was seeking new resources for opening out his poetic style, he learned from Bishop's more colloquial manner and more quotidian mode of observation.[7] Rereading Bishop, Lowell remarks, "suggested a way of breaking through the shell of my old manner," a manner that had come to seem to him "distant, symbol-ridden, and willfully difficult" (*Collected Prose* 227). Bishop's way of being "strange and imponderable" rather than "difficult" proved to be a highly attractive mode of moving beyond New Critical prescriptions in both her own and subsequent generations. In the work of younger poets like Sandra McPherson, Brad Leithauser, and Alfred Corn, one finds an apparent modesty of voice and vision, along with a subdued verbal wit and a descriptive precision derived from Bishop's practice.[8] For these poets, as for Lowell, Bishop's work offers the possibility of a poetry without rhetoric, without the inflations of Lowell's apocalyptic mode or the artificiality of neometaphysical modernism, at the same time that it remains true to an ideal of exacting craft.

The transition in Bishop's style, though, should not obscure an underlying consistency. Whether the scenes or narratives are imagined or observed, Bishop's poems work by straightforwardly presenting scenes or narratives whose significance the poet resolutely refuses to reveal. Bishop's reluctance to moralize or draw conclusions has drawn both praise and blame; what Ashbery particularly admires, A. Alvarez deplores: "Reading her poems is like listening to highly imaginative bed-time stories and hearing everything but the plot; it is touching, disquieting, but queerly inconclusive" (Alvarez 325). Certainly, Bishop's disinclination to moralize is one of the chief points of difference between Bishop's style and that of her mentor Marianne Moore, with its often pointed predications.[9] The signature gestures of closure in Moore are the rhetorical question, the QED, and the epigram: "why dissect destiny" (52); "What is / there in being able / to say that one has dominated the stream" (39); "This then you may know / as the hero" (9); "if you demand . . . you are interested in poetry" (267); "we prove, we do not explain our birth" (80); "Ecstasy affords / the occasion and expediency determines the form" (88). Bishop's closing questions, on the other hand, are often far more than rhetorical; her characteristic strategies of closure revolve around the image, taken in the sense of "an intellectual and emotional complex" (Pound, *Selected Essays* 4) and the posing of undecidable alternatives: "The Lent trees had shed all their petals: / wet, stuck, purple, among the dead-eye pearls" (*CP* 100); "more blue than that: / like tatters of the *Morpho* butterfly" (*CP* 131); "It would be hard to say what brought them there, / commerce or contemplation" (*CP* 12); "The sun climbs in . . . faithful as enemy, or friend" (*CP* 39).

In what follows I use a series of Bishop's poems to explore the ways in which a consistent strategy of reticence and withholding intersects with a changing use of tropes of similitude. While Bishop's reticence, her penchant for showing as against telling, and the apparently modest scale of her work have been the aspects of her achievement most influential on other poets, it seems to me that the complex strategies of similitude she employs are what gives her work the depths that recent critics have been concerned to explore, and on which they base their claims for ranking her as a major poet. Tracing the workings of similitude in Bishop's poetry reveals at once a poetic more complex, and more skeptical, than that of most of her heirs, or of other contemporary poets who, though less directly influenced by her, adopt similar stances of indirection and limitation. In the course of her early work Bishop seems to put aside her attraction to symbolist modes of representation, her attraction to an antimimetic poetry that aims at the creation of aesthetic worlds; as I've remarked with regard to "Brazil, January 1, 1502," her later work is not without its warnings regarding the dangers of this habit of thought. But beneath this transformation, the pull of what a critic like Harold Bloom might term the "heterocosmic" impulse remains strong in Bishop's work, and in tracing that force I think we will also uncover a deeply hidden but powerful attraction to apocalyptic modes of imagining. It's the hiding of that attraction to apocalyptic rhetoric, I propose, that generates much of both the difficulty and the power of Bishop's poetry.

"The Monument" is Bishop's closest approach to an ars poetica. The poem, from Bishop's first published volume, seems to put forward a poetic of impersonality, ambiguity, and organic form close to that of the then-reigning New Critical paradigms. As an ars poetica, "The Monument" bears a didactic burden, yet the poem turns out to be strangely uninstructive; many questions are asked in the poem's course, but they receive only oblique answers, if any. Indeed, the whole endeavor of the poem seems to be toward forms of knowing that entertain alternatives without needing to decide them. Cast in the form of a dialogue between a knowing instructor and a resistant pupil who is also a kind of Idiot Questioner, the poem seems to stake the claims of an aesthetic mode of apprehension against the scientific and ethical. The questioner asks a set of questions prompted by a scientific-historical and an ethical reason: "Where are we? . . . What is that? . . . what can it prove?" The instructor answers only by patiently continuing the process of observation, and to the reader it's apparent that the instructor's careful scrutiny yields a knowledge more significant than the questioner's irritable reaching.

The poem seems to begin at some point after the lesson has started; it appears that the first effect of the lesson will be to render its object visible: "Now can you see the monument?" The thirty lines of detailed description that follow function to create the object described, making it present to both the reader and the interlocutor of the poem (the voice that appears in quotation marks). The description begins in metaphor:

> It is of wood
> built somewhat like a box. No. Built
> like several boxes in descending sizes
> one above the other.
> Each is turned half-way round so that
> its corners point toward the sides
> of the one below and the angles alternate.
> [CP 23]

This metaphor is quickly converted into the language of direct apprehension; we would do well, however, to remember that "Each" refers back to the metaphorical "boxes," so that, in a recognizably symbolist fashion, the entire description is based on the original metaphoric move. Throughout, the chief speaker repeatedly draws attention to the role of the observer in producing the observed:

> The view is geared
> (that is, the view's perspective)
> so low there is no "far away,"
> and we are far away within the view.
> [CP 23]

The interlocutor's questions, on the other hand, are relentlessly literal-minded:

"Why does that strange sea make no sound?
Is it because we're far away?
Where are we? Are we in Asia Minor,
or in Mongolia?"
[CP 23]

The questioner asks after the geographical-political coordinates of
the space; the instructor's reply turns the question to its human and
imaginative determinants:

An ancient promontory,
an ancient principality whose artist-prince
might have wanted to build a monument
to mark a tomb or boundary, or make
a melancholy or romantic scene of it . . .
[CP 24]

This reply equates by apposition topography and political bound-
aries in a way that aligns the instructor's mode of vision with that
of the mapmakers alluded to in "The Map": "More delicate than
the historians' are the map-makers' colors" (CP 3). As the phrase
continues, the categorizing specificity demanded by the questioner
yields to the activity of imagining alternatives. Marking and making,
dynastic and aesthetic, are dissolved into a flow of possibilities that
is interrupted rather than coming of itself to a stop; the ellipsis
promises a further and indefinite expansion of the "or" syntax at
work here. It is not clear, even, that a monument was what was
aimed at; the "artist-prince" only "might" have intended to create
a monument. Nevertheless, when the questioner, who seems, under
the instructor's tutelage, to have become at least a bit more obser-
vant, asks "What is that?" the instructor confidently replies, "It is
the monument."

In contrast to the instructor, for whom the monument is "like"
boxes, the questioner, characteristically, takes the metaphor liter-
ally: "It's piled-up boxes." Seen literally, the monument and its space
hold little interest:

"Why did you bring me here to see it?
A temple of crates in cramped and crated scenery,
what can it prove?
I am tired of breathing this eroded air,
this dryness in which the monument is cracking."
[CP 24]

Presumably, to respond to these questions in the terms in which they are posed would be to grant the authority of the instrumental or ethical reason that asks them, and so the instructor's response to these questions is not to answer them but to try to shift the discussion back to the nature of the object itself. In the last of the poem's three sections, the instructor's voice alone appears, celebrating this monument in a description that seems an "imaginative" counterpart to the "physical" description of the first section:

> It is an artifact
> of wood. Wood holds together better
> than sea or cloud or sand could by itself,
> much better than real sea or sand or cloud.
> [CP 24]

The poem here recalls Wallace Stevens's "Anecdote of the Jar," whose eponymous object likewise sets itself against nature; the jar is "like nothing else in Tennessee," just as the space of the monument, being made of wood, is in some way "better than real sea or sand or cloud." As the "gray and bare" jar nevertheless makes "the slovenly wilderness / Surround that hill" (76), so the monument attracts the emblems of nature into its orbit: "once each day the light goes around it." And though Bishop's monument is a more festive affair than Stevens's jar, it shares the ambiguous gendering of its predecessor; the jar is both phallically assertive ("tall") and femininely concave, while the monument may be a "solid" construction, like her imaginary iceberg "erected indivisible," or "hollow," sheltering within it something perhaps too fragile to bear the elements, or the light.

Both poems invoke a decidedly modernist sort of artwork, a seemingly autonomous aesthetic object. Like Stevens's jar, Bishop's monument is an artifact, but if Stevens's jar is an emblem of the radically antinatural, Bishop's monument is presented in language that recalls that of New Critical organicism. While the description in the first section of the poem is conducted in passive and copulative constructions—"is of wood," "is turned," "is set," "is one-third set"— in the final section the monument suddenly comes to life. "It chose that way to grow," remarks the instructor; its decorations "give it away as having life, and wishing; / wanting to be a monument." The volition earlier attributed to the "artist-prince" who "might have wanted to build a monument" is here transferred to the monument itself, which thus invokes the central paradox of the organic notion of the work of art; it is an artifact, a built thing, that nevertheless has its own imperatives, its own dynamic of growth. The monument offers a "shelter" that protects and extends the temporal existence of something valuable.[10] At the same time, "what is within" this shelter "cannot have been intended to have been seen"; Bishop posits a decidedly modern separation of impulse and effect. Whatever is commemorated by this monument is itself unavailable, and so the monument comes to resemble the impersonal artwork of a modernist statement like T. S. Eliot's "Tradition and the Individual Talent."

Bishop's poem, one should remember, was written while Eliot was at the height of his critical influence; the term *monument* seems indeed to call out to a famous passage in Eliot's essay: "The existing monuments form an ideal order among themselves, which is modified by the introduction of the new (the really new) work of art among them" (5). This sentence may help to explain the rather odd choice of verb in Bishop's closing command, "Watch it closely." One might have expected *examine, look at,* or some similar term denoting the sort of attention we give to a static object; we *watch* what has the potential for change. So in "The Man-Moth" we are told that this poet-figure will yield up his "tear" only "if you watch" (*CP* 15). The curious apposition in the preceding sentence, in which the monument "is the beginning of a . . . monument," also takes us back to Eliot. The monument, while it may be a tomb, is also an origin, in something of the way that Eliot's "monuments" are self-replicating and capable of change; like Eliot's, Bishop's monument is not fixed and final but capable of transformation. The monument, in this final section of the poem, becomes comprehensively endowed with a kind of life, and so the kind of attention we are asked to give it at the poem's close is the kind of attention we would give to a living thing. If in recent years we have come to read Eliot's advocacy of artistic impersonality as a defense against a painful personal history, so we might also see Bishop's attribution of life to an artifact as a means of evading questions of human agency. "The Monument" seems itself to put forward a poetic of reticence and withholding, in which the poet can conceal herself behind the objecthood of the artwork.

The mode of close watching to which we are directed is one that rises from observation to speculation, from the declarative statements of the opening section to the *or*'s and *may be*'s that subsequently enter the poem. What seems crucial is that we refrain from deciding on any of the alternatives offered, just as the poem refrains from making any choices among them, and refrains as well from answering directly any of the questions asked by the second speaker. Bishop's monument speaks through its scroll-work, but it speaks just as much through its silences. The poem means to teach its reader a kind of tact when addressing an artwork; and it means, above all, to propose that the best responses to questions are often those that do not so much answer as change the terms of the discussion.

"The Weed" seems a kind of counterpoem to "The Monument," but one equally implicated in the aesthetic of silences and the topography of hidden spaces proposed in its companion. "The Monument" sees a world of dryness, barrenness, and artificiality and pronounces it good; "The Weed" presents a narrative of fertility, variety, and motion and seems to recoil from it. As Robert Parker points out, "The Weed" explores the uneasy territory of feeling associated with the fear of and repulsion from pregnancy (8–16), surely among the most powerfully taboo feelings a woman can express. At the same time, this little parable refrains so powerfully from offering interpretations of itself that the reader need never confront this feeling; the poem's edgy strangeness can be seen as an effect of "metaphysical" style rather than of a concealed burden involving the poet's anxieties about inhabiting a female body. While the poem seems to record an episode of unsuccessful repression, of fertility conjoined with pain, it also seems to keep its own counsel with determination and success.

"I dreamed" begins the poem, at once linking itself with a long tradition of dream-vision poetry, but also invoking Freud, for this vision of posthumous quiet is a wish fulfillment, an expression of that principle of inertia Freud came to term the death instinct:

> I dreamed that dead, and meditating,
> I lay upon a grave, or bed,
> (at least, some cold and close-built bower).
> In the cold heart, its final thought
> stood frozen, drawn immense and clear,
> stiff and idle as I was there;
> and we remained unchanged together
> for a year, a minute, an hour.
> [CP 20]

This "final thought," "frozen . . . immense and clear," recalls the imaginary iceberg Bishop associates with both the soul and the imagination. This comfortable arrangement, which recalls Wordsworth's description of his childhood notion of the grave as "a place of thought where we in waiting lie," is disrupted by "motion," the undesired growth of the weed:

> A slight young weed
> had pushed up through the heart and its
> green head was nodding on the breast . . .
>
> The rooted heart began to change
> (not beat) and then it split apart
> and from it broke a flood of water.
> [CP 20]

The imagery here suggests the process of pregnancy, in which the "head" of the fetus likewise "change[s] its position mysteriously" shortly before the "water" breaks. The heart's "frozen" thought is rendered fluid by this splitting and escapes "through the fine black grains of earth." This "stream" of racing images seems to encapsulate experience; these drops are perhaps analogous to the mammoth's tear, a precious possession that the speaker wishes to hold back, to retain:

> A few drops fell upon my face
> and in my eyes, so I could see
> (or, in that black place, thought I saw)
> that each drop contained a light,
> a small, illuminated scene;
> the weed-deflected stream was made
> itself of racing images.
> [CP 21]

But these scenes flee, and the poem ends with a confrontation between speaker and weed:

> The weed stood in the severed heart.
> "What are you doing there?" I asked.
> It lifted its head all dripping wet
> (with my own thoughts?)
> and answered then: "I grow," it said,
> "but to divide your heart again."
> [CP 21]

"To divide" is another way of saying "to break"; here as elsewhere in the poem Bishop deliberately refuses pathos. She picks a more

technical rather than the idiomatic term, as if to conceal or cam-
ouflage the emotional burden of the poem, part of which is, clearly
enough, a fear of and shying away from emotional experience. Ex-
perience is here associated with the body; it's worth noting that the
speaker claims the "thoughts" (product of the melting of the frozen
"final thought") for her own but refers to the parts of her dream
body impersonally, *the* heart, *the* breast, *the* ribs. Indeed, a good
part of the threat of the weed's little speech is in its referring to
"*your* heart," forcing the speaker to acknowledge that she cannot
remain detached from the heart and what it represents. The poem's
power lies in Bishop's anxieties about the body, about being female,
but also lies in the energy with which those anxieties are concealed
and displaced; the poem seems to ask its readers to take the depth
of that concealment as an index of the power of the anxieties.

Parker reads "The Weed" itself as a critique of or dissent from the
organicist doctrine of the artwork associated with romanticism, and
he is certainly right to see one of the concealed burdens of the poem
as a fear of poetic creativity. Looking at "The Weed" in conjunction
with "The Monument," however, may help us to qualify Bishop's
dissent from organicist ideas. "The Monument," as I've tried to
demonstrate, celebrates an artwork in terms that paradoxically see
it as both living and constructed; the monument has volition and
the capacity for change at the same time that it is set against nature,
specifically contrasted with "real sea or sand or cloud." The weed-
poem of "The Weed," on the other hand, is a natural growth, a direct
outpouring from "the region of the heart," rooted in the physical
body. What Bishop fears, then, is a poetry that is natural and spon-
taneous; to write from the heart, from nature, would be to write as a
woman, to pour forth from the heart in the manner of the sentimen-
tal women poets popular in Bishop's youth: Millay, Wylie, Teasdale,
Ella Wheeler Wilcox. "The Weed" embodies a fear of writing—
but of a particular kind of writing—a writing that would illuminate
what she wishes to leave dark, a writing that would be emotive and
overflowing rather than, in accord with modernist precept, "hard
and dry."

A similar set of anxieties about the female body, and about the poet's
relation to a "nature" associated with the female body, recurs in
"At the Fishhouses," which like "The Weed" is structured around
an opposition between an "illuminated scene" and a knowledge
acquired in darkness. "At the Fishhouses" seems at first straightfor-

wardly to follow the "Tintern Abbey" pattern of landscape description rising to reflective meditation on the human relation to nature. But just as Wordsworth's poem manages to subvert, by its baffling hesitations, qualifications, and counterturns, the model it seems to be in the process of creating, so Bishop's poem is careful to position itself at a distance from the reflective conclusions it offers. In doing so, it establishes a distance as well from Marianne Moore's "A Grave," a poem Bishop obviously had in mind. Moore's poem is centered upon moments of deliberately reductive declarative syntax: "the sea has nothing to give," "the sea is a collector," "it is neither with volition nor consciousness"; in "A Grave," conditional syntax operates negatively, as the sign of deluded perception: "as if there were no such thing as death," "as if it were not that ocean in which dropped things are bound to sink." Moore's poem, then, traces its lineage back to Wordsworth's "Peele Castle," in which an earlier, deluded vision of human reciprocity with nature is replaced by an awareness of nature's otherness and indifference to human concerns. One source of the difficulty of Bishop's poem is the way in which it tries to assimilate strategies deriving from "Tintern Abbey" to the strategies of "Peele Castle," which undoes much of what the earlier poem had constructed. Moore's poem, less conflicted about its parentage, uses similitude and conditionality as tropes of negation, marking the distance between the world and human ideas of it; in Bishop's poem, similitude functions in a significantly more ambiguous way.

The poem begins with an extended passage of low-key description; as in so many crepuscular poems, the observation of a scene just on the brink of disappearance prepares for a later movement from visible to visionary:

> Although it is a cold evening,
> down by one of the fishhouses
> an old man sits netting,
> his net, in the gloaming almost invisible,
> a dark purple-brown,
> and his shuttle worn and polished. . . .
>
> All is silver: the heavy surface of the sea,
> swelling slowly as if considering spilling over,
> is opaque, but the silver of the benches,
> the lobster pots, and masts, scattered
> among the wild jagged rocks,

is of an apparent translucence
like the small old buildings with an emerald moss
growing on their shoreward walls.
[CP 64]

Here an illumination powerfully reminiscent of Wordsworth's light
that never was produces from ordinary materials a transformed
scene that seems almost to have come from an earlier age, an age if
not golden at least silver. The world created by the poet is one of mir-
roring and similitude, obliquely echoing the closed circuit between
sea, building, and poet's state of mind presented in the opening of
"Peele Castle." Indeed, the comparisons employed in this initial sec-
tion of "At the Fishhouses" for the most part liken one element of
the scene to another; the "benches" and "lobster pots" are "like the
small old buildings," the fish tubs with their coating of herring scales
are likened to the "similarly plastered" wheelbarrows, whose "iri-
descent coats" are in turn echoed in the "iridescent flies crawling
on them." The poet seems to partake of the echoing responsiveness
of this world; as her "nose run[s]" and her "eyes water," she per-
haps is "spilling over" in a fashion similar to that which the sea is
"considering," a sort of pathetic fallacy in reverse.

A brief six-line section at the poem's center (there are forty lines
before it and thirty-seven after) quietly establishes a change in the
poem's direction:

> Down at the water's edge, at the place
> where they haul up the boats, up the long ramp
> descending into the water, thin silver
> tree trunks are laid horizontally
> across the gray stones, down and down
> at intervals of four or five feet.
> [CP 65]

The first section notes the gangplanks that "slant up"; here the poet
describes the "long ramp descending into the water." This brief
verse-paragraph brings together the two dominant color schemes of
the poem, the silver of the twilit landscape in the opening section
and the gray of the last section's submerged stones. Silver is the hon-
orific of gray, and so the distance seems small, and yet in its way
absolute, as the sense of human connection, however tenuous, of
the first section yields to a deep aloneness in the last. This interlude

perhaps marks too the moment in the poem where the light of sense goes out, where darkness falls and the poem shifts from perception to memory and "knowledge," for with the opening line of the final section the sea, which had been rendered "opaque" by the evening light, has become "absolutely clear."

This final section begins with a vatic rush of absolutes, in sharp contrast to the looping, hesitant syntax of the poem's opening half:

> Cold dark deep and absolutely clear,
> element bearable to no mortal,
> to fish and to seals . . . One seal particularly
> I have seen here evening after evening.
> [CP 65]

"This . . . is serious music," as the Irish poet Eavan Boland remarks, and it is broken off as quickly as it appears by the appearance of the seal, who seems to arrive, as Boland puts it, from "a whimsical bedtime story" (87). This hesitation, this need to temper the movement toward abstraction with a countermovement toward anecdote and irony, is as much a part of the meaning of the poem as are the statements that close it. The phrase that opens this section posits an absolute distinction between the "mortal," here a synonym for "human," and "fish and . . . seals," a distinction that is in turn placed in doubt by the poet's easy likening of the seal to herself as "a believer in total immersion." This is the only moment of this sort of cleverness in the poem, and it takes away figuratively what it seems to give literally; the seal's form of "total immersion" is rather a different thing from that prescribed by the Baptists. Where earlier in the poem watery eyes and overspilling sea seemed directly congruent, simile here becomes a figure for dissimilitude, marking the distance between human and animal, and the remainder of the poem follows a similar pattern of ambiguity and equivocation between likeness and unlikeness.

After this, the encounter between poet and sea is resumed, but again not without a moment of hesitation, a kind of drawing back or shrinking appropriate to contact with this unforgiving element:

> Cold dark deep and absolutely clear,
> the clear gray icy water . . . Back, behind us,
> the dignified tall firs begin.
> Bluish, associating with their shadows,

a million Christmas trees stand
waiting for Christmas. The water seems suspended
above the rounded gray and blue-gray stones.
[CP 65]

The firs are the most direct recollection of Moore in the poem; like the "firs" that "stand in a procession" and are "reserved as their contours, saying nothing," in "A Grave" (49), Bishop's trees are lightly personified, emblems of ceremony and self-containment in their association "with their shadows." Only after a gesture backward to these humanized presences can the poet direct her gaze steadily down into the sea:

I have seen it over and over, the same sea, the same,
slightly, indifferently swinging above the stones,
icily free above the stones,
above the stones and then the world.
If you should dip your hand in,
your wrist would ache immediately,
your bones would begin to ache and your hand would burn
as if the water were a transmutation of fire
that feeds on stones and burns with a dark gray flame.
If you tasted it, it would first taste bitter,
then briny, then surely burn your tongue.
It is like what we imagine knowledge to be:
dark, salt, clear, moving, utterly free,
drawn from the cold hard mouth
of the world, derived from the rocky breasts
forever, flowing and drawn, and since
our knowledge is historical, flowing, and flown.
[CP 65–66]

The sea is alien and inimical, and the poet can only imagine what touching or tasting it would be like: the thought experiment carried out in these "if" clauses brings back a metaphorical knowledge from a situation in which direct perception cannot be risked. The poet imagines testing the waters, but what she would find out would involve not the sea itself but her own bodily sensations of pain and bitterness; and the sea is described in these sentences only through analogy with another element, fire. The final sentence of the poem seems to offer something like a moral, or at least a conclusion, based on the encounter the poem records, but in fact this predication is heavily qualified and proves to be more of a puzzle than might at first appear. Early drafts read "This is what" rather than "It is like what," showing that Bishop herself was concerned to add a further layer of insulation between tenor and vehicle in the course of revision.

What seems clear enough at first is the characterization of knowledge as a cold, astringent, demanding medium that burns our mouths as it seems to nourish us (the sea being likened to the milk drawn from "rocky breasts"). Attending to the syntax makes us realize, however, that no real connection is established between "knowledge" and "sea"; the sea is being likened to our imagination of knowledge rather than to knowledge itself. If the opening section of the poem presents a world of similitude in which the human seems easily to find a place, the relation between human imagination and the world it inhabits becomes significantly more problematic in the course of the final section. The seal is directly likened to the poet, able to return her gaze, even as its name links it to the element it inhabits ("sea" and "seal"); the firs stand in a far more tenuous relationship of likeness to the poet, their way of "associating with their shadows" constituting an oblique reminder of separateness and death, those final facts of human existence. Finally, the sea is likened to an object of our imagining; we have traveled a long way from the responsive landscape of the first section. Boland defines the "theme" of the poem as follows: "An outward element—this almost intolerable water—will be shown, before the poem finishes, to correspond to the cold interiors of human knowledge" (87). But as knowledge itself recedes from our grasp behind a series of figures, the correspondence posited by the critic comes significantly into question. "Our knowledge is historical," the poet tells us, but does that make it similar to, or distinguish it from, the sea which is "derived . . . forever"?

Likewise, the emotional tenor of these final lines is difficult to pin down. Bishop seems to have been particularly interested in the notion of freezing to death; the speaker of "First Death in Nova Scotia" sees Jack Frost as somehow connected with her cousin's death, while "The Baptism" involves the death of a young woman who comes down with a fever after baptism by total immersion in freezing water. The story "The Farmer's Children" seems particularly suggestive in this regard; in it, a stepmother sends her two stepsons off to sleep in a barn, where they freeze to death. In "At the Fishhouses," the personification of the "rocky breasts" shades "the world" with a maternal quality but also hints that the world may be as indifferent a nurturer as the stepmother of "The Farmer's Children." Robert Lowell protested "the word BREAST," which he found "a little too much in its context perhaps" (letter to Bishop, 21 August 1947, Vassar College Library); presumably Lowell was put off by the suggestion of a monstrously extended maternal body. The suggestion is indeed disturbing and points toward a possible source of the ambivalence in the lines. The opening section of the poem seems to celebrate elegiacally the vanishing world of Bishop's Nova Scotia grandfather, whom she always recalls with warmth in her writings about her childhood. But looming up behind the figure of the grandfather is that of the poet's mother, here displaced into an image of a menacing natural world that nevertheless makes us wish to touch and taste it, a knowledge that is unbearably painful and yet makes one desire "total immersion" in it. For Bishop, knowledge of the mother must be double-edged: sought for to fill the vacancy of an orphaned childhood, terrifying in its connection to insanity.

The "dark and deep" woods Robert Frost once stopped by offered the poet an attractive oblivion; the "dark deep" sea Bishop confronts seems instead an invitation to a painful awareness. The language Bishop applies to her sea, its figuration as a kind of ice that burns, recalls Renaissance love poetry, with its rich vocabulary of paradox for describing the attraction of what causes pain, and recalls as well another poem of Frost's, a little poem similarly indebted to the language of courtly love:

> Some say the world will end in fire,
> Some say in ice.
> From what I've tasted of desire
> I hold with those who favor fire.
> But if it had to perish twice,
> I think I know enough of hate
> To say that for destruction ice
> Is also great
> And would suffice.
> ["Fire and Ice," *Complete Poems* 268]

Frost's jaunty eschatological speculations are far away in tone from the ending of "At the Fishhouses," but I think Frost can help us to see here the apocalyptic strain concealed in Bishop's poem; read beside Frost's famous poem, Bishop's ocean of fire/ice takes on some of the urgency and elevation of the romantic rhetoric of apocalypse.

Bishop is often described as a poet of the visual, whose precise observation is her signature trait, but "At the Fishhouses" seems to leave the visual behind as it ascends, in darkness, to a visionary perspective that encompasses "the world" in its glance. Bishop gives up the making of aesthetic worlds that was so conspicuous a property of her earlier poetry, but her attraction to world making remains, to resurface at moments like this one, where she replaces the world one can actually touch and taste with a world we can encounter only in imagination, only through the speculative experiments conducted in these "if" clauses. Bishop once referred to herself as a "minor female Wordsworth" (letter to Robert Lowell, 11 July 1951, Houghton Library), but "At the Fishhouses," as it moves from a world of fitting and fitted to a perception of the absolute otherness of the natural and a counterassertion of the mind's powers of mastery, explores a major Wordsworthian theme.

Many a visionary revelation has been bequeathed by the ocean's shore; an apocalypse in a dentist's office is a rather more uncommon thing. Even more explicitly than "At the Fishhouses," "In the Waiting Room" makes likeness and unlikeness its central terms of discovery, through which a recognition of "unlikely" similarity becomes a powerfully unsettling form of knowledge. This poem has of late become a privileged locus of revisionist reading, by which I mean interpretation that opposes the widespread image of Bishop as a descriptive poet with a corresponding demand for a recognition, in Lee Edelman's words, of "the rigor of her intellect, the range of her allusiveness, the complexity of her tropes" (181). Such a reappraisal is frequently linked with an account of Bishop's work that sees it as demanding feminist, or lesbian feminist, terms of appraisal, and here the freedom to discuss frankly the issues of sexual preference that critics have acquired since the poet's death has played an important role in changing our conception of her work. During her lifetime Bishop was rarely linked to the developing tradition of a feminist women's writing, despite the professions of feminism she made in the course of interviews; in recent years much critical energy has been devoted to finding in Bishop a more conflicted and skeptical attitude toward gender than earlier critics had remarked.

As I noted earlier, this is a process of "darkening" that resembles that undertaken in the Frost criticism, and again what enables it to a large extent are the gaps and silences prominent in the work of both poets. So Lois Cucullu, discussing the situation of the child

Elizabeth in "In the Waiting Room," puts a great deal of emphasis on the poet's omissions: "What is not said about the child hovers at the periphery of the poem—why no other family members are mentioned; why Elizabeth accompanies her aunt—creating a tension that is never resolved. The lack of information intensifies the child's isolation, making her all the more vulnerable in the reader's mind" (258). The poet's omissions provide a space that the critic can fill with a reading that stresses anxiety and uneasiness. Bishop withholds not just information, however, but also comment; the poem for the most part refuses to interpret the experience it recounts, and the poet as well refrains from placing the thoughts and feelings ascribed to the child of 1918 in the perspective of later knowledge, as if in some way to insist on the *presence* of the moment of crisis the poem records. The reader may choose to see this crisis either as successfully resolved in the grown-up persona that recounts it or as a persistent state that the poet has had to learn to inhabit.

The childlike quality of the speaker's voice in the poem has been frequently remarked. The short sentences and simple vocabulary contribute to this effect, as does the paratactic organization of the passage; the worlds of both waiting room and *National Geographic* are presented in terms similar to those of the travelogue in "Over 2,000 Illustrations and a Complete Concordance": "Everything only connected by 'and' and 'and'" (*CP* 58). The world the child perceives through the *National Geographic* seems, in this initial account, entirely unlike the world she inhabits; it is so thoroughly other that terms of response are scarcely available. The only comment the poem offers about these images is that the breasts of the "black, naked women" were "horrifying." Both the women and the "inside of a volcano" are "black," the Johnson couple are outfitted similarly; the elements of the magazine seem to resemble one another, but their only link to the child's world is through the dehumanizing strangeness of the resemblance between the women's necks and "light bulbs." The child's horrified response to the women's bare breasts seems the index of a scandalous difference, of a fear of the otherness represented by these women who seem more like objects than people.

If parataxis and dissimilarity govern the opening section, the crisis of the poem occurs at a moment in which difference becomes radically and uncomfortably compressed into identity. Heretofore, the child has been presented as autonomous and curiously self-sufficient.

It's more usually children who are accompanied to the dentist by adults than vice versa; Elizabeth's waiting for her aunt, and her rather grown-up ability to absorb herself in a magazine as a means of avoiding social contact and boredom, make her seem, despite her shyness, a composed and self-reliant figure. What shatters that composure is a moment in which reflection is short-circuited by an identification posited in the most radical terms:

> Suddenly, from inside,
> came an *oh!* of pain
> —Aunt Consuelo's voice—
> not very loud or long. . . .

> What took me
> completely by surprise
> was that it was *me:*
> my voice, in my mouth.
> Without thinking at all
> I was my foolish aunt,
> I—we—were falling, falling,
> our eyes glued to the cover
> of the *National Geographic*,
> February, 1918.
> [CP 160]

The child does not merely sympathize with the aunt's pain, does not merely imagine herself in her aunt's position, but seems to *be* her; the copulative is twice used, and the poet insists upon the physical, bodily nature of this identification: "in my mouth," "our eyes."

This sense of identification with the aunt is immediately matched, however, by a sense of self-alienation, by a division within Elizabeth; she loses her composure in more ways than one:

> I said to myself: three days
> and you'll be seven years old.
> I was saying it to stop
> the sensation of falling off
> the round, turning world
> into cold, blue-black space.
> But I felt: you are an *I*,
> you are an *Elizabeth,*

you are one of *them.*
Why should you be one, too?
[*CP* 160]

The child talks to herself, addresses herself as "you," a symptom of self-division reinforced by the gap between "I said" and "I felt," which mirrors the gap between what "I knew," the child's feeling of superiority, and the feeling of the aunt's voice being "in my throat." The child attempts to place herself, prevent herself from falling into the "black" space that has been identified with the otherness of the world represented in *National Geographic,* but is prevented by something that she "felt," by a sensation that seems at least in part physical. Being forced to acknowledge her identity with "*them,*" with the rest of humanity, inflicts a frightening sense of self-division upon the child. Similarly, the attempt to anchor her identity by saying her name only inflicts a further self-estrangement, for the "*Elizabeth*" that others refer to is a social construct, different from the child herself, only *an* Elizabeth.

As it proceeds the passage recodes various elements of the poem's opening through the new feelings initiated by this cry and the child's reaction to it. The "shy" child of the first section has here become a more deeply frightened one; where earlier her shyness seemed social in origin, here her reluctance to raise her eyes is rooted in deeper causes. Where the child of the first section "could read," here she "couldn't look any higher"; the mastery she earlier exercised through the glance is undone as she becomes implicated in what she sees. While the "trousers and skirts and boots" point in one way to sexual differentiation, in another the list, as it arrives at the "boots" (which recall the unisexual dress of Osa and Martin Johnson), collapses gender difference into identity, and humanness into objecthood. Where before, the waiting room had been filled with grown-up people, here people are reduced to an assemblage of parts and pieces, knees, articles of clothing, hands; people have been transformed into objects "lying under the lamps," almost as if their heads had been replaced by these lamps in a fashion similar to that in which the heads of the naked women had come to resemble light bulbs.

In the prose piece "The Country Mouse," which ends with a version of the incident recounted in the poem, the child asks herself, "How had I got tricked into such a false position?" (*Collected Prose* 33). The "position" of the poet, in relation to the child whose experience she describes, is similarly problematic. The child seems to fumble for a word, with an interruption by the grown-up poet; but it's unclear who finally provides the word: "How—I didn't know any / word for it—how 'unlikely'" (*CP* 161). This uncertainty parallels the sliding of tenses in this passage, in which the retrospect of "I knew that nothing stranger / had ever happened" is immediately followed by the present tense of "Why should I be my aunt, / or me, or anyone?" The adult's recollection of the child's feelings are suddenly replaced by the voice of the child's protest. The nature of that protest makes "unlikely" an especially "false" word to have chosen, for likeness—the likeness the child discovers between herself and "*them*"—is precisely what is at issue here. The succeeding lines, in their play on the likeness involved in rhyme, seem to underline the irony:

> How had I come to be here,
> like them, and overhear
> a cry of pain that could have
> got loud and worse but hadn't?
> [*CP* 161]

Rime riche, the overly exact rhyme of a pair like *here/hear*, always seems to strike a false note in English; it is a sign of insufficient differentiation. In this free-verse poem particularly, this odd homophonic rhyme seems to mark an unwanted similarity.

"How had I come to be . . . like them?" we may read this sentence as asking, and the child seems to expend an almost petulant energy in the various repetitions of this question. A number of critics have interpreted the burden of the poem as the child's sense of "connectedness," to use Bonnie Costello's term (119). Critics like Lois Cucullu and Lee Edelman imply a transformation of this sense into a feeling of solidarity along gender lines. The poem's persistent refusal to interpret itself, however, makes available another attitude toward the feelings of aversion and distress it so powerfully generates. In a draft of "The Country Mouse," the child remarks to herself, "I was in for it now. . . . I would get old and fat like that woman opposite me" (Elizabeth Bishop Papers, Vassar College Library). When the poet asks, "What similarities . . . / made us all just one?" this "just" indicates that the thought entails a sense of diminishment, one that makes the child resist this leveling equivalence of self and other. The young Elizabeth might be seen as rejecting with all her energies the horrifying knowledge that she is like the people with whom she shares the waiting room. This knowledge is presented in imagery that resembles that of "At the Fishhouses," where knowledge is represented as a burning, uninhabitable liquid:

> The waiting room was bright
> and too hot. It was sliding
> beneath a big black wave,
> another, and another.
> [CP 161]

Indeed, the entire world seems to become insufficiently distinct and separate, as the "night and slush" outside echo the "big black wave" breaking inside.

The feelings generated by Bishop's poem here recall those of Wordsworth's "Intimations Ode," which likewise explores the loss involved as a child's sense of separateness and immunity from the human fate fades into a sense of similarity to others and an acknowledgment of shared mortality. As in the "Intimations Ode," sympathy and pain are conjoined in Bishop's poem; human sympathy is the product of human suffering. But the thoughts Elizabeth has as she confronts the universality of suffering are anything but soothing. While Wordsworth wishes to persuade his readers that the fading of the visionary gleam is no reason to grieve, the Ode remains suffused with a longing for the feeling of absolute autonomy he describes in the Fenwick note: "I used to brood over the stories of Enoch and Elijah, and almost to persuade myself that, whatever might become of others, I should be translated, in something of the same way, to heaven" (*Poetical Works* 4:463). Bishop need not mount so elaborate an apology for the antisocial element of her vision; that element remains far more deeply hidden in her poem. Her reticence should not obscure, however, the side of the poem that strains away from the feeling of connection and sympathy, back toward a radically individualistic sense of separateness and mastery.

The poem is a good deal less explicit than the prose sketch, the drafts of which are in turn more explicit than the finished version. In the draft, the "fat and old" woman appears as an emblem of what it is that Elizabeth is; the figure has been almost entirely subtracted in the poem. The rhetorical question that ends the story, "*Why* was I a human being," seems more pointed than any of the many other rhetorical questions posed in the poem. The poem, then, artfully prolongs and varies the moment of crisis, partly by refusing to make its terms as straightforward, and the gain in aesthetic power is plain enough. As in "The Weed," Bishop takes an unpalatable feeling—in this case the hatred of being human, the hatred of feeling that one is connected in some way to the "fat," "old," and "false" creatures with whom one is surrounded—and embeds it in a narrative that refuses to interpret itself, that approaches this content obliquely. Wordsworth, expressing a similar content, resorts to an elaborate insistence on denying any sense of regret at the loss of the antisocial "splendor" he initially celebrates; Bishop equivocates, leaving her attitude toward the fall into connectedness significantly ambiguous. Sympathy grows out of pain, but sympathy is itself painful, and the child resists. "In the Waiting Room" shows that Bishop is not afraid to explore, even if only obliquely, a territory that borders on the egotistical sublime.

Bishop's tropes of likeness become, then, a means of exploring an array of issues regarding the self's relation to a range of others— nature, other people, other poets—and I hope the readings above have suggested something of the complexity and power of those explorations. Close attention to the dynamics of likeness and un- likeness in Bishop's work may help as well to displace, or at least qualify, the image of Bishop's modesty, in terms of both her am- bitions and the character of her self-assertions. I've discussed "At the Fishhouses" as if Bishop were including herself among those for whom the sea is a hostile, uninhabitable element, but her imaginings of unbearably painful contact are phrased in the second person: "if *you* should dip your hand in it . . . If *you* tasted it," leaving open the possibility that the poet, a "believer in total immersion," may find comfort where the reader finds pain. The meaning of Frost's "Fire and Ice" lies in the easy, familiar tone with which the poet professes his acquaintance with the agents of destruction, the equable and ap- praising eye with which he imagines apocalypse. Though Bishop's persona is hardly so self-assured as Frost's, she at least hints at draw- ing a distinction between the "you" and the "I" that are eventually united in the "we" of the closing lines, a distinction that places the reader on the outside, unable to bear the "total immersion" practiced by the poet. Slyly hidden though it may be, a distinctly unaccom- modating tone runs through Bishop's poetry, and readers have less reason to make themselves at home there than many have supposed.

It's disappointing, then, that the impact of Bishop's work on other poets has had little to do with the questioning conducted through her tropes of likeness. Willard Spiegelman defines Bishop's influence in terms of "domestic themes . . . and . . . colloquial diction" (158), and a number of more specific aspects of Bishop's style—short lines, plain syntax, indefinite closure—have become widespread characteristics of the contemporary lyric. These traits are elements of a more general disposition toward modesty of scale and avoidance of rhetoric that is at the root of Bishop's appeal to many contemporary poets. Those virtues are attractive even to poets whose sensibilities are markedly unlike Bishop's; scaling back the claims and ambitions of poetry shields the lyric voice from skeptical deflation in a world where, Theodor Adorno concludes, "the dimensions of poetry have shrunk" (*Aesthetic Theory* 24). Bishop's achievement is generally taken in contemporary practice to validate notions of craft, decorum, and attentive description, values inculcated in many an MFA program and subscribed to by many a mainstream poet, even where Bishop's influence is only oblique or unthought of.

Even in the work of Bishop's best and most conscious inheritors, it is these values that seem to constitute Bishop's legacy. Sandra McPherson, for instance, surely one of the best younger poets to have taken Bishop's work as a model, rarely uses figures of similitude, opting instead for a program of patient and exact description. Simile, in mainstream poetic practice, for the most part plays a decorative role, operating as an emblem of the poetic in what might otherwise seem lineated prose, for the imperatives of the plain style—unobtrusive craft, avoidance of rhetoric, and studied artlessness—leave poetry in constant danger of tumbling into the prosaic. Let us examine a poem by Sharon Olds, certainly one of the more prominent and highly decorated poets of her generation. "Sex Without Love" is perhaps a bit unusual in originating in thought rather than incident, but typical, I think, of mainstream poetic practice in the way it uses simile:

> How do they do it, the ones who make love
> without love? Beautiful as dancers,
> gliding over each other like ice-skaters
> over the ice, fingers hooked
> inside each other's bodies, faces
> red as steak, wine, wet as the
> children at birth whose mothers are going to
> give them away. How do they come to the
> come to the   come to the   God   come to the

still waters, and not love
the one who came there with them, light
rising slowly as steam off their joined
skin? These are the true religious,
the purists, the pros, the ones who will not
accept a false Messiah, love the
priest instead of the God. They do not
mistake the lover for their own pleasure,
they are like great runners: they know they are alone
with the road surface, the cold, the wind,
the fit of their shoes, their over-all cardio-
vascular health—just factors, like the partner
in the bed, and not the truth, which is the
single body alone in the universe
against its own best time.
[*The Dead and the Living* 57]

Figures of similitude abound in the poem, but it quickly becomes apparent that those figures have a descriptive rather than cognitive function. Comparing sexual partners to dancers or ice skaters merely compares persons engaged in one sort of activity to persons engaged in another. This is not to say, of course, that the poem lacks craft; the image of skaters gliding "*over* the ice" provides a nicely subdued hint of the human coldness of these loveless lovers, who do not genuinely interpenetrate even when "hooked / inside each other's bodies"; and the suggestions of athletic grace, concentration, and precision embodied in dancing and skating are picked up in the extended final metaphor at the poem's end. But neither simile involves the intellect; neither is a discovery. Likewise, "steak" and "wine" bring in secondarily a set of associations with sensual pleasure and satisfaction, but again those associations, linked to sexuality, are hardly surprising. The simile involving babies is certainly thought-provoking, but a little thought reveals that it is entirely gratuitous; since babies whose mothers are going to give them away are exactly as wet, no more and no less, as babies whose mothers are going to keep them, this elaboration serves no purpose but to remind us that sex without love may lead to unwanted pregnancy, a message better suited to public service announcements than poetry.

Again, I don't mean to deny the craft of the poem, which is very much evident in the extended closing simile, whose particular trick is to make over sexuality, which we normally think of as a pleasurable indulgence, into an ascetic discipline. Hanging the prefix "cardio-" out at the end of the line nicely conveys these loveless lovers' detachment of the heart (for which this is a decidedly detached locution) from other matters. But ultimately, the poem's challenge to conventional values, both sexual and poetic, is recontained through the distance and isolation in which the poem envelops these in some sense unimaginable persons. The poet professes to admire these exemplars of lucidity, who, unlike the rest of us, refuse to accept the "false," who "do not mistake" one thing for another. But ultimately, the poet consigns them to their aloneness, professing her incomprehension; she admits the superior truth of a lucid, unmistaken consciousness but prefers to remain within the emotive comfort of false beliefs. By the poem's end, its initial challenge to conventional values of emotional warmth and mutuality has been entirely defused.

Baron Wormser's "The Mowing Crew" manifests an even more radical defensiveness toward the operations of the intellect, suggesting that, at its extremes, the distrust of abstract formulation prevalent in mainstream practice may become generalized into a distrust of language altogether. The poem brings to mind immediately Robert Frost's poems on mowing, and behind them Andrew Marvell's mower poems, as well the biblical sources that underlie the analogy between flesh and grass. At the same time, the poem downplays its connection to this dense network of poetic associations, deliberately avoiding any appearance of being allusive or literary.

The mourners drive away
And talk about the graves.

Old man Shorey can't
Kept the mowing boys at work.
They take off
Their shirts and lie in the sun
Beside their machines
And go to sleep.

Young as they
Are, the grass doesn't bother them.
Their hair is girl-long,
They smile and spit.

Even when one of their own
Dies with his car on

The state highway, they don't
Seem to exactly believe it.

Standing at the graveside
They look placidly
At the dark, riven ground
And nod to each other
As if it were another
Hot day and they felt
Drowsy and wished to lie down.
[*Good Trembling* 47]

The poem certainly embodies a high standard of craft; cleanly writ-
ten and economical, almost entirely devoid of abstraction, it seems
a model of the aesthetic that values showing over telling. The fun-
damental metaphor is suggested with an inobtrusive piece of clever-
ness; the dangling syntax of "Young as they / Are," and the way the
enjambment alters the stress pattern natural in prose, encourage the
semantically impossible but poetically suggestive reading that this
clause modifies "the grass." Clever, too, is the slightly self-conscious
wit on display in the enjambment of "Dies with his car on / The state
highway," with its muted echo of the phrase "died with his boots
on." And another piece of deliberately awkward syntax, the split
infinitive of "to exactly believe,"[11] nicely catches the idiom of the
characters the poem presents, as well as mimicking, in the delayed
arrival of the verb, the resistance to belief it describes.

   The poem seems predicated on a notion of the superiority of in-
articulacy and silence to language. The mourners "talk about the
graves" rather than those who fill them, implying that language is
empty or beside the point; throughout the poem, the poet seems
to cast his sympathies with the apparently wordless "boys," who
"spit" and "nod to each other" but don't seem to talk, as if speech
were, like death, one of those aspects of the adult world "they don't
seem to exactly believe" in. Metaphor is used unobtrusively; both of
the "as" constructions in the poem function reflexively, likening the
"boys" to themselves. This further reinforces the sense of enclosure
within the body that the poem posits, and seems to admire, in these
figures, its implied assumption that people who do physical labor,
and are thus more in touch with the material world and the earth
itself, have a richer and more meaningful sense of life and death than
alienated intellectuals, even if they cannot articulate that sense. The

poem, then, seems to prefer the comfort of a lyrical ineffability to any sort of abstract utterance, and perhaps to any utterance at all; the Freudian notion of the death wish clearly informs the poem but is presented entirely without abstract formulation. An aesthetic of transparency shapes formal choices throughout the poem, in keeping with the distrust of reflective abstraction apparent on the plane of content; the poem's wordplay is deeply submerged.

The only prominent break in the idiom of naturalness the poem seems to aim for is the adjective "riven," a poeticism that no contemporary speaker would use in speech. But this piece of poetic diction is more, I think, than simply a flaw in the decorum of the poem; it's an indication of a more general anxiety about the poetic status of this utterance, a sort of return of the literariness repressed in the endeavor toward a transparent, conversational style. At this moment of heightened drama, the poet seems to lose faith in the aesthetic of transparency and falls back on a highly artificial piece of phrasing. It's a small moment, but one symptomatic of the dilemma of what I've been calling mainstream verse, caught between the contradictory imperatives of a focus on the rendering of experience that tends, because of the way it defines *experience,* to lead toward a prosy flatness and a need to assert the poetic status of its productions that leads toward obtrusive poeticism.

Neither Olds's poem nor Wormser's exhibits Bishop's influence in any direct fashion, but both represent a norm of practice heavily informed by the poetic strategies that Bishop is usually taken to exemplify. Powerful and unsettling as Bishop's work is, her influence, or more accurately the set of assumptions that the success of her work has been taken to underwrite, has not, I think, been an unequivocally productive one. Yet if her influence is the problem, it might also be the cure, for as I hope I have demonstrated, Bishop's poetic contains within it strategies that go far toward incorporating the demands of a skeptical lucidity with lyrical attitudes. Her contribution in this regard is generally taken to be her strategies of modesty and limitation, which obliquely undertake a skeptical deflation of a set of outmoded myths of cultural heroism inherited from romanticism and modernism.[12] As I hope I've demonstrated, however, the implications of Bishop's play with similitude and dissimilitude in some ways cut across those of her tactics of withholding; the "precious"[13] quality produced by her combination of precise observation and self-effacing presentation is undone by the tough-minded probing accomplished through her manipulation of tropes. Greater attention to the dynamic of Bishop's tropes of likeness might point toward ways in which contemporary poets can expand their horizons beyond descriptive lyricism and recover some of the challenge that Bishop's work, at its best, embodies.

Elizabeth

Bishop's

Silences

For the author of an enormous cosmologi-
cal epic based on conversations with spirits
through a Ouija board, James Merrill's begin-
nings as a poet were surprisingly conventional.
Merrill's first two volumes, *First Poems* (1951)
and *The Country of a Thousand Years of Peace* (1959), are typical
products of 1950s formalism: distanced, decorous, carefully crafted,
and highly impersonal. *Water Street* (1962) marks a turn toward
autobiography, a turn that coincides, to some extent, with an evo-
lution toward a more open, colloquial style that, while remaining
ostentatiously clever, is a good deal more offhand and less calculated
than Merrill's earlier idiom. Several subsequent volumes further the
autobiographical project, and indeed the first part of the trilogy,
"The Book of Ephraim,"[1] focuses as much on the impact of the
Ouija board sessions on the lives of Merrill and his partner, David
Jackson, as on the content of the revelation itself. As it progresses,
however, the trilogy becomes more urgently engaged with a set of
public and political issues; the poem explicitly presents itself as ex-

panding Merrill's horizons beyond the "CHRONICLES OF LOVE AND LOSS" (*CLS* 176) that had been his chief theme.

One could, then, plot the course of Merrill's career as a movement from impersonal to autobiographical to ethical and political subject matter, with a corresponding loosening of the stylistic rigidities of the early work. The trajectory would be, broadly, from private to public, from a poetry of aesthetic enclosure, hermetic and esoteric, to a poetry that, though in its Ouija board phase decidedly esoteric, nevertheless engages public issues in a more direct and accessible fashion. But this would be to simplify far too radically. Throughout Merrill's career, beside the self-revealing poems written in a looser, more direct style, appear others as formidably opaque and deliberately artificial as any in his first few volumes. Merrill's persistent attraction to the notion of a private art addressed to an elite and presented in a language thoroughly purified, in the Mallarméan sense, is an index of a general uneasiness about the poet's relation to his audience. In fact, Merrill's chief means of opening his style has been through ironic inversions of common idiom, in which the poet stands apart from the languages of public discourse even as he employs them; even the most accessible of Merrill's poems establish a wary balance between openness and distance. Rather than a progression from closed to open, private to public, Merrill's development is informed by a tension between public and private modes of expression from the moment, marked by *Water Street* (1962), that it assumes a distinctive and characteristic shape.

Throughout Merrill's work runs an uneasy fear that any publicly available language is necessarily inauthentic, which provides a deeper motivation than mere personal reticence for his attachment to strategies of indirection. This fear is focused in a passage in "An Urban Convalescence" in which Merrill advances and then retracts a decidedly "public" piece of phrasing. His thoughts are provoked by the razing of a building on his block in New York; the poet reflects on the social pathology that drives the constant erasure and re-creation of the city:

> It is not even as though the new
> Buildings did very much for architecture.
>
> Suppose they did. The sickness of our time requires
> That these as well be blasted in their prime.
> You would think the simple fact of having lasted

Threatened our cities like mysterious fires.
[WS 5]

But almost immediately, the poet turns round upon himself to reject this formulation of the problem:

> There are certain phrases which to use in a poem
> Is like rubbing silver with quicksilver. Bright
> But facile, the glamour deadens overnight.
> For instance, how 'the sickness of our time'
>
> Enhances, then debases, what I feel.
> [WS 5]

This moment of self-revision gestures toward an opening out from the closure of aesthetic objecthood within which the early poems had been confined; by representing within itself the process of revision the poem seems a less self-sufficient entity, more available to the reader. If earlier in the poem Merrill recoils from the image of his walls "weathering in the general view," here he invites the reader to see, in a sense, the plumbing of the poem, the process of producing and rejecting a phrase that normally remains hidden behind the finished work.

At the same time, it's important to note exactly why Merrill finds the phrase "sickness of our time" unacceptable. The expression is a decidedly public formulation, a property of the jeremiad writer. Merrill rejects it, not as one kind of poet might, because of its inadequacy to the public reality it means to represent, its substitution of a metaphysical principle for concrete causes, but because of its inadequacy to private feelings, because it "debases . . . what I *feel*." Merrill rejects a debased public language not in the name of truth to things as they are but in the name of truth to the private world of emotion. The poem ends, then, by looking toward the reconstruction not of the public realm whose damage the poem laments but of an interiorized "house" that is the product of individual experience:

>   back into my imagination
> The city glides, like cities seen from the air,
> Mere smoke and sparkle to the passenger
> Having in mind another destination
>
> Which now is not that honey-slow descent
> Of the Champs-Elysées, her hand in his,

But the dull need to make some kind of house
Out of the life lived, out of the love spent.
[*WS* 6]

This tendency to test issues of public concern by the measure of individual feeling characterizes the turn toward a more public subject matter and more accessible expression that occurs at this point in Merrill's career. He greets the Apollo moon landing, for instance, thus:

There on the moon, her meaning now one swift
Footprint, a man my age with a glass face
Empty of insight signals back through space
To the beclouded cortex which impelled his drift.
["Pieces of History," *BTE* 9]

For Merrill, the "swift footprint" (a mocking echo of Neil Armstrong's "one small step") is a definitive stamp of disillusionment, of the eradication of the natural wonder once represented by the pagan Artemis. Merrill likens himself to the astronaut, but the emptiness he feels arises from a radically different source; the "beclouded" earth represents both the aimlessness of the impulse driving the astronaut's exploration and the state of the poet's mind as he looks into the glass face of the television and sees himself, or at least a view that includes him in the beclouded world that looks on at the astronaut's exploits. At its extreme, this play of similitude and mirroring threatens to enclose the poet within a solipsistic space of reflection where, in characteristically symbolist fashion, the world outside the poet comes to be seen as little more than a projection of the poet's mental states.

Symbolism turns on an ambiguity between literal and metaphoric, or if ambiguity is too strong a word, on an extension and elaboration of metaphor to the point where it threatens to gain priority over the objects it modifies. As Christine Brooke-Rose points out, symbolism thus approaches a kind of zero degree of metaphor: "The poet imagines a scene and describes it literally, so that, strictly speaking, in the sense of words changing other words, there is no metaphor" (29). Merrill does not always push to the boundaries of metaphor in this way, but often enough a simple construct of likeness exfoliates into a richly imagined (or described) scene of its own, moving far from its metaphorical function. These lines from "Willowware Cup" describe an aged figure depicted on a teacup:

Soon, of these May mornings, rising in mist, he will ask
Only to blend—like ink in flesh, blue anchor

Needled upon drunkenness while its destroyer
Full steam departs, the stigma throbbing, intricate—

Only to blend into a crazing texture.
[*BTE* 36]

This extraordinarily condensed passage seems to encapsulate an entire narrative through a rapid series of substitutions. The fading of the cup's colors is likened to the spread of tattooer's ink through skin, but the metaphorical function of the image quickly moves to the background as it is elaborated into a richly detailed vignette: a drunken sailor receiving a tattoo in the shape of a blue anchor, meanwhile missing the sailing of the warship to whose crew he belongs. Richard Sáez, in his brilliant unpacking of this passage, suggests that the tattoo that comes to the poet's mind here belongs to a former lover (163). Absent confirmation by the poet himself, of course, the point is unknowable, but the critic's temptation to provide an autobiographical referent is an index of the powerful "reality effect" generated by the passage; indeed, this narrative moment seems vastly more real than what it ostensibly modifies, which after all is only the feelings ascribed by the poet to an image on a teacup. An easy commerce, or confusion, between figurative and literal likewise occurs at the heart of this vignette, where the presumably real destroyer is made grammatically to belong to the anchor, which is only a tattooed representation. Ordinarily, the modified object in a metaphor holds a kind of ontological priority over the modifying vehicle (de Man 6–9); when a poet describes his lover as like a flower, the lover is concrete and specific, the flower generic and, in a fashion, abstract. Merrill's metaphors frequently reverse this priority, a reversal that corresponds to the elevation, in his poetry, of aesthetic constructs over observed facts, his sense that "life [is] fiction in disguise" (*BTE* 14). This predilection underlies as well Merrill's taste for dreamscapes in his poetry, explicit in the case of poems like "The Mad Scene," "Dreams About Clothes," and section T of *The Book of Ephraim*, implicit in poems like "Part of the Vigil" and "Days of 1935." The dream offers the poet an opportunity to elaborate a world richly detailed and saturated with implication without subordinating himself to mimetic demands.

The poem "Childlessness," from *Water Street*, provides an excellent example of Merrill's symbolist mode, in which poems are constructed around the armature of a metaphor so far extended as to become, in a sense, the "reality" the poem attempts to represent. Extended metaphors are, of course, a common feature of the neometaphysical mode prevalent in 1950s poetry; Richard Wilbur's "Mind," for instance, performs a kind of tour de force in pushing past the limits a reader might have imagined possible a simile that is anything but intuitive:

> Mind in its purest play is like some bat
> That beats about in caverns all alone,
> Contriving by a kind of senseless wit
> Not to conclude against a wall of stone.

> It has no need to falter or explore;
> Darkly it knows what obstacles are there,
> And so may weave and flitter, dip and soar
> In perfect courses through the blackest air.
> [Wilbur 12]

The effect of wit arises here from the distance between the two elements of the simile, a distance played off against the manifold similarities the poet discovers, so that by the poem's final stanza the likeness has been so completely demonstrated that the poet can reverse his field:

> And has this simile a like perfection?
> The mind is like a bat. Precisely. Save
> That in the very happiest intellection
> A graceful error may correct the cave.
> [Wilbur 12]

While the central organizing metaphor of "Childlessness" is no less unlikely on its face than that of "Mind," Merrill draws no attention to the dissimilitude of its elements but rather assumes this highly arbitrary analogy as a given:

> The weather of this winter night, my dream-wife
> Ranting and raining, wakes me. Her cloak blown back
> To show the lining's dull lead foil
> Sweeps along asphalt.
> [WS 28]

Brooke-Rose notes that, in metaphors that work by direct substitution of one term for another (Simple Replacement metaphors, in her terminology), the use of the possessive adjective, as in "*my* dreamwife," particularizes the metaphoric element in a way that "assumes familiarity," that calls upon the reader immediately to recognize the statement as metaphorical (46). The introduction of the metaphor through apposition rather than through simile likewise concedes nothing to the reader; unlike Wilbur, Merrill makes no attempt to persuade the reader of the fitness of this central analogy. Wilbur accommodates his readers by implicitly making room for their initial skepticism; Merrill demands a reader willing to grant the poet his figurative premise.

The feeling of privacy generated by Merrill's poem arises, then, not merely from the veiling of a crucial datum of interpretation, the poet's homosexuality, but also from its strategy of metaphor; indeed, a striking number of Merrill's love poems, among them "The Mad Scene," "Part of the Vigil," and "The Kimono," begin with a similarly abrupt positing of a metaphoric *donnée* to which the reader must pay assent as the price of his or her entry into the poem. Intimacy of subject is reflected in an intimacy of expression; the metaphoric leaps that open the poems seem designed to weed out the reader unwilling to enter the self-enclosed aesthetic worlds the poems offer. In "Childlessness," this sense of intimacy is confirmed by further use of possessive pronouns and references to metaphorical objects whose real correlatives the poem leaves understood rather than stated:

> Outside, I hear her tricklings
> Arraign my little plot:
> Had it or not agreed
> To transplantation for the common good
> Of certain rare growths yielding guaranteed
> Gold pollen, gender of suns, large, hardy,
> Enviable blooms?
> [WS 28]

Here the metaphoric significance of "plot" seems both crucial and vaguely suggested. The poet's reference to "my little plot" gestures toward something apparently familiar to the poet but which the reader must supply by extrapolation; the verb "arraign" indicates that more than a piece of ground is at stake. This strategy of reference back to a ground of private feeling governs the poem's deployment of its imagery throughout:

> I lie and think about the rain,
> How it has been drawn up from the impure ocean,
> From gardens lightly, deliberately tainted;
> How it falls back, time after time,
> Through poisons visible at sunset
> When the enchantress, masked as friend, unfurls
> Entire bolts of voluminous pistachio,
> Saffron, and rose.
> [WS 28]

Merrill here raises subjects he touches on a good deal more directly, if telegraphically, in "Ephraim," where he refers to "The drug-addicted / Farms. Welkin the strangler" (CLS 55). The enchantress comes "masked as friend" at sunset because, as most city dwellers know, polluted air makes evening skies more richly colored. Merrill gestures here toward a large public issue, but through the medium of imagery drawn from the fairy tale; pollution is used as a metaphor for the poet's "tainted" emotional state.

The poem has the opportunity at this point to expand its focus outward to matters of public policy; what happens is rather the opposite: the poem moves inward, in an almost circular fashion, taking the result of one figurative series as input for another:

> These, as I fall back to sleep,
> And other slow colors clothe me, glide
> To rest, then burst along my limbs like buds,
> Like bombs from the navigator's vantage,
> Waking me, lulling me.
> [WS 28]

This image of aerial bombardment is generated not by narrative or discursive logic but rather by connection to the imagery used before; the sunset's colors are those of a bomb burst, and the falling bombs echo the falling raindrops. Throughout the poem, transitions are made in this fashion; one chain of imagery generates another, as the scenario of bombardment here produces its own aftermath:

> Later I am shown
> The erased metropolis reassembled

On sampans, freighted each
With toddlers, holy dolls, dead ancestors.
[WS 28]

No metropolis has appeared in the poem heretofore; it has been elicited by the image of bombing, and yet it is referred to by the definite rather than the indefinite article. It is a city Merrill knows, and expects his readers to accept as familiar. The strategy is characteristically modernist—the very title of *The Waste Land* is a classic instance—and serves both to include and to exclude, establishing intimacy with the reader who understands this elision of a longer specification into a symbol presented by a single image, distancing the reader unwilling to make the leap, and establishing in no uncertain terms that the poem's images refer to a vision within, rather than a reality outside, the poet.

In its final movement, the poem returns upon itself, taking up at its end an image introduced in the opening lines:

A world. The cloak thrown down for it to wear
In token of past servitude
Has fallen onto the shoulders of my parents
Whom it is eating to the bone.
[WS 29]

The definite article in "The cloak" again implies the reader's familiarity; indeed, the passage simply cannot be interpreted unless one refers the image back to its function in the earlier passage. The "cloak" of falling rain in the opening lines has become the water seeping through the ground in this final passage, a transformation readily enough understood, but only in reference to the previous use of the image; the poem uses, as if it were conventional and familiar, an emblem that it has itself established.

This sort of symbolist lyric, self-enclosed and self-generating, coexists in Merrill's oeuvre with its seeming stylistic opposite, ballads that, while they make little attempt to simulate the directness and naïveté (in Schiller's sense) of traditional ballads, nevertheless perform the ballad's task of story telling. Ranged between these two poles stands most of Merrill's work, manifesting various degrees of opacity and transparency. To some extent the privacy of Merrill's poetic is opened out by his ongoing elaboration of an autobiographical myth; as similar concerns recur in the poems, and as a life story is progressively revealed and filled in, the poems create a context for themselves, create an interpretive framework that to some extent retrospectively clarifies passages that had been opaque, and provides the poet a shorthand that allows him to achieve a high level of condensation. By *Braving the Elements*, this habit is so well established that Merrill can insert into "Days of 1935" a sort of parenthetical footnote to a poem that appears only later on in that volume: "(cf. those 'Days / Of 1971')" (17). So in "Lost in Translation" the poet remarks parenthetically "I wander through the ruin of S / Now and then, wondering at the peacefulness" (*DC* 10). Readers unfamiliar with Merrill's ongoing lyric autobiography will be reduced to guesswork on confronting these lines; those who know will recognize "S" as Strato, a former lover, and see that the "ruins" here are entirely figurative, a representation of the poet's present feelings about the affair. Stephen Yenser remarks, with reference to an earlier passage in "Lost in Translation," that Merrill "has come to write *as though* he could rely on the reader's acquaintance [with his family history]. His allusions conjure the familiarity they seem to presume" (12). This tactic of presuming familiarity with the poet's autobiographical myth is an extension of the strategy of using the possessive pronoun and definite article to a similar end in the presentation of metaphor.

What this tactic indicates as well is the erosion of a shared ground of culture between poet and reader. Merrill's is an erudite poetry that frequently makes allusion to standard monuments of Western cultural tradition. Those allusions are generally limited to works belonging to and preceding the high modernist period; although he makes substantial reference to popular culture, Merrill for the most part avoids assuming his reader's familiarity with any particular segment of contemporary cultural or intellectual production. Freud is often alluded to in Merrill's work, contemporary psychologists not at all; nineteenth-century opera is frequently invoked, twentieth-century opera scarcely ever. The one element of contemporary literary culture consistently alluded to in Merrill's work is his own poetry. I don't think this is in the least megalomaniac; what it means, simply, is that contemporary readers of poetry cannot be counted on to belong to the same universe of books and ideas; there is no body of contemporary culture and knowledge (with the exception, to some extent, of science) that readers can be expected to recognize, that the poet can take for granted. Under these circumstances, it seems only natural for the poet who seeks the compression and breadth that allusion makes possible to fall back on making his or her own work a central repository of allusive possibility.

The project of creating an autobiographical myth itself implies, however, a translation of private experience into public terms, no small order for a poet whose experience has been anything but representative, and whose horror of the debased languages of public discourse goes so deep. In "An Urban Convalescence," as noted above, Merrill enacts his dissatisfaction with available public terms by inscribing, then erasing, an instance of such discourse in his poem. In "Childlessness," conversely, at the moment in which the poem might fall into a recognizably public (in this case environmentalist) mode of address, the poet insulates his language from that possibility by translating his concerns into the language of the fairy tale, by representing a set of economic and political facts through the image of the "enchantress." But this tactic, Merrill must have seen, is in itself a kind of tour de force whose success depends on its placement within the sort of self-generating, self-referential framework elaborated by that poem. While mythic or folk-tale analogues continue to be important in Merrill's life writing, they have come to be shaded with considerable irony as Merrill uses them as much to mockingly draw attention to the distance between contemporary situation and mythic analogue as to liken one to the other; in this way, he ironically inverts the mythopoesis that characterizes 1950s formalist verse. And the language of public discourse, rather than being excised, as it is in various ways in "An Urban Convalescence" and "Childlessness," enters the poems, but enters them through the avenue of an ironic exploration, and exploitation, of cliché.

"The Broken Home," certainly among the richest of Merrill's autobiographical reflections, exemplifies this strategy of ironic distancing from both mythic analogue and the language of cliché. The broken home of the title, of course, is the first of many common idioms the poem holds up for scrutiny. That that idiom might have been spoken sincerely, if euphemistically, by his parents' generation but would hardly be used "straight" in his own social world serves to indicate both the distance from which the poet views the events he recounts and the gulf between the social mores, and thus the public language, of the 1930s and the 1960s, for Merrill was well aware that a new vocabulary for describing social facts implies a new set of attitudes toward those facts. At the same time, the definite article again assumes the reader's familiarity, and when this image makes its one appearance, in the last of the poem's seven sonnets, it has clearly expanded beyond its specific reference to Merrill's childhood to take on an emblematic quality. A kind of euhemeristic transformation seems to be taking place before our eyes as "the broken home" becomes separated as an archetype from "the real house" whose entirely other fate is also recounted.

The poem begins with a schematic representation of the poet's distance from "normal" family life, which he represents by an image that, gilt and framed, seems to have come as much from medieval religious painting as from contemporary life:

> Crossing the street,
> I saw the parents and the child
> At their window, gleaming like fruit
> With evening's mild gold leaf.
> [*ND* 27]

The poet, in contrast, huddles around an artificial light:

> In a room on the floor below,
> Sunless, cooler—a brimming
> Saucer of wax, marbly and dim—
> I have lit what's left of my life.
> [*ND* 27]

"Sunless," we realize, is a pun, a bad one, and the poet will test the limits of the reader's tolerance for bad puns at a number of points in the poem. What he seems to ask of his life, at this moment, is this:

> Tell me, tongue of fire,
> That you and I are as real
> At least as the people upstairs.
> [*ND* 27]

This has been taken by at least one commentator (von Hallberg 107) as an "ironic stab at his neighbors," an example of Merrill's "archness." Here, at least, I think the complaint is misplaced; Merrill has clearly shown the reader that the vision of this family presented by the poem is idealized, thoroughly unreal; it is the childless (gay) man's fantasy of what he does not and never will have. Merrill's next move in the poem, then, his effort to make his life real to himself, is to recast segments of his life story into quasi-mythic terms in an attempt to elaborate a counter myth to that of the harmonious family he has projected upon his neighbors.

The description of Merrill's father in the ensuing sonnet makes him seem larger than life; at the same time, one of its chief means of representation is the cobbling together of clichés, as if the man himself were somehow a fabrication of the received ideas of his era:

My father, who had flown in World War I,
Might have continued to invest his life
In cloud banks well above Wall Street and wife.
But the race was run below, and the point was to win.

Too late now, I make out in his blue gaze
(Through the smoked glass of being thirty-six)
The soul eclipsed by twin black pupils, sex
And business; time was money in those days.
[ND 27]

Merrill's punning etherealizes the language of his father's profession; from the poet's perspective the world of investments and finance seems as insubstantial as the clouds. The last line of the opening quatrain, though, is spoken in another voice, a ventriloquism, perhaps, of the father's tough-minded wisdom. A similar saying closes the second quatrain, though here the poet's distance is made more explicit. The phrase "time is money" posits a universal law; the poet's rephrasing denies its universality. "Time is money" again embodies the conventional wisdom of the hardheaded businessman, a wisdom whose truth the poet both acknowledges and distances himself from; his financier father may have transformed time into money, but time retained its own powers of transformation:

Each thirteenth year he married. When he died
There were already several chilled wives
In sable orbit—rings, cars, permanent waves.
We'd felt him warming up for a green bride.

He could afford it. He was "in his prime"
At three score ten. But money was not time.
[ND 27]

In this passage the trappings of haut bourgeois life take on a kind of uncanny menace. Describing the wives as "chilled" likens them to drinks or desserts, while the word's deathly resonances turn the father into a kind of Bluebeard. Under scrutiny, the phrase "permanent waves" too comes to seem disturbingly contradictory, suggesting an unnatural freezing of fleeting energies that echoes the father's battle to overcome time. The quotation marks around "in his prime" imply not simply that this is a stock phrase the poet separates from his own voice, but also that this is the way people in his father's world saw things, that his father's world implicitly accepted the right of any tremendously wealthy man of "three score ten" (again, a slightly archaic construction that belongs to the language of the father's rather than the poet's generation) to take a much younger bride. "He could afford it" means both that he had the money and that society would accept the marriage, perhaps the one because of the other. But the poet has the ironic last word here as he inverts his father's businessman's proverb, registering an ironic protest against the values his father represents.[2]

Those values are further scrutinized in the next sonnet:

> When my parents were younger this was a popular act:
> A veiled woman would leap from an electric, wine-dark car
> To the steps of no matter what—the Senate or the Ritz Bar—
> And bodily, at newsreel speed, attack
>
> No matter whom—Al Smith or José Maria Sert
> Or Clemenceau—veins standing out on her throat
> As she yelled *War mongerer! Pig! Give us the vote!*,
> And would have to be hauled away in her hobble skirt.
> [*ND* 28]

The sonnet presents the moment of the woman's suffrage campaign as seen from the poet's age, a perspective from which the passions and intensity of that earlier era seem far away; in 1962, one should remember, Merrill inhabited an America more like Lowell's "tranquilized fifties" than that of the fractious and chaotic decade the 1960s later became. "At newsreel speed" catches this perspective exactly, making the woman seem somewhat ridiculous, in the way that speeded-up figures in an old newsreel strike us as comic (Merrill was no doubt aware that the speeding-up effect occurs because the two eras simply run on a different time scale, sixteen as against twenty-four frames per second). The metaphor reminds us as well that our impression of such an incident indeed derives from newsreels, that our comic perspective on it is an artifact. The theatrical metaphor in "a popular act" mocks the stagy, publicity-seeking nature of this sort of demonstration at the same time that "act" might be taken without irony, the resolve of this "veiled woman" being contrasted to the passivity of the poet. The octave's final image is broadly comic, but reminds us again of the realities of women's disadvantaged position; "the hobble skirt" becomes a figure for all the restrictions placed upon women, as if this protester's having to be "hauled away" were not merely because of her violent outburst but also because her hobbling by social forms (beyond the forms of fashion) has made her incapable of locomotion.

The sestet reads this scene as an archetypal emblem, though the mythic continuity it posits is rather lamented than celebrated:

> What had the man done? Oh, made history.
> Her business (he had implied) was giving birth,
> Tending the house, mending the socks.
>
> Always that same old story—
> Father Time and Mother Earth,
> A marriage on the rocks.
> [*ND* 28]

The tonal nuances of the first line of the sestet would take a great deal of space to exhaustively unpack; what one can say briefly is that its evident mockery might be taken either way: as a ventriloquism of complacent male triumphalism or as sardonic irony; the nonchalance of the poet's "Oh" implies both that making history is simply the natural thing for men to do, and that it's no great accomplishment. The poet speaks from a moment in which the whole idea that history is made by great men seems increasingly questionable, and his rhyming of "history" with "story" encourages the reader to perform the feminist dissection of "history" into "his-story." In the final lines of the sestet Merrill obliquely returns to the subject of his own parents, seeing their "marriage on the rocks" as an instance of an archetypal situation. This archetype is handled, however, with a broad irony. "Father Time and Mother Earth" have fallen by the poet's time to the level of advertising images, while "on the rocks," like "broken home," is a euphemism employed by a society unable to bring itself to say "divorce." It's exactly this disinclination to confront matters directly, this way of seeing the conflict between the sexes as immemorial and irresolvable, the poet implies, that leads to scarred lives like his own. Bad language is a symptom of bad faith, a bad faith the poet's ironic reworking of cliché is meant to expose.

The fourth sonnet, while posing few apparent problems of interpretation, nevertheless carries a deeply hidden subtext within it, for it obliquely figures the poet's homosexuality, a fact he could represent, at this point, only sub rosa. This representation turns on an allusion to Freud's account of the Oedipal complex, an allusion made through a set of extravagantly bad, but also unobtrusive, puns:

> One afternoon, red, satyr-thighed
> Michael, the Irish setter, head
> Passionately lowered, led
> The child I was to a shut door. Inside,
>
> Blinds beat sun from the bed.
> [ND 28]

Perhaps the reader must be sensitized already by recognizing the pun in "sunless" to remark the similar pun in the fifth line of this sonnet. This line seems to encapsulate almost the whole of Freud's Oedipal myth, the son barred from the mother's bed by the threat of blinding/castration. And indeed the sonnet enacts a drama that suggests a castration or unmanning originating in an illicit desire for the mother:

> Under a sheet, clad in taboos
> Lay whom we sought, her hair undone, outspread,
> . . . . .
> Her eyes flew open, startled strange and cold.
> The dog slumped to the floor. She reached for me. I fled.
> [ND 28]

The shrinking of the setter, emblem of potency both because "satyr-thighed" and because its rigidity in point becomes a metaphor for erection, figures the poet's flight from heterosexual desire. This account of the etiology of homosexual object choice probably strikes a contemporary reader as outmoded, a feeling the poet now might well share. But the intensity of the writing, at the same time that the scene is distanced by a slight archaism of diction and syntax, indicates the poet's emotional investment in this very qualified self-revelation.

The sixth sonnet explicitly reflects on the poet's distance from the values of his parents, both from the public realm of politics and business represented by the father and from the private domestic world identified with the mother and devoted to procreation and nurture; like the earlier poem of that name, "The Broken Home" anxiously meditates on the poet's childlessness. The opening of this sonnet picks up from the preceding sonnet's ending:

They [the parents] are even so to be honored and obeyed.

> . . . Obeyed, at least, inversely. Thus
> I rarely buy a newspaper, or vote.
> To do so, I have learned, is to invite
> The tread of a stone guest within my house.
> [ND 29]

The poet's honoring his father and his mother "inversely" again makes an oblique allusion to his homosexuality; "invert" at the time was another term for "homosexual." Thus his self-comparison to Don Juan; while the poet hardly resembles this stereotypical seducer, he too stands outside society, is someone whose sexuality violates social norms and so invites the vengeance of the father. The poet, alienated from the ritual forms of public action, whose reduction to newspaper reading and voting reveals the emptiness of the public sphere, nevertheless sees in that very alienation the mark of his rootedness in his past; placelessness and isolation become a form, diminished as it may be, of connection and continuity. The sestet more explicitly recalls the themes of "Childlessness":

> Nor do I try to keep a garden, only
> An avocado in a glass of water—
> Roots pallid, gemmed with air. And later,
>
> When the small gilt leaves have grown
> Fleshy and green, I let them die, yes, yes,
> And start another. I am earth's no less.
> [ND 29]

Just as the public world has been reduced in the poet's representation to newspapers and voting, so the traditionally "female" world of nurture is represented by the poet's false starts at growing an avocado. Something of a fad in the 1960s, the avocado derives its name from a word for "testicle," and thus embeds an ironic reflection on the poet's lack of offspring within this little narrative.

The final sonnet of the poem's seven presents another of the poet's imaginary explorations of a scene; here the metaphoric broken home is described as if it were a physical reality: "A child, a red dog roam the corridors, / Still, of the broken home." The poet seems here to achieve some distance from his feelings by concretizing them in this image, then separating that image from an image of the "real" house:

The real house became a boarding-school.
Under the ballroom ceiling's allegory
Someone at last may actually be allowed
To learn something; or, from my window, cool
With the unstiflement of the entire story,
Watch a red setter stretch and sink in cloud.
[*ND* 30]

The imaginary house is described in the present tense as a persistent locus of memory or unconscious desire, haunted by the poet's earlier self; the unconscious, Freud posited, knows no time. The "real" house is depicted in a not unhopeful conditional mood; the "entire story" in the penultimate line refers most literally to the particular floor of the house as it cools off late in the day, but refers as well to the easing, both in the house itself and in the poet's life, of the tensions generated by the "old story" of sonnet 3, that of "a marriage on the rocks." This ending recalls that of Coleridge's "Frost at Midnight"; like that poem, Merrill's imagines the losses of the poet's early experience recompensed in some way by the richness of a child's happier circumstances. The recollection of Coleridge's poem, however, serves as well to remind the reader of the gulf between the poet's situation and Coleridge's; Coleridge is addressing his son, while the only figure the childless Merrill can imagine is "Someone." And yet, if Merrill's expansion of sympathy is less direct it is also wider; to feel that one's own unhappiness is made up for by the bright prospects of one's son seems narrower than a corresponding feeling about a stranger one has never and will never meet. "The Broken Home" revises "Frost at Midnight" by attaching that precursor to the patriarchal values of generational continuity, a set of values that the homosexual poet eyes skeptically throughout the course of the poem, and suggesting that the apparent disadvantage of the gay male—his lack of progeny—is in fact an advantage because it enables his sympathy to extend beyond the narrow confines of the family circle. This reversal, writ large, will become one of the structuring themes of the trilogy.

In his early poetry, Merrill enacts his distrust of public language by refusing for the most part to use it; his idiom is unabashedly literary, esoteric, and purified in the Mallarméan sense. With "An Urban Convalescence" Merrill allows a piece of public rhetoric to enter the poem, but only to enact the drama of its rejection, as the body rejects foreign tissue. "The Broken Home" perfects a new strategy, in which Merrill uses the language of cliché ironically against itself, through a burlesque punning that dissolves the dead metaphors and received ideas of public language into absurdity, or through reversals in which the seeming unconscious of some cliché is revealed. This way of turning commonplaces upside down enables Merrill to address public subjects without adopting the language of public address. Indeed, Merrill's handling of public language becomes the way that he treats public subjects; distancing himself from a mode of speaking becomes a way of distancing himself from the values that it represents. This is what distinguishes Merrill from other poets of his generation like Anthony Hecht and Richard Wilbur, who followed a similar path, beginning as neometaphysical formalists and maintaining course against the trend toward "open" forms that in the 1960s swept up many of their peers. Merrill's work, while exacting poetic craft has remained one of its prominent values, has been able to broaden its concerns through its carnivalesque transformations of everyday idiom.

The question remains, however, of the poet's relation to those who live by the wisdom he so wittily subverts, a question that becomes increasingly urgent in the trilogy. The imagined someone invoked at the end of "The Broken Home" is perhaps an easy enough object of sympathetic interest, but the poet's relations to those nearer at hand are more problematic. Critics have complained of Merrill's "snotty" attitude (von Hallberg 108) toward some of his subjects, and even if one feels that the accusation isn't entirely just, the poet himself reflects anxiously on the question. In "Days of 1964," the final poem in *Nights and Days*, the poem's climax occurs at a moment when the poet's middle-aged housekeeper appears before him in an aspect that confounds the stereotypical categories to which he had assigned her. The poem opens with a description of the poet's neighborhood in Greece, including a hill nearby that seems to serve as general party spot and trysting place, "If not Olympus, / An out-of-earshot, year-round hillside revel" (*ND* 54). The second stanza introduces the poet's housekeeper, Kyria Kleo:

> Her legs hurt. She wore brown, was fat, past fifty,
> And looked like a Palmyra matron
> Copied in lard and horsehair. How she loved
> You, me, loved us all, the bird, the cat!

I think now she *was* love. She sighed and glistened
All day with it, or pain, or both.
(We did not notably communicate.)
[*ND* 54]

This description is neither flattering nor original; of course one's
Greek housekeeper is pious, fat, and warmhearted. At the same time,
Merrill is warning the reader not to take as truth the impression
this passage records when he remarks on the lack of communication
between the two. This lack is concretized in the incident that occurs
at the poem's middle, when the poet recalls laughing with the lover
to whom the poem is addressed over an encounter with Kleo earlier
in the day:

Poor old Kleo, her aching legs,
Trudging into the pines. I called,
Called three times before she turned.
Above a tight, skyblue sweater, her face
Was painted. Yes. Her face was painted
Clown-white, white of the moon by daylight,
Lidded with pearl, mouth a poinsettia leaf,
Eat me, pay me—the erotic mask
Worn the world over by illusion
To weddings of itself and simple need.
[*ND* 55]

Both parties, encountering one another outside the space of their
economic relationship, seem disoriented; Kleo fails to hear the poet's
call, or fails to recognize his voice, while the poet is startled to see
this woman whom he had cast in a maternal role ("She called me
her real son") in a very different garb, as a creature of erotic desire.
Later in the poem, the poet imagines the possibilities for misunder-
standing in another sort of encounter with Kleo. As the poet catches
out Kleo when encountering her outside what seems her natural,
domestic sphere, so the poet would be caught out were his poem
to travel linguistically into her language and off the page (the lines
imply that Kleo cannot read). It's not entirely clear what the poet
asks to be forgiven for—for likening her to "lard and horsehair,"
for having laughed about her with his lover, or for putting her into
a poem at all. But the poet is clearly anxious about the way he
represents her; if in the course of the poem she goes from maternal
stereotype to a figure whose desires will not be so easily defined and

categorized, she also becomes subject to a kind of mockery that is different from the bemusement of the initial description of her. The poet and lover might stand here for the poet and his reader, those on the inside of the ironies the poems direct toward received ideas, while Kleo stands for those outside the circle of intimacy created by the poet's ironies; the poet perceives in her made-up face the mask of erotic illusion, but this perception is not available to Kleo herself.

The poet does not inform us whether Kyria Kleo has ever had Merrill's poem read to her. Some idea, though, of what might happen were the poet's corrosive ironies to leak out of their aesthetic containers can be gathered from a story in the *New York Times* (November 25, 1988), titled "Poetic Injustice? A Grocer Sees Insults in an Ode" (Ravo). The story focuses on Merrill's poem "November Ode," which had appeared in the October 27 issue of the *New York Review of Books*. The poem takes as its subject the closing of a local grocery in Stonington, an event the poet views both elegiacally and ironically. The *Times* story notes that Merrill "has defended the work as a lament on the dissolution of older communities everywhere"; at the same time, the poem is thoroughly imbued with Merrill's characteristically arch tonalities:

> The blow has fallen, our dear dim local grocery
>   been shut down by the State—not yet for good, though
>   how, in whose wildest dreams, will it get
>   its act together?

Ronald Albamonti, proprietor of Roland's Market in Stonington, was not amused. Feeling himself the target of "a deliberate poke," in the reporter's words, from Merrill, the grocer "packed up the produce and sold Roland's, and now plans to leave the town that has been his home for all of his 40 years." Mr. Albamonti apparently even contemplated a libel suit, presumably around the issue of whether his customers had ever had to close "Republican eyes / to dead mouse and decimated shelves." And he further accused the poet of insensitivity in his description of an employee: "He also criticized Mr. Merrill for writing about a 'handsome, cock-eyed daughter (in law?)'—a reference, he believes, to a clerk with an eye muscle disorder. 'It was devastating to her,' he said." Presumably, the grocer was stung as well by Merrill's remark that "the son picked to succeed him never lived up to the / seigneurial old man." The reader familiar with Merrill's work would likely take both of these characterizations in a somewhat different sense than an outsider. Insiders would see any passage about a son's failing to live up to the legacy of a father as a projection of the poet's own anxieties about failing to carry on the traditions and lineage of the "seigneurial old man" who founded Merrill, Lynch. On the other hand, readers who have been alerted by past acquaintance with Merrill's predilection for punning would see something more in the odd epithet "cock-eyed" than a physical description; the poet, through a pun on a vulgar term, hints that the clerk is flirtatious, perhaps even promiscuous. It's not at all clear, on reflection, that the operators of Roland's Market would think themselves any more kindly treated were they more familiar with Merrill's output.

The story ends with a remark by Mr. Albamonti that points up the gulf between the poet's ideal audience and the audience he inadvertently found in this case: " 'He feels he can hide behind the word "metaphor," ' Mr. Albamonti said. 'If he can live with himself, well . . .' " Indeed, "metaphor" is the dividing line between insider and outsider, and functions in this way like irony; the line between those who understand a metaphor and those who don't parallels that between those who get a joke and those who don't. Metaphor is a tool for creating intimacy, as the philosopher Ted Cohen points out, but any intimacy implies a corresponding exclusion. The mechanism is exemplified at the end of "November Ode," where Merrill includes the operators of the failed grocery along with himself as "victims of a force that in guises far more ghastly / elsewhere upon our planet squanders its fruits" and ends the poem with a kind of prayer:

> let us give thanks for what we've been spared,
>   and let what is lost
>
> (says the adage) be for God. Varying eerily
>   from truth to truth, his voice—and never more than
>   when speaking American—sounds like
>   that of the people.

Again, Merrill's solidarity in victimization with the grocers, tailors, and cobblers displaced by capitalism's destructive transformations of older communities turns on an opposition to, and a distance from, something he calls "the people." In one sense, of course, Merrill takes the phrase ironically, "the voice of the people" being an instance of politician's cant, but the phrase also communicates a sense of alienation from the poet's fellow citizens as he watches the metamorphosis of "neighbors into strangers," in the words of stanza 14. The poem appeared in the last year of the Reagan presidency, when indeed both the landscape and the public discourse of the United States seemed to have altered beyond recognition in a magically brief span of time. The "we" of the poem moves from the narrowly specific, the first stanza's "our dear dim local grocery," to the broadly inclusive, stanza 13's "what don't we learn to live without?" The range of the "we" narrows, however, in the subsequent stanza:

> we must ourselves go forth in hollow-eyed addiction
> to malls where all is maya, goblin produce,
> false-marble meats, tinned tunes, the powder
> promises of *Cheer*.

The readers the poem imagines are not those who, patronizing the "antique store or real estate office," are "charmed / by what these offer."

The poet places himself and his reader, then, between the gentrifiers who belong to the new world and the Dickensian figures associated with the grocery, with whom he shares a sense of belonging to a world that is disappearing day by day, without, like them, being frozen in time, unable to adapt:

> There my
> three were suspended:
>
> the aproned boy, head raised as if checking an order,
> the young woman at her counter, the old one,
> shawl held tight, mute in the gloaming still—
> their living simply
>
> switched off at the source by the electric company?

The poet's irony, in a sense, saves him. Robert von Hallberg discusses Merrill's characteristic attitudes as an attempt to embody in poetry the values of a particular class, though the class with which von Hallberg finally identifies the poet is not that of finance capitalists into which he was born but that of the self-styled aristocracy of camp: "From the camp viewpoint, politics is stylelessly overladen with content; it can be ignored because the camp sensibility is premised, as Susan Sontag has noted, on detachment. Merrill—and not just in his campier moments—claims an aristocratic aloofness from political activity" (110–11). Certainly in this case, such a judgment, while pointing to a real aspect of the poet's tone, is too harsh. The poet's solidarity with these figures is necessarily limited, and one suspects the poet would consider it vulgar and dishonest to forget the gulf between him and them, to pretend to more sympathy than he can genuinely feel, or to a greater share in their plight than really belongs to him. That gulf is represented in the poem by the oblique angle of his vision of this scene:

> Why, only
> mornings before, a rip in wintry
> blankness let me peer,
>
> Peer like Thoreau, cheek to the skylight of his glaucous
> parlor, down at wall-eyed denizens by cold
> and apathy hypnotized.

The poet's view of them seems almost hallucinatory, as if imagined, and yet originates in a violation of their privacy as he presses his cheek to the glass for a glimpse at the interior. For a poet whose work is filled with screens, veils, and masks, who maintains his own reticences so tenaciously, peeping through a hole is a powerfully transgressive act; the intimacy it creates is also a violation. At the beginning of "November Ode" Merrill implicitly aligns himself with those whom he describes "closing Republican eyes" to the progressive disarray of the market (though, of course, the poet here gestures as well toward the malign neglect that characterized the Republican president's stewardship of the nation); at its center he sees through the mask the market displays to the world; at its end he resigns himself to a diet of "maya," indecent illusion, but it's hardly surprising that he attempts to penetrate no further into the lives he glimpses through the window.

Private and public remain carefully and uneasily balanced throughout Merrill's work. This balance appears in one sense as the coexistence in the work of a directly autobiographical impulse alongside another impulse toward a figurative elaboration so rich as to appear almost autonomous, in which the importance of the represented object diminishes as attention shifts to the process of figuration. The poet's ambivalence on both sides of this opposition may be measured by comparing two remarks by Merrill that curiously invoke the same myth. Judith Moffett, in an article largely devoted to taking Merrill to task for the "willful obscurity" of some of his work, quotes the poet as saying to her, in regard to the difficulties his work poses to the reader: "You can call it the Sleeping Beauty Complex; let him hack his way through thorns and I'll be his forever after" (308). This statement oddly echoes a passage in "The Book of Ephraim," in which JM, envisioning the "doomsday clock" of the *Bulletin of Atomic Scientists*, looks ahead to a moment when "Powers / We shall have hacked through thorns to kiss awake, / Will open baleful, sweeping eyes, draw breath / And speak new formulae of megadeath" (*CLS* 55). Sleeping Beauty comes to the poet's mind when he describes his reader's relation to the poet's difficulty, and when describing humankind's penetration of the inner secrets of the atom. The will to hack through thorns is clearly an ambivalent quality, in the poet's estimation.

The contrast between these two passages points to some of the larger problems raised by the trilogy. On the one hand, *The Changing Light* takes up a set of issues that are familiar components of a certain left-wing, environmentalist political agenda: nuclear war, overpopulation, environmental degradation. These are the quintessentially global political themes, whose consequences go beyond even human affairs in a way that struggles involving rights, boundaries, and governments cannot. The poem attempts to rise to a perspective beyond the self, beyond even the human, and indeed the trilogy informs us that humans were not the first sentient beings to inhabit the planet. Yet at the same time, the political and social realities the poem confronts are increasingly, as it progresses, seen as a projection of enormous, occult forces to which the poet claims privileged access. The magical framework distances poet and reader from the imperative of action and instead focuses attention on the poet's initiation into and developing understanding of an elaborately delayed occult meaning, a process rather like that of Merrill's reader as he or she grapples with the periphrases and indirections of Merrill's style. As readers, we hack through thorns, expecting to find a baleful princess of global doom, only to discover instead the poet, once again securely at the center of the story.

Thinking about the trilogy should begin with the chief poetic impulse behind it, Merrill's impulse to broaden the basis of his poetry by reaching, as he puts it in "Ephraim," "heights up there beyond the heights of self" (*CLS* 66). It may be true, as Mutlu Konuk Blasing has remarked, that "no one has accused James Merrill of being postmodern" (299), but the drama of much of his work turns on the highly "postmodern" theme of the dispersal and decentering of the self. "The Broken Home" shows how a self is constructed aversively, out of a turn away from the values associated with a language that is rejected on aesthetic as much as moral grounds, but like the poem that self is fragmented; the poem's ending fails to integrate its various sections of narrative, and the moment of coherence and understanding available at its end occurs not for the poet but for a figure sharply separated from him. Images of fragmentation and self-division recur throughout Merrill's corpus, from *Nights and Days* on. "The Thousand and Second Night" translates self-division into grotesquely physical terms: "I woke today / With an absurd complaint. The whole right half / Of my face refuses to move" (*ND* 4). The poet wishes to be restored to his original wholeness: "I want *my* face back." But this desire is expressed immediately after a passage in which the poet has implicitly likened himself to Hagia Sophia:

> The building, desperate for youth, has smeared
> All over its original fine bones
>
> Acres of ochre plaster. A diagram
> Indicates how deep in the mudpack
> The real façade is. I want *my* face back.
> [*ND* 5]

What lies behind the mask is the oxymoronic "real façade," and what the poet perceives and fears is not merely the alienation from self brought on by middle age but the realization that there is no authentic self to return to, that beneath any mask lies nothing more than other masks. Cured of his paralysis, the poet remains fragmented, self-divided:

> These months in Athens, no one's guessed
> My little drama; I appear my own
>
> Master again. However, once you've cracked
> That so-called mirror of the soul,
> It is not readily, if at all, made whole.
> [*ND* 7]

"It" might refer either to the face (the soul's "mirror") or to "the soul" itself—as in the earlier passage, mask and reality become confused, suggesting that the soul is as frangible, and as deceptive, as the face. In this fractured state, the poet finds himself correspondingly alienated from the founding expressions of humanist culture:

"The day I went up to the Parthenon / Its humane splendor made me think *So what?*"

Similarly problematic relations between desire, illusion, and expression continually undermine the self presented in the poems. When the speaker of "The Mad Scene" (*ND* 37) responds to the question "Why did I flinch?" with "I loved you," it's not clear whether he flinched because or in spite of his love; the relation between desire and its expression becomes problematic. This is a pure instance of William Empson's seventh type of ambiguity, in which two irreconcilable alternatives are simultaneously entertained, the prevalence of which in twentieth-century poetry Empson ascribes to the psychic fragmentation of modern life (viii–ix). The disjunction between desire and expression gives rise to manifold deceptions and self-deceptions, and yet Merrill tries hard not to see through them, not merely out of a refined distaste for raw reality but because he fears that the coherence of his desires and impulses will be revealed as illusory. In the passage earlier cited from "Days of 1964," Merrill describes Kyria Kleo's makeup as "the erotic mask / Worn . . . by illusion / To weddings of itself and simple need," but at the end of the poem he describes his lover as "masked . . . in laughter, pain, and love." The love between poet and lover (for it is ambiguous whether this mask is one adopted by the lover or one projected by the poet) is likened to Kleo's crude disguise, the affinity of souls threatened by a reduction to "simple need."

At the same time, Merrill sees the structures of bureaucratic life impinging on the terrain of the self as well. In the second section of "Up and Down," the poet and his mother open a safe-deposit box in an "inmost vault" of "Mutual Trust": "She opens it. Security. Will. Deed" (*BTE* 56). The poet brings forth a constellation of terms— *trust, security, will,* and *deed*—that have migrated from the realm of human feeling to that of legal fiction. *Will* and *deed,* particularly, seem between them practically to sum up the notion of a centered subjectivity, the forming of intentions and their expression in acts; yet the will and the deed involved here have become detached from human agency, have been reduced to paper, to statements in an institutional discourse at the farthest remove from the origins of these terms in human spontaneity.

Section W of "The Book of Ephraim" brings to the fore Merrill's concern with finding an alternative to a poetics based in the self. At the section's center is a conversation between JM and his nephew Wendell, an art student, in Venice. This incident seems unlikely to be biographically based; Wendell is described as the son of "JM's niece" Betsy Merrill Pincus (*CLS* 13), but Merrill has no such niece (Yenser 222). Merrill devises the scene in order to reflect on his own endeavor in the poem, to think through some of his own ambivalences. Wendell shows JM his sketchbook, which to the poet's eye combines refined technique and grim subject matter:

> Page
>
> By page my pleasure in the pains he took
>
> Increases. Yet pain, panic and old age
> Afflict his subjects horribly. They lie
> On pillows, peering out as from a cage,
>
> Feeble or angry, long tooth, beady eye.
> Some few are young, but he has picked ill-knit,
> Mean-mouthed, distrustful ones.
> [*CLS* 79–80]

The poet tries to protest on behalf of the humanist viewpoint, but Wendell remains unconvinced:

> "The self was once," I put in, "a great, great
> Glory." And he: "Oh sure. But is it still?"
> [*CLS* 80]

While the poet here seems to speak on humankind's behalf (as he will do again in the pleadings with Gabriel in *Scripts for the Pageant*), the verdict on humanity Wendell pronounces doesn't seem all that far from the one arrived at by the trilogy; what differs between JM and Wendell is their response, artistically, to this perception. Having found that the deceits and illusions of the self make it a shaky foundation for poetic construction, the poet seeks his "heights" in an otherworldly realm; as Merrill remarked to an interviewer, "Well, don't you think there comes a time when everyone . . . wants to get beyond the self?" (*Recitative* 66).

The urgency with which many poets, from the 1960s on, have been seeking alternatives to a poetry of the lyric self has been amply documented by a number of recent studies. One strain of 1960s poetry sought, as Paul Breslin describes it, to "exorcise the socialized part of the self" (*Psycho-Political Muse* 9) and thus to uncover a deeper, unconscious voice that precedes the constitution of the individual ego; another found in ideological engagements, whether defined in directly political terms or along the lines of race, gender, and sexuality, access to a voice that addressed issues and a readership conceived of in terms broader and more public than those of lyric. For Merrill, neither of these approaches held any attraction, despite his having in his poems conducted a critique of inauthentic selfhood as searching as any in the works of his more explicitly political colleagues. Merrill's skepticism, as poems like "Mandala" show, could not be turned off to allow the poet direct access to a "deep image," arising from the unconscious, to replace his hermetic and highly self-conscious symbols. Gay identity certainly becomes in the course of Merrill's career an increasingly open and constitutive part of his work, but more in the sense of an intimacy-producing shared secret with his readers than as part of a militant politics of visibility, as in, for instance, Allen Ginsberg. The poet who neither reads the paper nor votes hardly seems a likely candidate "to speak to multitudes and make it matter" (CLS 82). Indeed, this phrase from section W of "The Book of Ephraim" seems to indicate in the puzzle of its own syntax Merrill's skepticism about such an endeavor. The "it" lacks an antecedent, so that the reader is never told precisely what might "matter"; this "it" is instead impersonal, as if the poet were implying that the very project of addressing a broad public would necessarily entail the impossibility of anything specific's being communicated.

"The Book of Ephraim" opens with the poet's apology for failing to write so as to "reach / The widest public in the shortest time" (CLS 3). More is at stake, however, than disseminating the otherworldly revelation:

> I had stylistic hopes moreover. Fed
> Up so long and variously by
> Our age's fancy narrative concoctions,
> I yearned for the kind of unseasoned telling found
> In legends, fairy tales, a tone licked clean
> Over the centuries by mild old tongues,
> Grandam to cub, serene, anonymous.
> Lacking that voice, the in its fashion brilliant
> Nouveau roman (even the one I wrote)
> Struck me as an orphaned form, whose followers,
> Suckled by Woolf not Mann, had stories told them

In childhood, if at all, by adults whom
They could not love or honor.
[CLS 5–6]

The poet turns away from Woolf, mistress of interiority, and the
theme of damaged relations between generations that he shares with
the novelist, to imagine a tone that embodies the communal au-
thority of tradition; indeed, he describes the poetics of interiority as
issuing from a breakdown in cultural transmission between genera-
tions. A poetics of interiority must manufacture its own authority
as it goes along, continually persuading the reader of its sincerity by
its skeptical self-scrutiny; thus all those moments in Merrill's poetry
where he stops to undo some fiction he has passed upon himself.
But this mode of establishing authority is necessarily provisional,
moment to moment; the writing acquires its authority precisely in
the act of seeming to question it. One can hardly blame Merrill
for supposing this mode to be unsustainable over the length of *The
Changing Light*. At the same time, while Merrill imagines this voice
drawn from tale and legend, the novel that was to have embodied it
is lost, appearing in "The Book of Ephraim" only in summary and
paraphrase; nor does the poet seem much to rue that loss. Failing
to achieve the impersonal voice he wishes for, the poet essentially
makes do with the familiar tactics. Thus the substantial degree of
irony directed at Ephraim and his revelations, and passages like the
opening of section I, where JM tells his "ex-shrink . . . the whole
story" (CLS 29), assuring the reader that the poet hasn't lost his
trademark skepticism, or the ending of section D:

—For as it happened I had been half trying
To make sense of *A Vision*
When our friend dropped his bombshell: POOR OLD YEATS
STILL SIMPLIFYING

But if someone up there thought *we* would edit
The New Enlarged Edition,
That maze of inner logic, dogma, dates—
Ephraim, forget it.
[CLS 14]

At least in "The Book of Ephraim," Merrill uses all his resources
of irony to put plenty of distance between himself and the century's
other prominent example of a poet in touch with a spirit otherworld.
Though Yeats's spirits once told him that they came to give him

metaphors for poetry, Yeats rather more often struck the tone of the ending of "All Souls' Night," where he announces "I have mummy truths to tell." R. P. Blackmur, in his acute essay on Yeats's use of "magic" as an organizing principle for his poetry, while being in many ways unsympathetic to this aspect of the poetry, nevertheless recognizes the situation that drove Yeats to desperate expedients: "All this is to say generally . . . that our culture is incomplete with regard to poetry; and the poet has to provide for himself in that quarter where authority and value are derived" (82). Yeats sought to improvise a framework for that authority and value through magic, but as Blackmur judges, correctly I think, what is left over generally derives its persuasive force not through that framework but through the presentation of character or some telling form of language that translates the magical into more generally available terms of observation (88). Merrill's problems in reconstituting some basis of authority and value are even more acute than Yeats's, given that the various aristocratic nostalgias which retained at least a vestigial persuasiveness in Yeats's time are hardly viable in contemporary America. "The Book of Ephraim," which was originally conceived of as a free-standing poem rather than as a component of a longer opus, works by means of the sort of moment-to-moment tact, the deft balancing of skepticism and assent, that informs Merrill's lyrics. Early into *Mirabell*, however, the powers behind the board announce their demand for "POEMS OF SCIENCE" (113), a demand that fundamentally alters the dynamics of the poem.

Magic and science, viewed as strategies for organizing the poet's perceptions, would seem to be diametrically opposed. Magic, as Blackmur points out, is a quintessentially private discipline (90), available only to the inspired adept, while science is a rational, publicly available discourse. What increasingly joins them, in the course of the latter two books of the trilogy, is metaphor, in that both the magician and the scientific portions of the "lessons" at the board are treated as bearing the sort of provisional relation to "reality" we term metaphorical, and in their functioning as metaphors for one another. Early on in *Mirabell* JM imagines that the POEMS OF SCIENCE will arrive directly rather than through the mediation of the Ouija board: "I supposed vaguely / That inspiration from now on would come / Outright, with no recourse to the Board" (*CLS* 109). But the board, in the scheme of the poem, comes to represent language itself, the peculiarly human instrument into which the spirits' revelations must be translated, and no direct, inspired communication ever becomes available. Indeed, the theme of a good part of the first several *Books of Number* is Mirabell's search for a language with which to communicate to JM and DJ; initial misunderstandings threaten to scuttle the project before it is well started. After their introduction to Mirabell, JM calms DJ's fears about encountering fallen angels by reassuring him: "Something tells me that all this Flame and Fall / Has to be largely metaphorical" (*CLS* 114). The insistent awareness of the metaphorical nature of the revelation is one of the means Merrill employs to distance himself from Yeats. Later in the poem the reader learns that DJ is something of an incarnation of Yeats (*CLS* 217); DJ's role as foil to JM reflects the way Merrill wishes to position himself in regard to his equivocal precursor. DJ is plodding, literal-minded, prone to overly immediate responses. It's DJ who must be reassured, as in the passage just quoted, that there's no real danger in communicating with the bat-creatures, DJ whose fears of "RADIATION" must be calmed by a reminder that "THIS IS ALL IN A MANNER OF SPEAKING" (*CLS* 421).

Soon enough, however, JM is more frustrated than reassured by the heavy veil of metaphor that cloaks the narrative of the bat-spirits. Having learned that the bat-creatures both inhabited the earth and dwelled inside the atom, JM probes further:

> That ozone layer is the Van Allen belt,
> Right? But *three* Edens? Adam and Eve, you said,
> Were universal principles at war,
> So what could possibly have come before them?
> Eden, no doubt, is also a child's name
> For the first matter, lost in flood or flame.
> Surely underneath such fables lie
> Facts far more thrilling—won't you specify?
> [*CLS* 121]

But the response he receives makes clear that the specification he demands cannot be accomplished in human language:

> A moment's baffled hesitation, then:
>
> ELEMENTAL FORCE EVOLVING FORMS THE VARIOUS MYTHS
> AS TAILS FELL AWAY HOW SHD I SPEAK COMMAND ME
>   O SCRIBE
> [*CLS* 122]

For Merrill, no revelation can be direct; all must be translated through the mechanism of metaphor, and the poet resigns himself to this necessity, establishing with Mirabell a convention around these moments of translation:

> Our peacock, we have noticed, more and more
> Embellishes his text with metaphor.
> Some aren't bad; he likes to signal them
> With a breezy parenthetic (m).
> [CLS 173]

As Mirabell becomes more humanlike, learns "manners," he becomes a more frequent user of metaphor. Indeed, the utopian future Mirabell projects for humankind turns on the elevation of "PURE REASON" to the space currently occupied by revealed faith:

> WE HAVE PULLD DOWN THE SUPERANNUATED CHURCH
> & RAISED AN ALTAR TO THE NEW HOUSE GODLET: PURE REA-
> SON
>
> . . . . .
>
> NOW METAPHOR IS THE RITUAL OF THIS NEW REASON
> & OF WHAT RITES? THE RITES OF LANGUAGE
> [CLS 239]

Mirabell insists, in other words, that the revelation he bears is non-mystical, is mediated rather than direct and absolute. The story of the trilogy, then, becomes one familiar to Merrill's readers, a story not so much about the progressive revelation of doctrine but about the poet's education in and through metaphor. As in "Days of 1964," the poet learns not to look behind the masks, learns to accept the play and contingency of metaphor; the literalizing gaze is likened to the light of a nuclear blast in the account of the Russian bomb test in *Scripts*:

> A PURE
> WHITE LIGHT, THE NEGATIVE OR 'EYE' OF BLACK
> BURST ON US   The *bad* white, the metaphor-
> Shattering light? AMORAL   YES MY DEARS
> [CLS 456–57]

Poet and reader undergo an analogous discipline in learning to check the impulse toward literalization, to forgo the desire to sort metaphor into its literal and figurative portions.

So the board, which bears upon it the raw material of language, remains the instrument by which the pair receive their revelation, and Merrill is fond of reminding the reader of the disparity between revelation and instrument. The capitals used to indicate transcriptions from the board are the most obvious instance; more telling are those moments when the reader is abruptly reminded of the ramshackle conduit through which the revelation flows: Merrill constantly refers to the physical apparatus of the cup and board, and at one point the spirits inform DJ and JM that "HEAVEN . . . CD FIT IN THIS CUP OR BE VASTER / THAN EARTH ITSELF" (CLS 264). The latter quotation, from *Scripts for the Pageant*, perhaps suggests Merrill's reading in popular accounts of quantum mechanics. From the quantum perspective, much in the scientific description of the natural world becomes sublimed into metaphor; so physicists no longer worry whether light comes in waves or particles but simply state that, measured one way, light behaves as a wave and measured another, as a particle. This principle of complementarity, the simultaneous truth of irreconcilable alternatives, is writ large in the division of *Scripts* into three sections, YES, &, NO, reflecting these three elements of the board itself; not yes *or* no but yes *and* no, opposites held together by the board's only piece of syntax. Indeed, this phrase becomes in *Scripts* a kind of comic refrain with which the poet's quest for certainties and fixed answers is periodically reproved. For the poet, then, science and magic are merely two of the "languages" celebrated in this passage from book 1 of "Ephraim":

> We were not tough-
> Or literal-minded, or unduly patient
> With those who were. Hadn't—from books, from living—
> The profusion dawned on us, of "languages"
> Any one of which, to who could read it,
> Lit up the system it conceived?
> [CLS 31]

Almost everything in the two latter books of the trilogy can be seen in either light, from either perspective; the evaporation of doctrine into double-sided metaphor leaves the poem bearing an ethical content but largely lacking in metaphysical sanction for it.

The passage from "Ephraim" quoted above occurs at the end of the section in which JM's "ex-shrink" has diagnosed the board business as a "folie à deux." JM plays with the idea, admitting that

Ephraim's realm of knowledge seems suspiciously congruent to that of his two mediums:

> As through smoked glass, we charily observed
> Either that his memory was spotty
> (Whose wouldn't be, after two thousand years?)
> Or that his lights and darks were a projection
> Of what already burned, at some obscure
> Level or another, in our skulls.
> [*CLS* 31]

At this point, JM simply decides that, if Ephraim is a projection, let him long be so:

> *He* was the revelation
> (Or if we had created him, then we were).
> The point—one twinkling point by now of thousands—
> Was never to forego, in favor of
> Plain dull proof, the marvelous nightly pudding.
> [*CLS* 32]

Later, we learn that Ephraim is something of a projection of the powers above him, one peculiarly adapted to the tastes and interests of DJ and JM. Indeed, Merrill posits this translation into terms the receiver can understand as a principle of all occult revelation: "TO EACH EPIPHANY / ITS OWN" (*CLS* 359), as the spirits say. But here, it seems to me, is where some of the deliberate oddities of the poem's informing design come back to haunt it.

It's one thing to speculate, as the poet does in section I of "Ephraim," that the spirit world with which one is in contact seems to reflect one's own knowledge because it is indeed a projection of oneself, and quite another thing to propose that this is so because the spirits have translated their discourse into terms uniquely suited to the receiver. Part of the problem, certainly, is the coziness of the setting, the very fact that the material of a cosmological epic is being communicated, as the poem puts it, "at the salon level" (*CLS* 72). More troubling, it seems to me, is the set of problems this introduces on the plane of both content and response. As I noted above, the poem insists on the metaphoric nature of its metaphysical content, which implies that the poem's meaning is to be sought, if anywhere, on the ethical plane; the poem is wisdom literature, whose metaphysical trappings exist to buttress and ground the ethical content.

The poem's ethic, alas, seems quite as intimately adapted to the knowledge and values already held by DJ and JM as its cosmological scheme. The problem lies not so much in the particular values espoused, problematic as they may be, as in the implication that these values have some kind of supernatural sanction. That gay men gain access, by their refusal of reproduction, to a range of valuable feelings denied to people who follow more conventional life patterns is an entirely plausible notion, and suitable for poetry (CLS 156); the difficulty comes in the implication that heaven agrees. While the reader is encouraged to view the celestial machinery of lab souls and cloning as a metaphor, the judgment the machinery implies— that most of humankind is brutish and underdeveloped, and that therefore famine and other natural disasters are nothing to mourn— remains as a kind of absolute, which the poet, after an initial coyness, seems to have little trouble adopting. My complaint, I wish to make clear, is not with the particular ethical content the poem embodies but rather with the failure of skepticism that takes place around it. The reader comes to be in an odd position; the more the reader shares the values the poem embodies, the more tempted he or she will be to literalize its cosmic framework, which is precisely, Merrill indicates, what an ideal reader would not do. The intimacy-producing function of metaphor is thus curiously short-circuited.

Merrill's lyric poetry met, and meets, its audience on the ground of a shared preference for figurative over literal language, a preference that grows from a shared skepticism about the possibility, or the desirability, of seeing through appearances to the real. That skepticism springs from a distrust of the self, widely experienced among poets in the 1960s, that drove many of Merrill's peers either to a primitivist poetic that attempted to reach down to preindividual depths of experience, or to a poetic that involved an overcoming of the self through ideological attachments.[3] Merrill responded instead by installing the poet's distrust as a leading theme of the work, by investigating the self's constitution not merely through inauthentic experience but through inauthentic language as well. With *Mirabell* and *Scripts*, Merrill shifts tactics, and in the process, I think, narrows his appeal. While Merrill acknowledges that the occult machinery of the poem is problematic, that seems to me ultimately much less of an obstacle to response than the positing, without a sufficiently reflective irony, of certain values as central to the poem's experience. One scarcely needs, in reading the poem, to believe that winged creatures precipitated a nuclear conflagration in China eons ago;

the poet himself doesn't seem to believe it. On the other hand, the reader's sharing of the belief that the most useful leaders are those who ensure the most rapid thinning of their population's numbers seems distinctly less optional. I want to emphasize that it's not the belief itself, in poetic terms, that I see as problematic, though I don't happen to share it, but rather its being posited as a given rather than as something that has to be earned through the discipline of skeptical questioning in which Merrill's lyric poetry is so rich. Merrill's epic ultimately collapses, I think, under the weight of its unexamined assumptions. On the other hand, it could hardly have been written at all had it operated on the principles of hermeneutic suspicion that drive the lyrics. The poet's problem, one that cannot be willed away or overcome by individual virtuosity, is the problem that Blackmur starts out from in his discussion of Yeats's magic, that "our culture is incomplete with regard to poetry" (82), a statement even more true now than when Blackmur made it. Merrill's difficulties in the later volumes of the trilogy arise from the lack of a positive ground of shared belief and values underpinning contemporary intellectual culture; almost nothing can genuinely be taken for granted. Merrill's lyrics have shown how powerful a poetry erected on a shared ground of irony and self-distrust can be. The failure, magnificent as it may be, of so talented a poet at epic may simply indicate that epic remains outside the cultural possibilities of our age.

John Ashbery came of age as a poet in a literary world shaped by the aftermath of the modernist "revolution." To a poet starting out in the late 1940s and early 1950s, that revolution would have appeared not only in the form of the existing monuments of high modernist writing but also in the body of criticism designed to make the difficult poetry of the modernists accessible. I refer, of course, to what has been called, by its own practitioners and by literary historians, the New Criticism. The New Critics devised a set of reading strategies that helped make the dense, allusive, and elliptical styles of modernism legible to a broad reading public, and, by no means coincidentally, they consolidated the cultural authority of modernism by installing it (and themselves) within the academy. Those developments made the universities sites for producing readers conversant with the techniques and sympathetic to the values of modernism, and so prepared an audience for Robert Lowell and other 1950s poets, like Richard Wilbur, John Berryman, and Anthony Hecht, who began their careers under the spell of Eliot. Indeed, the criticism shaped the poetry as well as the audience; Lowell, for instance, describes his own excited reading of critical essays when he was a young poet: "When I was twenty and learning to write, Allen Tate, Eliot, Blackmur, and Winters, and all those people were very much news. You waited for their essays, and when a good critical essay came out it had the excitement of a new imaginative work" (237). For Ashbery, however, Lowell's rise, and the synergy between academic criticism and poetry it represented, felt stifling rather than invigorating. In an interview with John Koethe, Ashbery describes his sense of alienation from the critical climate that fostered Lowell's work:

> *Koethe:* What was it then that made people like you, Frank O'Hara, and Kenneth Koch more comfortable with people in the music and art worlds than with people in university or literary circles?

> *Ashbery:* I think around 1950, with the rise of Robert Lowell, everything became much more codified and academicized. It seems that the fifties were stricter and more structured than the forties and thirties. Randall Jarrell said in an essay I once read that "in this post-Auden climate, it seems that a coat hanger could write a marvelous poem about the delights and torments of being a college professor." [Koethe 79–80]

Ashbery forgoes the conventions, and thus to some extent the audience, generated by the academic appropriation of modernism. The difficulty of his poetry arises in great measure from this decision not to write the sort of poem Lowell was writing, not to produce within the paradigms offered by the New Criticism.

But Ashbery's reaction to the academic poetic and critical establishment of the 1950s and 1960s is complicated by that establishment's identification with an experimentalist aesthetic. Confronting an avant-garde that has become an establishment, Ashbery knows, is vastly different from confronting an establishment plain and simple, and this awareness runs through the often absurdist logic of "The Invisible Avant-Garde," a lecture he delivered at the Yale Art School in 1968. In it, the poet seems at times positively nostalgic for the good old days when the experimental artist was ignored, rejected, or denounced as a lunatic. In the early modernist period, Ashbery implies, the job of the avant-garde artist, though hard, was essentially simple: one knew where the cutting edge was and what it might take to be on it, and the outrage of the public provided a reliable index to one's success in extending the boundaries of art. With modernism's move from the margins to the center, however, Ashbery sees the contemporary avant-garde paradoxically as threatened by public acceptance. Hostility toward experimental art having been replaced by an avid embrace of aesthetic transgression, the element of risk that produced the aesthetic *frisson* of avant-gardism is in danger of disappearing.

Ashbery's talk begins with an admission that he is, in the very act of discussing the problem, exemplifying it:

> The fact that I, a poet, was invited by the Yale Art School to talk about the avant-garde, in one of a series of lectures under this general heading, is in itself such an eloquent characterization of the avant-garde today that no further comment seems necessary. It would appear then that this force in art which would be the very antithesis of tradition if it were to allow itself even so much of a relationship with tradition as an antithesis implies, is, on the contrary, a tradition of sorts. At any rate it can be discussed, attacked, praised, taught in seminars, just as a tradition can be. ["Invisible Avante-Garde" 389–90]

An academic lecture series on the avant-garde is not merely an index but a cause of the situation Ashbery surveys, a situation that threatens to reduce him, if only in jest, to silence. The existence of an avant-garde "tradition" is more than an oxymoron; it puts into question the very existence of the avant-garde. Ashbery contrasts this situation to that prevailing at the time he began writing poems: "When I was a student and beginning to experiment with poetry . . . it was the art and literature of the Establishment that were traditional. There was in fact almost no experimental poetry being written in this country" (390). Ashbery describes this state of affairs as "bleak" (390) at the same time that he credits it with generating "tremendous excitement": "Most reckless things are beautiful in some way, and recklessness is what makes experimental art beautiful" (391). The artist had it better when he or she had it worse. So far, "The Invisible Avant-Garde" seems a direct inversion of an earlier genre of avant-garde manifesto; rather than decrying the ignorant, ossified public's rejection of experimental work, Ashbery laments the public's too-ready assimilation of the new as a threat to the sensation of risk that must accompany experimentation.

Ashbery goes on to inquire about the origins of the situation he surveys, in which the experimental artist is threatened by acceptance and "it seems no longer possible, for an important avant-garde artist to go unrecognized. And, sadly enough, his creative life expectancy has dwindled correspondingly, since artists are no fun once they have been discovered" (392). Ashbery notes that this state of affairs is usually blamed on "the media," but he rejects that explanation and proposes instead that a natural appetite for heroism has impelled the rapid decline in the "period of neglect" a new artist must suffer: "Events during the first decades of this century eventually ended up proving that the avant-garde artist is a kind of hero. . . . So that, paradoxically, it is safest to experiment" (393). Here, perhaps, is one factor behind the deliberately paradoxical argumentation of Ashbery's talk: a reluctance to pitch his discussion in terms of heroism, a desire to break down the binary logic of the modernist manifesto that conduced so powerfully to constructing an image of the artist as hero. Ashbery's argument comes full circle, to the logically absurd proposition that it is "safest to experiment." The avant-garde, in this formulation, becomes entirely absorbed into tradition, the excitement of risk it once embodied entirely dissipated in regimented innovation.

Yet Ashbery struggles to find opportunity in this bleak situation, though his optimism seems qualified: "On the other hand, perhaps these are the most exciting times for young artists, who must fight even harder to preserve their identity" (393). The talk ends with a series of lengthy quotations from the early-twentieth-century Italian-German composer Ferruccio Busoni, a deliberately eccentric choice of ally, whom Ashbery admires for his ability to have inhabited a situation polarized between the expressionist avant-garde, on the one hand, and "pedantic neo-classicists," on the other, while producing music that "has the unique quality of being excellent and of sounding like nobody else's" (394). Ashbery's image of the authentic artist, then, is not so much one who is on the outside or the margin but one who is *between*, who resists the dogmatisms of both the vanguard and the establishment. Indeed, Ashbery's assessment of the situation of avant-gardism rejects modernist assumptions of progress in the arts, along with the heroic self-image encouraged by such assumptions. The modernist rhetoric of innovation, breakthrough, and advance works by implicit analogy to the development of technology, with its powerfully cumulative and linear logic. Ashbery's analysis, though its absurdist flavor certainly bears noting, turns ultimately on a circular or dialectical model of successive negations, in which the avant-garde, which begins as the antithesis of tradition, comes to constitute a tradition itself, and thus is transformed into its opposite. His response to this problem is not to posit a series of ever more radical breaks with the past designed to repeat the avant-garde's initial transgressive success, but rather to question the ongoing viability of the distinction between vanguard and tradition.

It is scarcely surprising, then, that Ashbery and his work played no role in the "war of the anthologies," the controversy between formalists and the proponents of "open" forms that dominated the American poetic landscape in the early 1960s. Whatever their points of dispute, both sides in that battle agreed on a progressive account of literary history that focused on poetic technology: whether the combatants opted for "open" forms or "fixed" forms as the better way of embodying and extending modernist literary values, both viewed the formal disposition of poetic work as its crucial defining feature. When, in the 1960s and 1970s, a number of onetime formalists, like James Wright and W. S. Merwin, abandoned forms for free verse, their conversions were in most cases absolute. Ashbery, however, has mixed free verse and fixed forms throughout his career. Fixed forms, in his view, provide an antidote to the mode of colloquial sincerity currently widespread in American poetry (Remnick 61); at the same time, he treats the forms he employs with a great deal of irony. He favors forms, like the pantoum and the sestina, that advertise their own arbitrariness; invents his own, rather gimmicky forms, as in the group of one-line poems in *As We Know*; or in "The Songs We Know Best" writes a poem to the tune of a schlocky pop song.[1] He uses traditional forms in ways that undermine their authority. But using them at all involves a rejection of the notion of a progressive advance in poetic technique that definitively outmodes traditional options. For Ashbery, no stylistic choice, whether of diction, form, or genre, is dictated unequivocally by the development of the medium.

Even though Ashbery shared with the Beat and Projectivist camps a disaffection from the reigning academic modernism, he rejected both the progressive model of literary change they espoused and the heroic self-image they cultivated.[2] Ashbery did not appear in the leading antiformalist anthology, Donald Allen's *The New American Poetry*. And I suspect he had Allen Ginsberg, leading figure in the anti-formalist opposition, in mind when in "The Invisible Avant-Garde" he remarked: "In both life and art today we are in danger of substituting one conformity for another, or, to use a French expression, of trading one's one-eyed horse for a blind one. Protests against the mediocre values of our society such as the hippie movement seem to imply that one's only way out is to join a parallel society whose stereotyped manners, language, speech and dress are only reverse images of the one it is trying to reject" (393). Ashbery here expands the frame of reference outward from art to life, and in the process invokes a characteristically 1960s anxiety over the encroachments of mass society upon the preserve of the individual. Whether formulated in the terms of Herbert Marcuse's One-Dimensional Man, David Riesman's Lonely Crowd, Theodor Adorno's Authoritarian Personality, or Max Weber's various writings on institutionalization and the routinization of charisma in bureaucracy, the disappearance of difference into conformity, on the one hand, or into the space of illusory freedom opened by "repressive tolerance," on the other, was a dominant theme of both intellectual and popular reflection. For Ashbery, then, the question of the possibility of the avant-garde is not merely aesthetic, it is "a question of survival both of the artist and of the individual" (393). Despite his sense of urgency, however, Ashbery elects not to confront the so-called establishment head-on in his poetry; where Ginsberg inveighs directly against the "Moloch" society he sees around him, Ashbery names the monster only in a burlesque tone:

> The rise of capitalism parallels the advance of romanticism
> And the individual is dominant until the close of the nine-
>   teenth century.
> In our own time, mass practices have sought to submerge the
>   personality
> By ignoring it, which has caused it instead to branch out in all
>   directions
> Far from the permanent tug that used to be its notion of
>   "home."
> ["Definition of Blue," DDS 53]

Poetry's answer to "mass practices" cannot be a straightforward counterattack; poetry must rather provide within its own practices the image of a possible alternative. Ashbery would no doubt want it to be said of his own poetry what he wrote of Frank O'Hara's: "It does not advocate sex and dope as a panacea for the ills of modern society; it does not speak out against the war in Vietnam or in favor of civil rights; in a word, it does not attack the establishment. It merely ignores its right to exist, and is thus a source of annoyance to partisans of every stripe" ("Frank O'Hara's Question" 6). In his poetry, Ashbery seeks a way to reinvent some of the oppositional energy with which avant-gardism was originally invested, a way to resist the institutional form of modernism that had come to constitute the poetic mainstream, while at the same time avoiding the romanticism of rebellion encouraged by a merely negative stance. Translating from political to poetic, Ashbery resists the pressures of conformity by ignoring the stylistic taboos erected by both New Criticism and Beat or Projectivist poetics.

Ashbery's rejection of the audiences trained by the New Critics and by their opposite numbers in the counterculture, however, raises for him an urgent collateral problem, that of finding an audience at all. Ashbery addresses this problem by re-creating what one might paradoxically call an old-fashioned type of vanguard formation, one that depends heavily on personal acquaintance and word-of-mouth dissemination of reputation, circulates its work in fugitive small magazines, and is linked to like-minded practitioners in other arts. Ashbery, it is true, began his public career by winning the Yale Younger Poets Prize, a thoroughly mainstream honor, and one that launched many of the most widely recognized poets of his generation, including Adrienne Rich, W. S. Merwin, James Wright, and John Hollander. But the circumstances of his receiving the prize (judged that year by W. H. Auden) may in fact have persuaded Ashbery that he would have to build an audience not through an appeal to established standards of poetic performance but rather in the earlier avant-garde fashion of assembling a coterie. The manuscript of *Some Trees* had been screened out early in the process of judging, and his winning the award depended on his personal acquaintance with Chester Kallman, Auden's companion: "I submitted the volume to the Yale Younger Poets and it was returned by the Yale University Press, not forwarded to W. H. Auden, the judge. He had decided not to award the prize that year because he didn't like any of the manuscripts that had been sent to him. At that point a mutual friend of ours mentioned that I had submitted mine and he asked to see it directly and accepted it" (Gangel 11). The volume received only one favorable review in a periodical, Frank O'Hara's gracious piece in *Poetry*, and took eight years to sell out its eight-hundred-copy pressrun, circumstances that made it plain to Ashbery that mainstream avenues for the dissemination of poetry were for the most part closed to him (Tranter 95). Ashbery's recognition, for at least the first fifteen years of his career, moved in slowly expanding circles from the group of poets and artists, including O'Hara, Kenneth Koch, James Schuyler, Jane Freilicher, and Larry Rivers, with whom he was associated. Ashbery's pamphlet of poems, *Turandot*, was published by the Tibor de Nagy Gallery, and it was John Myers, Nagy's partner in the gallery, who first applied the label "The New York School of Poets" in *Nomad*, a fugitive small magazine published in California (Sommer 298). Although Ashbery's sweep of the three major book prizes with *Self-Portrait in a Convex Mirror* in 1976 made him almost instantly one of America's best-known poets, through the period in which his style was maturing Ashbery's audience was a coterie, neither within the mainstream that Lowell dominated nor a part of that mainstream's antitype, the Beat and Projectivist opposition headed by Allen Ginsberg.

Poetry, Ashbery remarks in an interview, is "not a cottage industry in America but a college industry" (Sommer 299), and the New Criticism, perhaps inadvertently, did much to make that possible. One of the chief mechanisms by which it made modernist difficulty teachable was the explicitly dramatistic mode of reading it encouraged, in which the key interpretive terms became *speaker* and *situation*. This principle is spelled out in the introduction to Cleanth Brooks and Robert Penn Warren's widely used textbook, *Understanding Poetry*:

> All poetry, including even short lyrics or descriptive pieces . . . , involves a dramatic organization. This is clear when we reflect that every poem implies a speaker of the poem, either the poet writing in his own person or someone into whose mouth the poem is put, and that the poem represents the reaction of such a person to a situation, a scene, or an idea. In reading poetry it is well to remember this dramatic aspect and to be sure that one sees the part it plays in any given poem. [23]

Reading according to the master terms *speaker* and *situation* helped smooth over the jagged and problematic discontinuities of much modernist writing, enabling apparent breakdowns in coherence to be recoded as dramatic representations securely under the control of the poet's formal impulse. So, in their discussion of T. S. Eliot's "The Love Song of J. Alfred Prufrock," Brooks and Warren appeal to the paradigm of speaker and situation to salvage a notion of the poem's unity from its own disjunctions: "The transitions here appear, at first glance . . . violent. This apparent violence disappears, however, as soon as we realize that the relations between the various scenes, ideas, and observations in the poem are determined by a kind of flow of associations which are really based on the fact that they develop and illustrate the fundamental character and situation of Prufrock" (591). The violent and apparently arbitrary transitions that characterize modernist style are here brought back within the confines of the New Critical dictum of organic unity. If, as Brooks and Warren remark, the poem's "primary difficulty for the reader is the apparent lack of logical transitions" (595), New Critical reading accommodates poem to reader by filling in that absence, thus pacifying the threatening "violence" of the poem. *Speaker* and *situation*, then, become important critical tools in producing a "college industry" of modernism, and it is on the reading practices engendered by these categories that Ashbery's resistance to the institutionalization of the avant-garde focuses.

Ashbery's manipulation of pronouns plays a leading role in his dismantling of the speaker-situation model. Personal pronouns shift and blur, and impersonals and relatives such as *it* and *this* float through the poems detached from any easily ascertained referent. "I" often gives way without warning to "you" or "them," or one in a series of similar pronouns will suddenly seem to have a different antecedent from its companions. Ashbery remarks about this effect: "I guess I don't have a very strong sense of my own identity and I find it very easy to move from one person in the sense of a pronoun to another" (NYQ 25). The notion of persona or mask was a critical element in modernist poetics and the criticism it fostered; the persona posited an ironic distance between poet and speaker, through which the expressive impulse could be transformed into the impersonality that was so much a New Critical desideratum. Ashbery proposes, however, not ironic distance but an undecidable blurring or wavering, a confusion antithetical to the New Critical notion of speaker. Similarly, the broad gestures of Ashbery's vaguely defined impersonal and relative pronouns point to what might rather be called a *condition* than a *situation* conceived in the dramatistic terms of the New Criticism. Such gestures at once insist on the importance of the contexts they suggest and leave those contexts tantalizingly obscure, asking the reader to fill in the blanks opened in the poem. In doing so, the pronouns produce not the ironically distanced situations favored by New Critical reading but a wavering and indeterminate suggestion of identity between the contexts of poet, poem, and reader.

Donald Davie's remarks on wandering pronoun reference in Shelley's verse may help us imagine the reaction of a reader imbued with New Critical values to Ashbery's free treatment of pronouns. Citing a stanza from Shelley's "The Cloud," Davie notes that the passage "comes to grief on the loose use of a personal pronoun" (136), then goes on to lament that "this looseness occurs time and again." After quoting this further passage from the poem,

> The stars peep behind her and peer;
> And I laugh to see them whirl and flee,
> Like a swarm of golden bees,
> When I widen the rent in my wind-built tent,
> Till the calm rivers, lakes, and seas,
> Like strips of the sky fallen through me on high,
> Are paved with the moon and these.

he exclaims that "the grotesque 'and these' is an affront to all prosaic discipline." Affronts to discipline such as the lapses Davie identifies in Shelley generally brought down charges of "muddle" or "fuzziness"—perhaps the two most damning terms in the New Critical lexicon. Ashbery, however, has chosen to write as if entirely unafraid of provoking such charges; he employs pronouns in just the way Davie here protests.

"Soonest Mended" offers an excellent example of the deliberately vague handling of pronoun reference that characterizes Ashbery's style:

> Barely tolerated, living on the margin
> In our technological society, we were always having to be
>   rescued
> On the brink of destruction, like heroines in *Orlando Furioso*
> Before it was time to start all over again.
> There would be thunder in the bushes, a rustling of coils,
> And Angelica, in the Ingres painting, was considering
> The colorful but small monster near her toe, as though wondering whether forgetting
> The whole thing might not, in the end, be the only solution.
> And then there always came a time when
> Happy Hooligan in his rusted green automobile

Came plowing down the course, just to make sure everything
    was O.K.,
Only by that time we were in another chapter and confused
About how to receive this latest piece of information.
Was it information? Weren't we rather acting this out
For someone else's benefit, thoughts in a mind
With room enough and to spare for our little problems (so
    they began to seem),
Our daily quandary about food and the rent and bills to
    be paid?
To reduce all this to a small variant,
To step free at last, minuscule on the gigantic plateau—
This was our ambition: to be small and clear and free.
[*DDS* 17]

"The whole thing . . . everything . . . this . . . all this": the passage
is linked together by a chain of gestures toward some large, encom-
passing whole that conditions the utterance of the poem, furnishes
its context, at the same time that this context seems continually to
shift, one frame to replace another. The simile in the first sentence
exfoliates into a whole scenario (bounded by the frame of "the Ingres
painting"), which is in turn quickly swept away, as if the poem too
were "forgetting the whole thing." The frame then shifts from gilt
to newsprint with the arrival of Happy Hooligan, so it seems likely
that "everything" here is rather different from "the whole thing" put
aside in the previous sentence, while with the return of the "we" the
cartoon figure becomes enclosed within a "chapter" (of our lives?
of a serial?), suddenly telescoped from a space shared with us to the
flatness of the page. And yet the same operation is immediately per-
formed, if only provisionally, upon the "we" of the passage, who are
placed within a further expanded framework, becoming "thoughts
in a mind." Even the definite article comes into play as a means of
ambiguation. Terming it *the* gigantic plateau" implies the reader's
familiarity with the object, yet the poem does nothing to place the
reference; it becomes one more situation or frame of reference that
dissolves before it has stabilized.

    The fluid transformations of situation in the poem are matched by
its similar play with the speaking subject. The opening lines appar-
ently address a specific individual or group that shares a particular
experience with the poet; by the end of the passage quoted above,
however, it seems clear that the application of this "we" has become

generalized to include the poem's audience, all those who share the desire to "step free." Yet suddenly a "you" enters the poem, a "you" that seems sharply delineated and specific:

> a robin flies across
> The upper corner of the window, you brush your hair away
> And cannot quite see, or a wound will flash
> Against the sweet faces of the others, something like:
> This is what you wanted to hear, so why
> Did you think of listening to something else?
> [*DDS* 18]

As it continues, the poem seems to oscillate between according the "you" a separate identity and folding it back into the "we":

> These then were some hazards of the course,
> Yet though we knew the course *was* hazards and nothing else
> It was still a shock when, almost a quarter of a century later,
> The clarity of the rules dawned on you for the first time.
> *They* were the players, and we who had struggled at the game
> Were merely spectators, though subject to its vicissitudes
> And moving with it out of the tearful stadium, borne on shoul-
>   ders, at last.
> [*DDS* 18]

A typically Ashberyan play with pronoun reference in this passage sets up a further play of distance and proximity between "we" and "they." Tracing back, one finds that the "it" in the final line refers to "the game"; one usually thinks of a game's being over when players and spectators leave the stadium, but here the game itself is what moves out of the stadium, as if the stadium were simply one more of the framing structures that dissolve or give way in the course of the poem, leaving the "we" in a position similar to the "players" to which it had earlier been opposed. As when the poet imagines "us" as "thoughts in a mind," this passage figures the position of marginality posited in the poem's opening as both attractive and disturbing. Being out of the game provokes anxiety while at the same time opening a potentially liberating distance from the "struggle."

The play between the elements that inhabit the poem's "we" receives a further turn as "I" and "you" engage in a moment of dialogue:

                    Better, you said, to stay cowering
Like this in the early lessons, since the promise of learning
Is a delusion, and I agreed, adding that
Tomorrow would alter the sense of what had already been
    learned,
That the learning process is extended in this way, so that from
    this standpoint
None of us ever graduates from college,
For time is an emulsion, and probably thinking not to grow up
Is the brightest kind of maturity for us, right now at any rate.
[*DDS* 18–19]

This dialogue, however, diminishes rather than confirms the distinc-
tion between these two speakers, as if this "you" and "I" were akin
to Prufrock's, a figure for some division within the self. The final
appearances of the first-person plural seem deliberately to expand
and contract at once its range of reference:

And you see, both of us were right, though nothing
Has somehow come to nothing; the avatars
Of our conforming to the rules and living
Around the home have made—well, in a sense, "good citi-
    zens" of us,
Brushing the teeth and all that, and learning to accept
The charity of the hard moments as they are doled out,
For this is action, this not being sure, this careless
Preparing, sowing the seeds crooked in the furrow,
Making ready to forget, and always coming back
To the mooring of starting out, that day so long ago.
[*DDS* 19]

"Both of us" narrows the pronoun to "I" and "you," while the final
passage seems once again to open out to include the poem's readers,
all those who share the circumstances of their lives with the poet.
A similar expansion of reference takes place in "Prufrock" as the
"we" introduced in the final lines seems to exceed the "you and I" of
the opening, which denominates only Prufrock himself. Prufrock,
however, remains defined by his distance from the "human" society
around him, while in Ashbery's poem, in the last of its many re-
visions and reframings, the lines of demarcation blur between this
"we" and the "society" in opposition to which it is defined in the

poem's opening. Prufrock's final "we" functions as if the poem had suddenly reached out to take you with it as it goes down gasping, while "Soonest Mended" shuttles fluidly among that pronoun's various possibilities. "Prufrock" reaches out of the frame it has constructed, but only to drag the reader in, while "Soonest Mended" continually puts into question what is inside and what is outside the frame. The marginalized poet has become a "good citizen," but only "in a sense."

A comparison with what David Trotter, in his outstanding study of modernist poetry *The Making of the Reader*, calls "external reference" may help to illuminate the function of Ashbery's sweeping, inclusive impersonal and relative pronouns. Trotter defines "external reference" as the use of a relative term—possessive, demonstrative, comparative—that refers not to something already specified in an utterance but to "an object or person or event in the environment of the utterance," and thus "call[s] upon the reader to supply information from his or her own experience" (14). In Trotter's account of *The Waste Land*, Eliot's use of external reference—"this red rock," "this card," "that corpse," "that noise"—"revive(s) for his readers a perception of wholeness and immediacy" (45). The relative terms project the image of a knowable world whose relations to the speaker can be specified, even when the particular objects of reference cannot. The pub-talk of Eliot's working-class women may at first seem baffling in its heavy use of the unspecified "it": "And if you don't give it him, there's others will, I said" (*The Waste Land* l. 149). "If you don't like it you can get on with it, I said" (l. 153). "It's them pills I took, to bring it off, she said" (l. 159). "Well, if Albert won't leave you alone, there it is, I said" (l. 163). But while Eliot fails to provide the antecedents his women gesture at, the reader nevertheless has little difficulty supplying them. The device, while seeming on the one hand to point up the poverty of these women's language, on the other makes for an effect of community and intimacy; these women can take things for granted with one another, understand one another's oblique hints and pointings, and as we understand them as well, we become included in this linguistic community.

If Eliot's external references may be said to create, from an initial perception of fragmentation, a sense of a whole, a world whose relations to the poet are known and measurable, Ashbery's have just the opposite effect; they project a world that is fundamentally unknowable, beyond the power of the poet to name or describe. "Loving

Mad Tom" provides a characteristic example of Ashbery's use of
the undefined "it":

> Then to lay it down like a load
> And take up the dream stitching again, as though
> It were still old, as on a bright, unseasonably cold
> Afternoon, is a dream past living. Best to leave it there
> And quickly tiptoe out. The music ended anyway. The occa-
>   sions
> In your arms went along with it and seemed
> To supply the necessary sense. But like
> A farmhouse in the city, on some busy, deserted metropolitan
>   avenue,
> It was all too much in the way it fell silent,
> Forewarned, as though an invisible face looked out
> From hooded windows, as the rain suddenly starts to fall
> And the lightning goes crazy, and the thunder faints dead
>   away.
> [HD 16]

In this passage the pronoun seems to live a weird, independent exis-
tence, cut loose from responsibility to reference, continually shifting
ground. Whatever "it" stands for seems to be what we would ordi-
narily call the subject of the poem, yet that subject remains obsti-
nately indefinite. This vagueness presents the particular occasion of
the poem as if it were already familiar, as little in need of specifica-
tion as the "it" of "it is raining"; indeed, the final "it" of this passage
could be, syntactically, either a third-person pronoun or part of an
impersonal construction. Ashbery's unspecified "its" move too fast
for us to get our bearings; they point to a situation that can be ges-
tured at but not articulated. The New Criticism implicitly identified
"situation" with dramatic scene, a bounded and framed space held
at a distance from the poet. Ashbery's "it" wavers between naming
a specific situation the poet can observe and apprise, and naming an
encompassing condition that the poet cannot stand outside of and,
for that very reason, cannot formulate discursively. What remains
of the poet's attempt to do so is a trail of abandoned references
that trace the path of his efforts to grasp in language the fluid and
fragmentary world he confronts.

This foredoomed effort to follow the transformations of a shifting
and unstable object characterizes Ashbery's use of syntax as well.

The New Criticism's dramatistic mode of reading made modernist experiments with the fragmentation of syntax safe for readers; shorn of ontological implications, discontinuity could be recuperated as a dramatic effect. Ashbery's mature work evades this sort of reading by offering not a paucity of syntax but an excess; Ashbery's sentences tend to extend themselves until the original impulse is lost or entirely transformed. I quote from "Summer":

> And suddenly, to be dying
> Is not a little or mean or cheap thing,
> Only wearying, the heat unbearable,
>
> And also the little mindless constructions put upon
> Our fantasies of what we did: summer, the ball of pine needles,
> The loose fates serving our acts, with token smiles,
> Carrying out their instructions too accurately—
>
> Too late to cancel them now—and winter, the twitter
> Of cold stars at the pane, that describes with broad gestures
> This state of being that is not so big after all.
> [DDS 20]

Semantically, this sentence traces a circular path from the death that is "not little" to the "state of being that is not so big," just as the poem itself turns on several meanings of the word *reflection*. Much more important to the experience of reading a sentence like this, however, is the richness and complication of the delays that intervene between these mirroring statements. Each element of the sentence seems to receive a full elaboration, to the detriment of the impulse that would organize it into a representation of a single, unified thought or action. "To be dying" is defined both positively and negatively, with the speaker rejecting three potential adjectives. The syntax of "And also" is equivocal; this "And" seems at first parallel to the opening "And" in a construction that makes us expect a copulative/predicate clause to follow, but even if we supply the ellipsed verb, the predicate never arrives. Following the colon, "summer" seems to initiate a catalogue of items in apposition to "constructions," but the "and" in "and winter" implies the phrase "summer . . . and winter," which brackets the items between, as if they were in apposition not to "constructions" but to "summer." Or, this final "and may be another in the series "And suddenly . . . ," "And also." What is important is less the particular possibilities suggested by the syntax than the way that the syntax suggests numerous possibilities without providing sufficient information to resolve them.

In their involuted and elaborate transformations, such sentences break down the linear thrust of subject-verb-object structure. The world they create is dynamic, but its dynamism is impersonal—the reader encounters not subjects performing actions but a range of actions whose agents and predicates seem multiple and elusive. If the subject-verb-object model corresponds to classical causation, in which a single agent acts to produce a single effect, Ashbery's syntax reflects a world of overdetermination in which any effect can be explained multiply, breaking down the direct relation between agent and action. The subject (in both the grammatical and philosophical senses) is marginalized, releasing an explosion of syntactical energies that overflows the bounds of correct and logical syntax. The New Critics delighted in teasing out ambiguities, but saw those ambiguities as building to form coherent, if paradoxical, structures; their notion of ambiguity was ultimately spatial. Ashbery's syntactical puzzles, however, arise in the form of sentences that seem to change their projected shape in mid-stream, just as this sentence from "Summer" seems destined to fall into a parallel construction but gets distracted and never arrives. Ashbery's ambiguities are fluid rather than structured; they refuse to respond to the sort of treatment New Critical close reading would subject them to.

New Critical reading practice was adept at connecting distant subjects and predicates to their verbs and filling in ellipsed syntax, but tended to see as "muddle" the syntactical fluidity of a Shelley or a Tennyson. Though not himself a New Critic, F. R. Leavis classically expresses the dissatisfaction of the academic canonizers of modernism with the self-generating quality of Shelley's mode of composition in this discussion of "Ode to the West Wind":

> In the growth of the "tangled boughs" out of the leaves, exemplifying as it does a general tendency of the images to forget the status of the metaphor or simile that introduced them and to assume an autonomy and a right to propagate, so that we lose in confused generations and perspectives the perception or thought that was the ostensible *raison d'être* of imagery, we have a recognized essential trait of Shelley's: his weak grasp upon the actual. [206]

As this quotation makes clear, Shelley's sins, in Leavis's eyes, go beyond syntax to matters of representation; Shelley's disordered syntax argues a more general disorder of categories. Later in the same essay Leavis remarks in disgust about another passage, "The metaphorical and the actual, the real and the imagined, the inner and the outer, could hardly be more unsortably and indistinguishably confused" (212). For Leavis, the essence of good imaginative hygiene is the rigid policing of these boundaries. For Ashbery, however, one's grasp upon the actual can never be anything but weak in Leavis's terms, as metaphor, imagery, and thought are the only tools we have available for the task; all the poet can do is "braid . . . my own / Snapped-off perceptions of things as they come to me" (SP 44). Indeed, in discussing his intentions, Ashbery employs mimetic terms in a way that overturns the mimetic premises from which Leavis writes: "As with the abstract painters, my abstraction is an attempt to get a greater, more complete kind of realism"(TCO jacket). "[Shifting pronouns create] a kind of polyphony in my poetry which I again feel is a means toward greater naturalism" (NYQ 25). Only by violence, obviously, can realism and naturalism—even granting those terms their broadest, least technical sense—be employed to refer to Ashbery's declared aim of "reproduc[ing] in poetry . . . the actions of a mind at work or at rest" (NYQ 18). Both terms imply the possibility of verifying a representation against "the actual." Mental processes are not open to this sort of inspection—no one can say to the poet, "You don't really think like that." By appropriating these terms Ashbery effectively denies the existence of an "actual" available to perception outside of mental representations; his is a world internalized in much the way Leavis complains of in Shelley. For Ashbery, representation of the world begins and ends in representation of the thoughts by which we apprehend it.

Thus Ashbery's practice of metaphor seems deliberately to call into question the priority of the actual to the metaphors it generates. Frequently, his metaphors involve tenor-vehicle mismatches so extreme as to suggest that the metaphor's job of communicating information about the thing it modifies has been all but abandoned:

> the ground on which a man and his wife could
> Look at each other and laugh, remembering how love is
>   to them,
> Shrank and promoted a surreal intimacy, like jazz music
> Moving over furniture.
> ["A Wave," AW 69]

A metaphor like this is at the farthest possible remove from the metaphysical conceit, whose revival was one of the striking stylistic features of the work of Lowell and other mainstream practitioners of the 1950s and 1960s. The conceit, as in Donne's famous comparison of two lovers to the legs of a compass, brings together two physically unlike but intellectually comparable items; after overcoming the initial perception of strangeness, the reader can formulate quite clearly the like qualities that make the metaphor appropriate. The likeness between shrinking and promoting, on the one hand, and moving, on the other, however, cannot be apprehended intellectually; the metaphor refuses to subordinate itself to the "actual," refuses to yield up the terms of likeness into which it can be translated. In other cases, the poems present the reader with richly elaborated metaphors while failing to supply the "actual" items the metaphors were meant to modify:

> Like a rainstorm, he said, the braided colors
> Wash over me and are no help. Or like one
> At a feast who eats not, for he cannot choose
> From among the smoking dishes.
> ["Worsening Situation," *SP* 3]

The first simile here seems straightforward enough in structure, even if its content remains puzzling; "braided colors" seems to be a metaphor for an "actual" term that is not provided. The syntax of the second sentence, however, remains grammatically incomplete, leaving the metaphor incomplete as well. The vehicle here is sharply etched, but the reader receives no guidance as to its application; the poet seems more interested in presenting this vignette than in using it to inform us about something else. Like his pronouns, Ashbery's metaphors often seem to live an independent existence, divorced from the explanatory functions that, in Leavis's view, are metaphor's *raison d'être*.

Syntax and diction together create the illusion of voice, but just as Ashbery's syntax sometimes seems, in its apparently aimless exploration of syntactical possibility, to arise more from autonomous operations of language itself than from an individualized speaker, so his diction seems as well to range so broadly across levels of language as to break down any notion of a speaker who might be characterized through lexical usage. Ashbery takes to an extreme a

device Donald Davie remarks in Auden's work, a deliberate oscil-
lation "between a colloquialism which is slang and a literary pomp
which is exotic," thus "exploiting a source of calculated impurity
of diction" (26). In a few lines, Ashbery is capable of moving from
"Puaagh. Vomit. Puaaaaagh. More vomit" to "these abstractions /
that sift like marble dust across the unfinished works of the studio"
(*SP* 15). At times, as Byron and Auden did, Ashbery uses this strategy
to achieve an effect of raciness and urbanity, an expert play upon
the various registers of language; but at other times the effect seems
decidedly more extreme, as if the poet were prey to a compulsive
urge to impersonation. Given the range of voices that inhabit the
poems, it hardly seems accurate to speak of the poet's choosing or
adopting them; he seems rather possessed by these voices, which are
often not characters but categories. Rather than evoking an indi-
vidual's idiosyncratic speech, the poems instead frequently contain
passages that fall into the patterns of stereotypical, anonymous dis-
courses. So in "Grand Galop" a speaker informs us that "today's
lunch is Spanish omelet, lettuce and tomato salad, / Jello, milk and
cookies. Tomorrow's: sloppy joe on bun, / Scalloped corn, stewed
tomatoes, rice pudding and milk" (*SP* 14); while in "The Skaters"
the answer to "Any more golfing hints Charlie?" is "Plant your feet
squarely. Grasp your club lightly but firmly in the hollow of your
fingers. / Slowly swing well back and complete your stroke well
through, pushing to the very end" (*RM* 58). While both Byron and
Auden employed up-to-the-minute colloquialisms to strike the tone
of smart conversation, Ashbery often uses an outdated slang, delib-
erately distancing the colloquialism of the poem from the language
we might expect to hear the poet use in conversation:

> It looks as though the storm-fiend were planning to kick up
>   quite a ruckus
> For this evening. I had better be getting back to the tent
> To make sure everything is shipshape, weight down the canvas
>   with extra stones,
> Bank the fire, and prepare myself a little hardtack and tea
> For the evening's repast.
> ["The Skaters," *RM* 56]

This is neither contemporary idiom nor even the way somebody's
grandfather might talk; it seems closer to the kind of humorous rep-
resentation of the language of a person who has become frozen in
time that one encounters in movies or TV commercials. Certainly

not the poet's voice, neither is it the voice of another speaker; it is, rather, a representation of a representation, doubly removed from the voice of any actual speaker. Though Ashbery cites Auden as the inspiration for his use of slang, he often uses colloquialism in ways substantially different from Auden's, to undermine rather than enhance the impression of voice.

Yet the illusion of voice is far from entirely erased from Ashbery's poetry, as we may fairly say it is from that of the most radical of contemporary Language writers. While at times the language of the poems appears generated out of nothing more than a principle of unlimited freeplay, one nevertheless finds, juxtaposed with passages of broadly distanced irony, a language that seems expressive, that seems to invite us to take it as personal and immediate. A further look at the opening of "Definition of Blue" may help illuminate this characteristic strategy, in which a burlesque tone slides into something more recognizably Ashberyan without any clear indication of transition:

> The rise of capitalism parallels the advance of romanticism
> And the individual is dominant until the close of the nine-
> teenth century.
> In our own time, mass practices have sought to submerge the
> personality
> By ignoring it, which has caused it instead to branch out in all
> directions
> Far from the permanent tug that used to be its notion of
> "home."
> [*DDS* 53]

The opening lines, as David Bromwich points out, feel like a parody of a lecturer ("Poetic Invention and the Self-Unseeing," 122), or perhaps a page from that "pocket history of the world" Ashbery describes in "Grand Galop," "so general / As to constitute a sob or wail unrelated / To any attempt at definition" (*SP* 16). And yet by the time we arrive at the "permanent tug," we encounter a typically Ashberyan paradox, one that dissolves fixity—"permanent," "home"—into gesture and impulse: "tug." Though the voice of the lecturer resurfaces at moments in the poem ("But today there is no point in looking to imaginative new methods"), no clear demarcation ever emerges between the lecturer's and the poet's voices. The degree of irony to be accorded any particular statement thus becomes difficult to judge, and it becomes anything but clear that we are not to take the opening lines as an "authentic" statement of the poet's beliefs. Parody depends on some notion, even if only implied, of what a nonparodic statement would sound like; in Ashbery's writing, the distance between parodic and nonparodic verges on the unmeasurable.

An examination of "Daffy Duck in Hollywood" may help to make the workings of this tactic clear. The title of this poem from *Houseboat Days* promises a performance like the earlier "Farm Implements and Rutabagas in a Landscape," in which Ashbery elaborates a sestina-length scenario, involving the "Popeye" comic strip characters, that seems to bear no reference whatsoever to anything outside itself, that seems as much pure poetry, in its way, as any Mallarmé sonnet. "Daffy Duck in Hollywood," similarly, at first appears to follow no organizing principle but the wild and senseless aggregation of images, delivered in an idiom that similarly collages archaic constructions sprung from chivalric romance with a sort of pedantic slanginess, as if someone for whom English is a foreign language were trying to write in a racy vein by using a dictionary of colloquialisms:

> Something strange is creeping across me.
> La Celestina has only to warble the first few bars
> Of "I Thought about You" or something mellow from
> *Amadigi di Gaula* for everything—a mint-condition can
> Of Rumford's Baking Powder, a celluloid earring, Speedy
> Gonzales, the latest from Helen Topping Miller's fertile
> Escritoire, a sheaf of suggestive pix on greige, deckle-edged
> Stock—to come clattering through the rainbow trellis
> Where Pistachio Avenue rams the 2300 block of Highland
> Fling Terrace. He promised he'd get me out of this one,
> That mean old cartoonist, but just look what he's
> Done to me now! I scarce dare approach me mug's attenuated
> Reflection in yon hubcap, so jaundiced, so *déconfit*
> Are its lineaments—fun, no doubt, for some quack phrenolo-
>   gist's
> Fern-clogged waiting room, but hardly what you'd call
> Companionable.
> [*HD* 31]

This style of chaotic juxtaposition produces an effect of agitation and urgency, which in turn is continually undercut by the humor generated in the collision of elevated language with the mundane.

Daffy Duck's voice seems consistent in its cycle of inflation by allusion to chivalric romance, followed by farcical deflation, while at the same time these contrasts seem far too great to subsume under any notion of a coherent speaker. The title, "Daffy Duck in Hollywood," in its specification of speaker and situation promises a dramatic monologue, but what the poem delivers cannot be brought together within Brooks and Warren's notions of "fundamental character and situation."

The poem's contrasts reflect those of its source, which is not so much Tex Avery's 1938 cartoon "Daffy Duck in Hollywood" as Chuck Jones's celebrated "Duck Amuck" of 1953. In "Duck Amuck," Daffy swashbuckles onto the screen wielding a rapier, as if to reprise his 1950 role, "The Scarlet Pumpernickel." The setting, without Daffy's noticing it at first, shifts to a barnyard, where, after an ineffectual attempt to apprise the cartoonist of the problem, Daffy chooses to switch rather than fight, changes to overalls, and throws a hoe over his shoulder. Throughout, the scene keeps shifting in this fashion, with Daffy always a step behind. By the middle of the cartoon nothing is safe; Daffy's body is replaced temporarily by a monstrously absurd contraption, and his voice is reduced for a time to a series of animalistic grunts and squawks. Like the Daffy of the cartoon, Ashbery's character is at the mercy of disconcertingly rapid changes of scene which leave the speaker disoriented and strange to himself, unable to face his own "reflection." Yet, at about its middle, the frenetic motion of the poem gives way to a moment of syntactical calm:

> I have
> Only my intermittent life in your thoughts to live
> Which is like thinking in another language.
> [HD 32]

If the poem, to this point, has embodied the predicament of the mind assaulted by the chaos of discourses that compete for priority in our culture, here it stands back to reflect on that predicament. Of course, a cartoon character lives only an "intermittent life" in the thoughts of others, but here Ashbery generalizes this condition with an oblique echo of a passage from "Soonest Mended" quoted earlier: "Weren't we rather acting this out / For someone else's benefit, thoughts in a mind / With room enough and to spare for our little problems" (DDS 17). While in "Soonest Mended" marginalization seems potentially liberating, a way to "step free" of the narrow concerns of the self, in the later poem it is shaded with some of the pathos generated by the most extremely marginalized character in English poetry, Milton's Satan, as Daffy continues:

> While I
> Abroad through all the coasts of dark destruction seek
> Deliverance for us all, think in that language . . .
> [HD 33]

On first thought Daffy seems to get the worst of the comparison these lines propose. But if the distance between the earlier and the contemporary culture hero allows us to measure the diminishment of our own civilization in comparison to Milton's, it also invests with a certain grandeur the duck's struggle to prevail against the shocks and indignities inflicted by an unseen tormentor, a tormentor who is in fact his creator as well. It's by no means certain whether the joke here is on him or on us.

In the poem's brief final section the agitation of the first part is finally stilled and a number of typically Ashberyan constructions appear:

> Some
> There were to whom this mattered not a jot: since all
> By definition is completeness (so
> In utter darkness they reasoned), why not
> Accept it as it pleases to reveal itself? As when
> Low skyscrapers from lower-hanging clouds reveal
> A turret there, an art-deco escarpment here, and last perhaps
> The pattern that may carry the sense, but
> Stays hidden in the mysteries of pagination.
> Not what we see but how we see it matters; all's
> Alike, the same, and we greet him who announces
> The change as we would greet the change itself.
> [HD 34]

"As when" is a common opening gambit for Ashbery's sentences, and "the mysteries of pagination" falls into a pattern common in his work, in which an abstract noun is modified by an oddly concrete genitive. And the poem closes with a passage that seems to echo, tonally, a great many other endings in Ashbery, in which an acceptance of limits enables a felicity unavailable to striving:

Life, our
Life anyway, is between. We don't mind
Or notice any more that the sky *is* green, a parrot
One, but have our earnest where it chances on us,
Disingenuous, intrigued, inviting more,
Always invoking the echo, a summer's day.
[HD 34]

This closing section sports a number of inversions (e.g., "bivouac we") reminiscent of the verbal habits of the Daffy Duck voice, yet this ending seems very different in tone from the broadly ironic opening. How has this voice entered the poem? I propose that the often highly conventional-seeming endings of Ashbery's poems are enabled by the fracturing and displacement of voice—of which "Daffy Duck in Hollywood" is a particularly baroque example; Ashbery is able to employ highly traditional forms of lyric closure because the play of voices in the poems prevents these passages from being read directly as expressive utterances by the poet—saves them, that is, from sentimentality.

Again and again, even the most discontinuously organized of Ashbery's poems arrive at some traditional form of elegiac terminus: a phrase or image that seems to sum up the poem as a whole, a natural image, an epigrammatic reflection, or a gesture that suggests a return to beginnings:

And yet it results in a downward motion, or rather a floating one
In which the blue surroundings drift slowly up and past you
To realize themselves some day, while, you, in this nether world that could not be better
Waken each morning to the exact value of what you did and said, which remains.
["Definition of Blue," *DDS* 54]

There are still other made-up countries
Where we can hide forever,
Wasted with eternal desire and sadness,
Sucking the sherbets, crooning the tunes, naming the names.
["Hop o' My Thumb," *SP* 33]

And then somehow the loneliness is more real and more human

You know not just the scarecrow but the whole landscape
And the crows peacefully pecking where the harrow has
      passed.
["Lithuanian Dance Band," *SP* 53]

At sunset there is a choice of two smiles: discreet or serious.
In this best of all possible worlds, that is enough.
["The Serious Doll," *HD* 51]

> The night is itself sleep
And what goes on in it, the naming of the wind,
Our notes to each other, always repeated, always the same.
["A Love Poem," *AWK* 101]

While these endings are not without their Ashberyan oddities, they nevertheless fall into a number of recognizable paradigms for poetic closure, much more so than Ashbery's transitions correspond to familiar modes of transition. In part, this habit makes possible his characteristic fusion of elegiac lyricism and a jagged, discontinuous surface. Endings like "the crows peacefully pecking" write a satisfying finis to poems that might otherwise feel deprived of closure, given the tenuousness of their internal structure, in which neither narrative movement nor an apparent discursive logic seems to dictate the flow of transitions. Again, Ashbery's strategy of equivocation permits the poet to inhabit the elegiac mode while avoiding the charge of sentimentality the skeptical consciousness stands ready to make. The seemingly arbitrary arrival of these elegiac moments distances them from the poet, as if they were merely thrown up by the same energies of language that have generated the jagged structures of the body of the poem. At the same time, the ending casts its humanizing glow over the rest of the poem, making its puzzlements legible within the context of the affective state they can, retrospectively, be seen as leading up to.

Ashbery's endings, though, are merely a special case of a more general strategy, in which a language of lyric pathos wanders unmoored through the poems. This language is on occasion introduced by conventionalized emotive gestures:

Alas, the summer's energy wanes quickly,
A moment and it is gone.
["Soonest Mended," *DDS* 17]

Ah, but this would have been another, quite other
Entertainment, not the metallic taste
In my mouth as I look away . . .
["A Man of Words," *SP* 8]

O we are all ushered in—
Into the presence that explains.
["The Preludes," *AWK* 91]

These markers—"Alas," "Ah," "O"—create a momentary sense
of a lyric subject whose feelings might be communicated by the
poem, while in a good many passages Ashbery verges on an almost
Tennysonian lushness:

You have built a mountain of something,
Thoughtfully pouring all your energy into this single monu-
    ment,
Whose wind is desire starching a petal,
Whose disappointment broke into a rainbow of tears.
["These Lacustrine Cities," *RM* 9]

          But the summer
Was well along, not yet past the mid-point
But full and dark with the promise of that fullness,
That time when one can no longer wander away
And even the least attentive fall silent
To watch the thing that is prepared to happen.
["As One Put Drunk into the Packet-Boat," *SP* 1]

          Feelings are important.
Mostly I think of feelings, they fill up my life
Like the wind, like tumbling clouds
In a sky full of clouds, clouds upon clouds.
["Poem in Three Parts," *SP* 22]

          Why must you go? Why can't you
Spend the night, here in my bed, with my arms wrapped
    tightly around you?
["No Way of Knowing," *SP* 57]

As quickly as one impulse works to dismantle lyric subjectivity,
another reassembles it from its components. But again, only its scat-
tered and transitory nature allows this lyric impulse to exist at all.

If we were to take passages like these as directly expressive, they would court the charge of sentimentality. Sentimentality was a leading object of modernist scorn, and the remedy usually prescribed for it was irony. Brooks and Warren give a clearly tendentious, if ostensibly evenhanded, treatment of the question:

> We rarely find the ironical poet . . . falling into sentimentality; other faults he may have, but this fault his irony usually protects him against. It is easy to see why. The sentimental poet is nearly always straightforward and direct. When we feel that he is caught off guard and takes his subject or himself too seriously without previous consideration—when we feel that he is "carried away" by his own enthusiasm, we say that he is sentimental. [595–96]

Ashbery departs from institutionalized modernism in his use of an almost Victorian language of sentiment, but at the same time that language is saved from sentimentality by its being bracketed, so to speak, by a language of irony. As this expressive language passes through the poems—appearing, having its moment, then giving way—the reader is dissuaded from identifying the sentiments it expresses with those of the poet. Pathos appears, but it is a disembodied pathos that floats free from a subject that might experience it, just as Ashbery's sentences wander away from their grammatical subjects. The New Criticism preferred the ironic to the sentimental speaker, but refused to ironize the concept of speaker itself. Ashbery thus carries out a two-pronged attack on the New Critical notion of speaker: he ironizes the idea of speaker, fracturing and scattering poetic voice, while conversely reintroducing a language of sentiment. Ashbery's work is both more and less "direct," more and less sentimental, than New Critical prescription would allow.

This continual erasure and restoration of voice results in the previously remarked blurring of boundaries between parodic and nonparodic. In its usual operation, parody acts as a kind of exorcism, giving the definitive send-off to a style or a mode of expression that has gone stale, that no longer commands aesthetic faith. Ashbery, however, describes his own practice of parody in almost precisely the opposite terms:

> *NYQ:* You do seem to use parody and certain types of diction or jargon, really, in a wry way. There is a humorous or satirical aspect to things that you write.

JA: Yes, but it's not so much satirical as really trying to re-vitalize some way of expression that might have fallen into disrepute. [*NYQ* 30]

The boundary between parodic and nonparodic is a founding taboo of style, and Ashbery's breach of it seems to be behind the angry accusations of insincerity leveled by his detractors. Robert Richman, for instance, complains of the poetry that "the emotions, like the images, seem to be used or false" ("Our 'Most Important' Living Poet," 63), while Claude Rawson intends his description of Ash-bery's handling of parody to be anything but flattering: "In the high self-conscious mix of postmodern Shandyism, the ubiquitous ele-ment of parody, instead of implying rejection, tends to cherish what it mimics along with the mimicking self" (182). Behind complaints such as these lies an assumption that it remains possible to express "emotions" in poetry in a direct and untroubled fashion. For Ash-bery, however, sincerity is by no means an easy or unproblematic matter in a "technological society" that pushes lyricism to the mar-gins; as he puts it, "You can't say it that way any more" (*HD* 45). Ashbery's poetic is rather the product of a perception closer to that of Adorno, who sees the ruthless rationalization of modern society as destroying "the traditional concept of the poetic as something elevated and sacred" (*Aesthetic Theory* 24). For Adorno, poetry's response to the loss of certainty it has suffered cannot be a retreat into nostalgic repetition: "If [poetry] wants to survive it must aban-don itself without reservation to the process of disillusionment that has devoured the traditional concept of the poetic" (24). Ashbery knows that this situation cannot be canceled by a simple act of will. The confusion between parodic and nonparodic, ironical and sin-cere, which has so upset some of Ashbery's critics, provides a means by which lyricism is allowed to survive, protected from the on-slaught of disillusionment, but only at the price of self-estrangement, of camouflaging itself so that it seems almost indistinguishable from its opposite.

The reading I present here might be seen as attempting to recon-cile the very different accounts of Ashbery given by critics such as Marjorie Perloff and Helen Vendler, to place the poet *between* two attitudes toward his work, as he placed himself between the neo-metaphysicals and the neo-avant-gardists at the outset of his career. Perloff counts Ashbery as an exemplar of the "poetics of indeterminacy"; for her, his writing represents the achievement of an absolute impersonality, in which the freeplay of the signifier scatters any vestiges of a lyric subject. Vendler, on the other hand, sees Ashbery through the lens not of Derrida but of Keats, as a lyric singer directly within the romantic lineage (*The Music of What Happens* 224–26). Each has seen a share of the truth, to paraphrase Ashbery, although it seems to me that Vendler has hold of the more significant, and less obvious, truth. Perloff's discussion of Ashbery assimilates him to the heroic mode of early modernist avant-gardism, a mode Perloff has been anxious, in her championing of the Language poets, to validate. But as we've seen, Ashbery in his own statements reveals a profound distrust of the impulse to avant-garde heroism. Certainly, the poet of linguistic freeplay exists in Ashbery, but exists in combination with, and in some sense permits the existence of, the Keatsian lyricist. Ashbery himself says that "all my stuff is romantic poetry, rather than metaphysical or surrealist" (*NYQ* 30): not metaphysical, like the 1950s formalists led by Lowell, nor surrealist, the genealogy Perloff would construct for him. The opprobrium which the academic canonizers of modernism heaped upon the romantic impulse paradoxically enables its revival to perform a subversive function; declaring oneself a romantic marks in a forthright way one's distance from New Critical orthodoxy.

Yet Ashbery's romanticism remains tempered by the presence in his poetry of all those moments that trouble and question the pure voice of the lyric singer. The poetry becomes, then, imbued with a kind of second-order pathos, in which its difficulty—its moments of fragmentation and opacity—reads as an index of the frustrations of the poet's situation. The poet's urge to speak clearly and directly to an audience must struggle against his uncertainty about who the audience is, against the fear of sentimentality that haunts lyric discourse in a world dominated by technocratic rationality, against the ironic intrusions of degraded language, from bureaucratese to advertising to cartoons, upon his linguistic consciousness. Ashbery never forgets that, in Walter Benjamin's words, "the climate for lyric poetry has become increasingly inhospitable" (109), and the poems never allow the reader to forget this. But even the most fragmented and recalcitrant moments of Ashbery's writing have buried within them a poignancy born of their own lack of expressiveness. The expressive mode surfaces from time to time, but the condition of its doing so is the incorporation of the antipoetic into the poem and the consequent alienation of the expressive mode from the speaking voice. On this slender and dangerous middle ground, between a sentimental lyricism and a radical impersonality that would be no more than a surrender in the face of the antipoetic, Ashbery's work takes its stand.

John

Ashbery's

Difficulty

THE RETURN

OF THE REPRESSED:

LANGUAGE POETRY

AND NEW

FORMALISM

In the early 1980s American poetry seemed to have passed beyond the era of contentious theoretical debate initiated in the 1950s by the Beat and Projectivist movements. James Breslin, surveying the American poetry scene in 1984, proposed as a metaphor not the "peaceful public park" of the "middle fifties" or the "war zone" of the "sixties," but "a small affluent town in Northern California," where "there are no ideological disputes" (250). While the general sense of comfort, complacency, and smallness, in both its good and bad aspects, evoked by Breslin's description remains characteristic of what one might broadly call the mainstream—those poets who teach in MFA programs, publish with trade and university presses, and appear in journals like *American Poetry Review*, *Ploughshares*, and *Antaeus*—in recent years this stable configuration of poets and audiences has been upset by insurgencies from both its metaphorical right and left. The loosely organized, free-verse "voice" poem, which dominates practically unchallenged an anthology like Daniel Halpern's 1975 *American*

Poetry Anthology, has suddenly found itself under attack by ideas of poetic form that question its theoretical foundations.

One band of insurgents has become known as New Formalists, the other as Language poets. They might seem at first to have nothing in common except an enemy, but both movements' defining themselves against the colloquial free-verse lyric that occupies the mainstream makes for some shared assumptions, despite the radical differences between their programs. Most broadly, both participate in that curiously persistent American poetic myth, already on its third go-round in this century, that one might term "technological determinism," which takes the decision to write in "closed" or "open" forms as the crucial, defining poetic choice. Both hold a fundamentally deterministic view of poetic form, seeing the formal strategies they employ as dictated inescapably by the nature of poetry, or of language itself, or by the direction of history (literary or other). Though their prescriptions differ radically, both propose themselves as antidotes to what they describe as the imprisonment of American poetry within a poetics of the private self. A focus on the technology of literature thus becomes the remedy to a focus on personality. And both have arisen and flourished largely outside the academy. It's one of the weird ironies of our moment that one finds an entrenched academic poetry dedicated to the ideals of spontaneity and direct expressiveness challenged on one side by poets who draw much of their inspiration from literary theory and philosophy, and on the other by poets advocating a return to convention and tradition.

Any disinterested observer has to be impressed by the energy and perseverance of the loosely confederated group of writers who have come to be known as Language poets. Since coming together in various locations some twenty years ago, the core group of founders and a circle of followers have formed an extensive network of like-minded practitioners, staged readings, published magazines, and founded publishing houses. They have done this with almost no help, or even attention, from the mainstream outlets and institutions serving poetry; the Language poets have not been adopted by any commercial publishing house, promoted or noticed in venues like the *New York Times Book Review* or even, for the most part, *American Poetry Review* or *Poetry*, or received grants and prizes from the usual foundations and committees. For a long time the Language writers existed outside or on the fringe of the academy, though recently a number of them have joined faculties and their movement has acquired some powerful academic boosters, most prominent among them Jerome McGann. Five years ago, a survey of the most significant developments in recent American poetry might well have omitted Language writing without risking charges of partiality; now, the vigorous backing of its academic supporters has made Language writing an important issue on the American poetic scene.

The Language writing movement presents itself as a revival of an earlier mode of avant-gardism, not merely in its establishment of alternative means of distribution but also in its self-conscious taking of aesthetic positions, its frequent production of manifestos and other statements. Mainstream poetic practice in America, as it flows through the creative writing programs, has little need of manifestos. Though a rhetoric of pluralism obscures the underlying conformity, the range of stylistic options and models employed in the mainstream is in fact quite narrow; differences in outlook and approach are rarely so dramatic as to involve fundamental disagreements of principle that would be worth arguing publicly. For many mainstream poets, interviews rather than essays are the chief avenue for articulating a poetics. While mainstream poets may disagree in their understandings, for instance, of the master abstractions, such as "voice," "image," "immediacy," and "concreteness" that structure mainstream poetic production, such disagreements are rarely so severe as to call for polemic; nor does it seem, in general, that the poets have devoted much theoretical reflection to these subjects.[1] The Language writers stand outside the consensus; they are self-conscious poetic revolutionaries of a sort familiar since Wordsworth. What distinguishes them from earlier poetic revolutionaries is their seeing the increase in difficulty attendant upon their innovations as in some ways an end in itself rather than merely a side effect of poetic experimentation. Hostile readers often accused poets like Eliot and Stevens of deliberate obscurantism, and while the snob appeal of baffling the complacent bourgeois reader was certainly a real part of the attraction of modernist experimentalism, the modernists, sincerely, I think, rejected the accusation of deliberately attempting to be unreadable, even if they felt, as Eliot did, that serious poetry in the modern era "must be difficult." For a Language writer like Bruce Andrews, however, "unreadability" is a goal in itself, intimately linked to a high and largely unexamined value placed upon the "new": " 'Unreadability'—that which requires new readers, and teaches new readings" ("Text and Context" 31).

What seems to have generated the recent interest in Language writing among academic critics, however, is not this relatively novel aspect of their work, but rather the explicitly political character of the aesthetic underpinning it. The Language writers obviously have their roots in the alternative poetries gathered in Donald Allen's 1960 anthology, *The New American Poetry*. But where the older poets in that anthology were often New Deal liberals, and the younger poets leftists of the Beat anarchist sort, the Language writers generally announce themselves as Marxist radicals. As McGann puts it: "The difference between pre- and post-1973 American poetry lies in the extremity of the ideological gap which separates traditionalists from the innovators in the post-1973 period. . . . L=A=N=G=U=A=G=E writers typically foreground their oppositional politics in ways that the New American Poets did not" (CPAR 627). Academic criticism has obviously been growing much more heavily politicized and ideologically self-aware in recent years; and though Language writing developed largely outside the academy, its fate surely depends in large measure on the extent to which it can capture the institutional readership represented by the university. While the insertion of modernist works into the curriculum that took place in the 1940s and 1950s in some ways only confirmed the triumph of modernism, to a significant extent it produced that triumph—or was, rather, the triumph itself. If Language poetry is to follow the path from marginality to centrality earlier taken by high modernism, its alliance with a newly politicized professoriat will be crucial.

Rationales for poetic experiment might be broadly described as falling into two categories, natural and cultural: either one asserts that the current modes of poetry are out of tune with the nature of language, the way men actually speak, or some similar natural ground, and proposes to bring them closer; or one asserts that the current modes reflect a debased cultural condition, or the values of a dying society, and proposes a renovation on the basis of that diagnosis. The Wordsworthian revolution, while of course bearing an enormous cultural component, presented itself as one based on a natural rationale; no one *speaks* the way Gray writes. Rimbaud's revolt, and somewhat more ambiguously the Pound-Eliot insurgency, might be seen as instances of culturally formulated stylistic revolutions. Though other factors were involved and adduced, certainly the poets' reactions, respectively, to the France that emerged from the defeat of the Commune, and more generally the Europe that plunged itself into the Great War, were the targets of a program of transformation that saw discarding the aesthetic forms of a "botched civilization," in Pound's phrase (*Personae* 191), as part of a larger struggle over social values.

Both forms of revolutionary rationale are represented in the Language movement's writing. As McGann remarks, the Language writers assume the Saussurean position that "declares 'reality' to be a function of the language(s) by which we speak of it" (PECF 446) and go beyond that proposition to subscribe to Derridean tenets concerning the inability of any speaker or utterance to fix the play of signification, an inability that leads to a deep and fundamental skepticism regarding the referential function of language. As Bruce Andrews puts it, "individual signifiers have no natural relationship to individual signifieds or mental imagery, and certainly not to individual referents" ("Constitution" 157–58). If referentiality is merely an exploded fiction, and the self simply a metaphor, then a writing that dispenses with referentiality, abandons the notion of lyric subjectivity, and discards any pretense of embodying an authorial intention will be more in tune with the true nature of language. Following out this logic, the Language writers produce work that pushes to an extreme the lexical and syntactical innovations of such modernists as Joyce and Stein (Harmon 106). If the freeplay of the signifier is at the heart of all language, then truth to the medium (a decidedly modernist value) will be best secured by a corresponding freeplay in every element of the work.

This "natural" rationale for experimentation slides over easily into the cultural rationale, along lines laid out by the poststructuralist sources of the Language aesthetic. Julia Kristeva puts it well: "Magic, shamanism, esoterism, the carnival, and 'incomprehensible' poetry all underscore the limits of socially useful discourse and attest to what it represses: the *process* that exceeds the subject and his communicative structures" (16); a critique of bourgeois instrumentalist discourse, in other words, is inherent in the hermetic nature of difficult poetry. Similar notions are elaborated in the critical writings of Language poets like Ron Silliman: "What happens when a language moves toward and passes into a capitalist stage of development is an anaesthetic transformation of the perceived tangibility of the word, with corresponding increases in its expository, descriptive and narrative capacities" (*NS* 10). The antidote, then, to the hegemonic operations of exposition and narrative would be writing like that of Silliman's *Tjanting*, which seems fairly effectively to have short-circuited those modes of discourse: "False start. Circadia. True start. Applause, ability. A run around a ring around of roses read. Gum bichromate. Jets swoop low over the destroyer amid bursts of anti-aircraft fire, dozens of bombs going off in the water, then rise up again & the audience cheers. Sandy analogy to the quick. The poem plots. Not this. Indented servant. Moot pleonast. Opposable thumb" (*In the American Tree* 141). For the Language writers and their academic supporters, assaults on the "descriptive and narrative" functions of language such as those staged by Silliman's work strike a blow against the ideological apparatus underpinning the capitalist state.

At its extreme, this argument for the political efficacy of experimental writing makes a decidedly dubious appeal to nature. Hannah Weiner, for instance, proposes that "disjunctive and non-sequential writing can change states of consciousness, awakening the reader to reality, and thus the need for political change. . . . it does this by forcing an aberration in the left brain language centers" (226). More typical of the cultural rationale, however, is the sort of argument against narrative summarized in this passage by McGann: "Narrativity is an especially problematic feature of discourse . . . because its structures lay down 'stories' which serve to limit and order the field of experience, in particular the field of social and historical experience. Narrativity is . . . an inherently conservative feature of discourse" (CPAR 638). If narrative is inherently conservative, then the abandonment or sabotaging of narrative challenges the foundations of the existing order. McGann's characterization of the political operation of Silliman's work might be generalized to that of the entire movement: "As a writer his struggle against these exploitive social formations appears as a critique of the modes of language which produce and reproduce the 'reality' of a capitalist world and history" (CPAR 640). Language writing thus appeals to the leftist academic critic as an instance of politically engaged creative work that operates not within the outmoded discourse of a "vulgar" Marxism, nor along the lines of the group solidarity of an oppressed or marginalized cohort to which the critic does not belong, but in a set of terms made available by a commitment to Western Marxist and poststructuralist theoretical positions, exactly the theoretical matrix within which the critic functions. So Andrew Ross celebrates the appearance, in the work of the Language poets, of a "new hardheadedness in cultural and social matters" (365), as distinct, presumably, from the dogmatism of the party intellectual or the sentimentality of the spokesperson for the disadvantaged.

This coincidence of theoretical tenets has its limiting as well as its generative aspects, however. Both the natural and the cultural rationales for Language writing beg some obvious questions, questions that critics like McGann and Ross, perhaps because of the proximity of their own assumptions to those of the poets, fail to ask. The "natural" rationale views language as having a particular nature, one described in deconstructive terms as polyvalent, disseminated, and decentered; the job of the text, then, in reflecting that nature, is to "order itself in such a way as to multiply . . . generative 'polyentendres'" (PECF 449). But if this is indeed the nature of language, then all writing, not merely Language writing, is polyvalent, disseminated, and decentered, and no special efforts on the part of the poet are necessary to achieve this condition. McGann remarks that in Charles Bernstein's poetry "relationships and forms of order can only be had if they are actively made by the reader" (CPAR 638), but if two decades of deconstructive and reader-response criticism have established anything, it is that this holds true for all literature, indeed for all writing of any kind. McGann demonstrates the point himself when he reads Robert Frost's "Stopping by Woods" as if it were Language poetry (MRP 627–30). The point of this exercise, presumably, is to clinch McGann's case for the centrality of reception history in interpretation; only reception history, he implies, can save us from such absurdities as taking the "though" in "His house is in the village, though," as the name of the village. But demonstrating that Frost's poem can yield as many "polyentendres" per line as any by Bernstein undermines the case McGann makes elsewhere for the necessity of Language writing, and for its radical difference from more conventional forms of writing.

What this reveals as well is the high and unargued value McGann places upon self-consciousness; presumably, what differentiates Frost and Bernstein is the latter's superior awareness of the many possible ways of reading his poetry, as opposed to the logocentric naïveté implicitly assigned to the former. McGann probably had some such notion in mind when he remarked of "procedural writing" that its "acts of intervention . . . are conscious of their own relative status" (CPAR 637). Though the demands made by the self's exposure as a fiction mean that "acts" here must be "conscious," the passage nevertheless implies that the value of Language writing proceeds from its authors' self-consciousness about their position and their activities. The suspicion is confirmed later in the same essay, when the novel, victim of its own mystifications, is contrasted unfavorably with poetry: "The novel, dominated as it is by referentiality and narrativity, is always moving within the medium of its own self-occlusion. The function of poetry is to provide an example of language in conscious pursuit of complete self-transparency" (CPAR 641). Here again, in canonically deconstructive fashion, language has a mind of its own, but despite McGann's care to subtract any mention of the author from passages like this, it seems that for him the value of Language writing is intimately bound up with the intense self-consciousness of its practitioners.

This valuation raises questions of its own. For the moment, though, I want to focus on the radically dualistic schema employed in the critical discourse around Language writing, in which a bankrupt traditionalism is opposed, in starkly Manichaean fashion, to the authenticity of the experimentalists. Ron Silliman sounds a characteristic note when he states that "the mechanisms of public canonization are pathological and its proponents are malignant" ("Canons" 152). McGann's version of this tone is less melodramatic but equally alarmist: "So false and self-conflicted seem the ordinary public forms of discourse—in the media, the policy organs of government, and the academic clerisy—that the artistic representation of such discourse must either be subjected to their one-dimensionality or it must activate a critical engagement" (CPAR 643). This binarism is translated straightforwardly into political terms: "Oppositional politics are a paramount concern, and the work stands in the sharpest relief, stylistically, to the poetry of accommodation" (CPAR 626). So McGann reads the rift between Language writing and "traditionalist" verse in terms of apocalyptically imagined political alternatives. This ascription of absolute political virtue to the "experimentalists" and absolute political bankruptcy to the "traditionalists" underlies the curious lack of skepticism with which he evaluates the claims of Language writing. Like other contemporary historicists, McGann is nothing if not critical when examining the self-understandings of earlier poets, subjecting their work to rigorous demystification; the very title of McGann's *The Romantic Ideology* makes plain his characteristic attitude. When it comes to Language writing, however, the critic deploys a highly conventional vocabulary of appreciation, describing Silliman's *Tjanting*, for instance, thus: "The chief effect is a brilliant sense of immediacy which is not, however, fixed or formalized" (CPAR 639). Or, take Andrew Ross's praise for Barrett Watten: "For once, there is the sense that a fair deal has been struck; the labor of composition is somehow equal to the labor of reading,

After

the Death

of Poetry

and so the readers share meaning rather than merely responding to the writer's meaning, or else producing their own at will" (76). That "somehow" begs an enormous number of questions, and a skeptical observer might ask how either alternative, "merely responding" or "producing . . . at will," could ever be possible; even the most passive or "wild" reading, one would have thought, is still to some extent an interactive process. I don't mean to be ungenerous; anyone who's ever talked or written about poetry has probably been driven to language as empty as this in describing what he or she admires about a particular work; I'm no exception. But we're a long way here from the "new hardheadedness" Ross celebrated earlier.

For the most part, the poets themselves are refreshingly honest about problems and contradictions that academic critics pass over in silence. Jackson Mac Low, for instance, in his statement " 'Language-Centered,' " acknowledges that "the many works thrown under this rubric are no more 'centered in language' than a multitude of other literary works" (23); he acknowledges, in other words, that the radical separations engineered by the critics are finally arbitrary. Mac Low likewise raises questions about the political valence, or at least the political efficacy, of "language-oriented" work in an exchange with Bruce Andrews:

> *Jackson Mac Low:* Now you might say . . . don't write in the transparent modes, even if in directly critical and negating ways . . . because that only encourages the hegemony. But I question very strongly that that all should be abandoned. . . . What do you think of a tandem project of this sort?—that it does encourage the bastards?
>
> *Andrews:* I feel that it only encourages the bastards *in me* [laughter]. . . . I'm suspicious about the efficacy here.
>
> *Mac Low:* So am I. But nevertheless, I feel sometimes I ought to speak in a way that a larger number of people here and there might be interested in; you might not just have the converted, but those on the line, etc.—by bringing in a lot of things that are efficacious, in the sense of a rhetorical poetry . . . a more basic poetry. [Bernstein, *The Politics of Poetic Form* 39–41]

Bruce Boone shares the anxiety Mac Low expresses here regarding the efficacy of the exclusively formal strategy of opposition practiced by the movement: "Our left writing of the 70s has had its characteristic deformation. It has become 'textual' at the price of abandoning any specific political tasks. As techniques of randomness have come to characterize this writing project, its social functions are no longer clear" (123). What these statements reflect is a set of long-standing questions that arose in the course of modernism over whether content or form is the more appropriate locus for oppositional practices. Silliman, while defending the specificity of the "ideological struggle" waged by the mostly white, middle-class practitioners of Language writing, nevertheless notes that "in poetry, there continues to be a radical break between those networks and scenes which are organized by and around the codes of oppressed peoples, and those other 'purely aesthetic' schools" (*NS* 31). Silliman's clarity, with its suggestion of the possibility of alternative modes of struggle, contrasts markedly with the mixed imperatives of an academic critic like Hank Lazer, who applauds the development of a multiethnic poetry on the one hand, and on the other seems distressed that these poets don't, in accordance with his own notion of the politics of form, write Language poetry ("The Politics of Form and Poetry's Other Subjects," 524–27).

Setting aside the question of the political specificity of Language writing as opposed to writing produced by members of oppressed groups, one might still question Language writing's oppositional claims. Even granting that contemporary forms of language are the products of hegemonic capitalist rationality, it doesn't follow that smashing those forms will smash capitalism. Moreover, the proposed cure is disturbingly similar to the symptoms of the disease. Andrew Ross describes the benefits of the "new sentence," an epithet adopted from Silliman, as "multiplicity of points of view, the restricted pleasure of 'jump-cutting,' narrative experimentation, the capacity to accommodate a limitless variety of information, marked discourses, voice, personality, and so on" (375). However, these same "aesthetic advantages" are also enjoyed, to an exceptional degree, by MTV, whose status as a locus of oppositional practice is dubious, to say the least. Here again, one of the poets, Bruce Andrews, is a good deal more skeptical than the academic critics:

> Writing can attack the structure of the sign after declaring that settled system of differences to be repressive. But there's an ironic twist here. The Blob-like force of interchangeability & **equivalence** . . . precedes us: it has actually carried quite far the erosion of the system of differences on which signification depends. . . . So to call for a heightening of these deterritorializing

> tendencies may risk a more **homogenizing** meaninglessness . . .
> an 'easy rider' on the flood tide of Capital. ["Constitution" 159]

In a cultural situation such as ours, it's hard to draw clear distinctions between practices that merely reflect the general psychic and social disintegration wrought by capitalism, practices that critically represent that disintegration, and practices that might potentially contest it or offer alternatives. But at a time when the seemingly omnipresent discourse of advertising is aggressively dissolving our sense of traditional narrative forms, one must query the exclusive claims to political efficacy advanced on behalf of a mode of writing for which, in McGann's words, "the time is always the present" (CPAR 637).

The binaristic thinking of critics like Ross and McGann compels them to see John Ashbery as having taken a wrong turn in his career—as being, ultimately, a failure or a sellout. The critics' need to delegitimate Ashbery's project is acute, for Ashbery provides an alternative model of a practice that has a genuine claim to the label "innovative," even "oppositional," and yet rejects the presuppositions that stand behind the critics' support of Language writing. Any reader who cares deeply about poetry is likely to be almost as dissatisfied with mainstream "workshop" practices as the Language writers and their critical promoters, but Ashbery's long history as an experimental writer, and the importance of his work to many of the Language poets, mean that he cannot be dismissed simply as a "workshop" poet. Ashbery thus threatens to throw into question the absolute dichotomies that underpin the critical valorization of Language writing. While the academic promoters of Language writing divide all poetic practice into "contestatory" and "accommodational" styles, Ashbery has used "compromise" as a favorable stylistic description (Sommer 302). And while the critics find the Language poets' highly politicized self-understandings congenial, Ashbery, though he was an "Artist for Carter" in 1980, has expressed his distaste for poetry directed primarily toward political ends (Koethe 183, Sommer 307) and belongs to an earlier avant-garde model of resistance by nonparticipation, as opposed to the Leninist vanguard role assumed by the Language writers. On the other hand, Ashbery continues to generate enormous hostility among conservative critics, which is at least one mark of experimental authenticity.

Ashbery's role in keeping alive experimental possibilities in the 1950s and 1960s is too important for them to erase or pass over in silence (Shoptaw 61–64), so Ross and McGann must separate Ashbery's work into a "good" experimentalist period and a "bad" accommodationist period. For these critics, Ashbery's most valuable work is *The Tennis Court Oath*, a book from which the poet has in large measure distanced himself (*NYQ* 16). Ross, in his anxiousness to discredit the "compromise" style of the later Ashbery, is forced to make free with the facts: "Poetry published by the major presses is generally, as one might expect, more easily 'consumed' than less well distributed writing; to give just one example, the John Ashbery published now by Viking/Penguin is easier to 'read' . . . than the John Ashbery of, say, the Ecco Press, from the seventies" (370). Whether Ashbery's recent work is easier to "read" may be questioned. Ashbery himself thinks that it is "just as random and unorganized" as his earlier work (Tranter 94), and the effect of greater ease may simply be a result of Ashbery's having by now educated an audience and acclimated it to his mode of writing. There's no question, however, that Ross's evidence here doesn't prove what he says it does. Ashbery published two books with Ecco Press in the 1970s: *Rivers and Mountains* and *The Double Dream of Spring*. Both volumes, however, were republications of books originally issued by Holt, Rinehart, and Winston and E. P. Dutton, respectively—exactly the sort of "major presses" that, Ross assures us, would never bring out a collection of experimental work. McGann, while he acknowledges Ashbery's "swerve away from the poetries of the fifties and sixties," tells us that "in those early years [1962–72] his innovative stylistic repertoire had been fully deployed" (*CPAR* 627), and since then the poet's work has narrowed to "suburban and personal interests" (*CPAR* 628). What is at stake, McGann remarks, "is not so much an issue of poetic style or poetic quality as it is a problem in ideology—the kinds of cultural ideas that are to be propagated through that crucial ideological apparatus, the academy" (*CPAR* 628). This statement rests on two questionable presuppositions. First, McGann assumes that the value of Ashbery's work reduces directly to its value in the academic setting, thus discounting in advance the cultural work Ashbery performs for his sizable extramural readership. And more significantly, McGann equates the explicit ideological commitments of the producer of a work to the ideological *effects* of that work.

Obviously, a full treatment of this question would involve the elaboration of a theory of value, which would in turn necessitate a consideration of the relationship between art and ideology; I can hardly provide such a theory here. But I think that I can state my difference with McGann and the contemporary work he champions briefly enough. McGann, as I've previously noted, posits two possible responses to inhabiting "an imperial culture like our own": one may either "oppose and change such circumstances, or . . . take them as given, and reflect (reflect upon) their operations" (CPAR 628). McGann's sneering parenthesis implies that reflection upon the current situation can do no more than reproduce it, an assumption by no means self-evident. His separation of reflection from opposition and change seems problematic as well; might not the one be a necessary precondition for the other? One might, indeed, characterize the limitations of the analysis McGann puts forward as a failure of reflection. As I have tried to show, Ashbery's development as poet arose from, and was conditioned by, an impulse to oppose a very specific set of practices, that of New Critical reading (and writing). While this opposition certainly had larger implications (it was, among other things, a swerve from the *Partisan Review*-style liberal politics of Lowell and his critical supporters), it was played out on a fairly narrowly defined, and specifically aesthetic, field. What disturbs me about both McGann's advocacy and the Language writers' self-understandings is the extremely high degree of generality at work, in which large abstractions like "narrativity," wielded by even larger abstractions like "capital," are posited as the privileged sites of political struggle.

Language writing, in McGann's account, is constantly seen as "disrupt[ing] certain traditional forms of meaning" (PECF 442), or "disturb[ing] the public order of language" (PECF 453), without the "traditional forms" or the "public order" being much further specified. McGann apparently feels that opposition at the highest level of generality is the most radical and the most genuine, so a poetry that abandons narrativity altogether must be more valuable than one that, as I hope my previous discussion of Ashbery has demonstrated about his work, employs disjunctive transitions but more familiar forms of closure. Given that narrative seems to have preexisted capitalism, however, it's open to question whether an all-out assault on it is an appropriate strategy to contest capitalism; at least one major Marxian critic, Fredric Jameson, assures us that the struggle against capitalism requires its own narratives (*Political Unconscious* 19–20). A more nuanced and precise reflection on current conditions might in fact help in shaping strategies of opposition and change. The extremely abstract and generalized understanding of the contemporary situation of writing prevalent among supporters of Language poetry has the bad effect of discouraging attention to the local and specific determinations and effects of particular poetic practices—determinations and effects that are often difficult to sort into the categories "contestatory" and "accommodational." The Language faction's discussion of these issues is pitched in terms that resemble the Cold War liberal discourse on mass culture, as it is persuasively delineated in Andrew Ross's *No Respect*. In that work, Ross evinces a formidable skepticism toward the intellectuals' vision of themselves as a small island of critical and independent thought bravely holding out against a tide of mass-produced, empty cultural objects designed for passive consumption. It's curious, then, that Ross's account of Language poetry trades so heavily in the forms of response he so lucidly questioned with regard to an earlier generation of critics.

Though I'm certainly aware that no single poem can adequately stand for a movement as broad and varied as Language writing, I put forth Charles Bernstein's "The Kiwi Bird in the Kiwi Tree" as a representative example of the kind of problems that arise in an attempt to embody the central tenets of Language writing theory in poetic practice. McGann places the poem among Bernstein's "most statemental [*sic*]" work (PECF 455–57); the poem was featured in a selection of Bernstein's poetry that appeared in *Rethinking MARX-ISM*. I quote from that text:

> I want no paradise only to be
> drenched in the downpour of words, fecund
> with tropicality. Fundament be-
> yond relation, less 'real' than made, as arms
> surround a baby's gurgling: encir-
> cling mesh pronounces its promise (not bars
> that pinion, notes that ply). The tailor tells
> of other tolls, the seam that binds, the trim,
> the waste. & having spelled these names, move on
> to toys or talcoms, skates & scores. Only
> the imaginary is real—not trumps
> beclouding the mind's acrobatic vers-
> ions. The first fact is the social body,
> one from another, nor needs no other.

The very title of the poem points toward the arbitrariness of the signifier; kiwi birds and kiwi trees (vines, actually) have no necessary reason to share a name. Neither does the poem's title seem to have anything to do with the poem itself; names and things are disjoined throughout. The whimsicality of the title, both in itself and in its relation (or lack of relation) to the poem, immediately puts one in mind of Wallace Stevens. But while a Stevens title of this sort tells its reader to expect a similar tone in the poem it introduces, Bernstein's title initiates no such contract; "The Kiwi Bird" is rich in a Derridean sort of linguistic freeplay but is hardly playful; it takes itself seriously indeed.

The poem begins with "I," as if to initiate a personal lyric, but this is the only instance of the pronoun in the poem; the suggestion of lyric subjectivity is as quickly spirited away as it is introduced. The syntax alternates from simple declarative sentences to fragments; what the poem largely avoids is complex subordinated constructions, which tend incorrigibly to produce the effect of subjectivity. The poem takes liberties with language throughout, splitting words apart at the ends of lines, punning constantly, echoing both popular phrases and poetic tradition. Although the effect is decidedly artificial (not a pejorative term in the Language poetry lexicon), Bernstein's puns and allusions have nothing of wit or cleverness about them. Puns usually operate to reveal, even if only facetiously, some hitherto unsuspected correspondence; Bernstein's puns are, deliberately and programmatically, fabrications rather than discoveries. Taken in connection with "downpour of words," "tropicality" serves to remind the reader that tropic and trope are etymologically cognate, as well as bringing to mind "topicality," but because the word is made up, the pun carries none of the sense of surprise and rightness that one could imagine a different kind of poet—Merrill, for instance—producing with a carefully prepared play on "tropical." Likewise, the splitting of "encircling" across a line break puts "cling" together with "mesh" to further characterize this fabric. The effect of this enjambment is entirely different from that usually aimed at when poets break a word across lines, which is either to make a joke about the constraints of form or to play off the meanings of the elements of a compound word against the meaning of the word as a whole, as in Ben Jonson's famous "twi- / Lights."[2] The splitting that produces "cling" from "encircling" has no semantic or etymological basis, and so it leaves the meaningless syllables "encir-" dangling on the line above; the effect is one of arbitrary and willful imposition rather than the discovery of latent implication that occurs in Jonson's lines.[3] The same could be said about

Bernstein's "vers- / ions." Isolating the first syllable of the word at line's end reminds us that "verse" has to do with turning, the turning at the end of each line (echoing the third line's "tropicality") as well as, in the context of "the mind's acrobatic vers- / ions," obliquely recalling the idiom *mental gymnastics*. Another kind of poet would have devised a phrase that used the term in an ordinary, idiomatic sense while also punning, in etymologically aware fashion, on it; this simultaneous satisfaction of two competing demands is the essence of wit. Bernstein, on the other hand, abandons any effort to adhere to common idiom in the search for multiple meanings; his puns, however polysemous, are single entendres.

My description of Bernstein's tactics as arbitrary and willful would not strike the poet, I suspect, as a criticism; Bernstein seems deliberately to avoid the belief in the occult rightness of connections established through pun or rhyme that characterizes what we usually take as "poetic" thinking. Indeed, the subject, so far as I'm able to determine it, of this poem is the simultaneous arbitrariness and inescapability of language. If one takes "Fundament beyond relation" to stand in apposition to "words," then words are seen as standing in so constitutive a relation (to beliefs, to reality) as to be beyond relation (in the sense of telling)—beyond the possibility, that is, of fully understanding and conceiving that relation, because the thing understood and the means of understanding are the same. Thus what seems "real" is in fact a construction, "less 'real' than made," and the "encir-cling mesh" of words surrounds us from our infancy (the root meaning of *infancy* is "speechless"). The poem, however, sees in this not a prison house of language but a generative structure; the "bars" are not those of a jail cell but those of a musical score, a structure within which "notes" may be placed. I won't attempt to expound fully the Lacanian resonances of "Only / the imaginary is real," but it's surely apparent that the sentence implies that we can have access only to representations and constructions, never to the unmediated "real" itself. "The first fact is the social body" is then itself ambiguous; the "body" may be either the body of the individual, which is necessarily shaped by, and understood through, the pressure of the social; or it may be the "body" of society, which preexists and conditions individual identity.

The poem, as I read it, is decidedly "statemental," in McGann's coinage. That in itself is hardly a fault, nor is it a fault that the poem's statements seem largely confined to accepted truisms of poststructuralist thought; that the *Essay on Man* and the *Essay on Criticism* are devoid of original thinking doesn't make Pope any less interesting a poet. The question that needs to be raised about a poem like "The Kiwi Bird in the Kiwi Tree," I think, is whether it fails of being adequately difficult. This may seem paradoxical, given that Bernstein and other Language poets deliberately aim to create difficulty, which would seem to be a readily attainable goal. But difficulty is not so easily achieved. The absence of any implicit standard by which a reading of the poem might be taken as adequate means that any reading might be valid, which makes the job of interpretation all too easy. Consider "scores" in line 10. The movement of the poem from "a baby's gurgling" might be seen as tracing the path of an individual's development, as a baby graduates from "toys" and "talcoms" (I confess that the misspelling baffles me) to the more active entertainments of "skates & scores." The term *scores,* of course, picks up the musical metaphor from the notes and bars of the previous sentence, may allude to the fascination with sports many of us acquire at some point in childhood, and may even refer to the period of adolescence, when boys become preoccupied with "scoring." More generally, the movement from "gurgling" to "scores" reflects the increasingly rigid and sharply categorized worlds we inhabit as we grow from infant to adult. But where nothing exists to impede the critical fancy, it's hard to feel that any act of interpretation has consequences; armed with the right critical equipment, an equipment easily enough acquired through some acquaintance with the critical prose of the movement, a reader can multiply interpretations indefinitely without the poem's providing any resistance.

Whatever meaning "The Kiwi Bird in the Kiwi Tree" has, then, is a matter of surfaces. There is nothing to penetrate because no meaning is hiding behind any other; all are equally available, and the poem offers no grounds for choice. But if this sort of poem is ultimately too easy to read, it's also too easy to write. To adopt a phrase from Coleridge, the best art seems to operate spontaneously under laws of its own devising; the problem with a poem like this one is that it has failed to devise a sufficiently rich set of rules for itself. The arbitrary treatment of all elements of language is here erected into a principle, but as I've previously remarked, the freedom from common idiom thus produced means that the poem's wordplay can achieve neither surprise nor that sense of rightness that arises when conflicting demands are simultaneously satisfied. When the poet is free to choose words without regard to goals other than polysemy, the polysemy that results scarcely seems an achievement. Ashbery speaks of attempting "to keep meaningfulness up to the pace of randomness"; Bernstein's poem, and much of the writing that goes under the "Language" rubric, may be looked at as either all meaning or all randomness, but the interesting area, and the area of genuine difficulty, lies between.

If both the practitioners and the critical promoters of Language poetry at least imagine its politics to be those of the radical left, the politics of the New Formalism have often been related to the wave of cultural and political conservatism that coincided with the rise of the movement in the early 1980s. Certainly the conservative arts journal *New Criterion* has played a role in promoting the movement by publishing many New Formalist poets and providing editorial space for essays like Brad Leithauser's "The Confinement of Free Verse" and Robert Richman's "Poetry and the Return to Seriousness," which attempt to publicize and provide a rationale for New Formalism. This association with conservative politics is hotly disputed by some apologists for New Formalism; Robert McPhillips, for example, points out that the political views expressed in New Formalist work are by no means necessarily conservative (RNF 76). Whether there might not be a deeper politics of form, in which even "pro-gay and anti-nuke" sentiments, expressed in a formally conservative fashion, could be seen as bolstering, rather than undermining, the status quo, McPhillips does not consider. Regardless, one might propose that the New Formalism, whatever the political allegiances of its practitioners, partakes of the public atmosphere of the 1980s, in which mushy liberal pieties, whether political or prosodic, had become so thoroughly entrenched that what once might have seemed unambiguously reactionary could present itself as daring and revolutionary. Indeed, the New Formalists are not shy about presenting their own movement as a poetic "revolution" (McPhillips, RNF 73).

As with the Language poets, there are varying degrees of militancy in the New Formalist camp, from moderates who practice both "closed" and "open" forms and simply argue for giving poets the option to choose whichever best suits their intentions, to radicals who, like some of the Language poets, posit a physiological basis for the necessity of their chosen forms. The polemical writing of the New Formalists appeals to both the cultural and natural forms of rationale; indeed, both may appear in the same essay. Brad Leithauser, in "The Confinement of Free Verse," begins by proposing simply that free verse "at the moment shows signs of exhaustion"

(4); this is the language of cultural rationale, which sees the present state of free verse as an instance of the cyclical abandonment and revival of literary conventions. By the end of the essay, however, Leithauser is reaching instead for the rather dubious support of neurology, entertaining at least provisionally the thesis put forward in Frederick Turner and Ernst Pöppel's paper "The Neural Lyre," in which the coauthors propose that poetic meter arises from particular features that are hard-wired into the brain. Leithauser, extending their argument, remarks that "the English language, and the bodies and brains of those who read and write it, may well be limited structurally so as to ensure that not only free verse, but every other poetic genre as well, will never match the breadth and vigor of the iambic line" (13).[4]

Taking something of a middle ground among the New Formalist polemicists is Timothy Steele, whose *Missing Measures: Modern Poetry and the Revolt Against Meter* stands as the most substantial attempt so far to place the New Formalism upon firm theoretical footing. Steele's method of pursuing this aim is curious, however; rather than presenting arguments in favor of using traditional measures, Steele devotes almost all of his nearly three hundred pages to an attempt to delegitimate free verse, apparently feeling that undermining the alternative will be sufficient to bring poets (and audiences) back to traditional prosodies. Steele presses his attack on a number of fronts; indeed, his book, while focusing on the development of free verse, is something of an indictment of poetic modernism *tout court*. Steele brings a formidable erudition to the task, even if that erudition is monotonously applied; passage after passage ends with Steele's informing the reader that this or that earlier poetic movement or group of poets, although sharing some of the goals of the modernists, nevertheless continued to write in traditional meters. This refrain, in fact, reveals one of the serious problems underlying Steele's argument; for all its erudition, Steele's writing curiously lacks a historical sense. In his long discussion of the way in which prose fiction in the last two centuries has usurped the territory, and the privileges, formerly accorded to poetry, he never mentions the spread of literacy, the growth of the middle class, or increasing urbanization, to mention only three of the factors that one might suppose have played a role in this development. And despite his explicit distance from the assumptions of the modernists, one can nevertheless see in the categories he employs the effects of the modernist redefinition of poetry.

Language

Poetry and

the New

Formalism

Like the Language poets, Steele is a rigid binarist; all poetry in his view is divided, absolutely, between formal and free. The various metrical systems of the world, the syllabics of Japanese and French, the accentual lines of old Germanic languages, the quantitative prosodies of the classical languages, and the accentual-syllabic meters of languages like modern English and German all, for Steele, fall into the category of "conventional" or "traditional" form (Steele is oddly silent on the subject of ancient Hebrew prosody; he refers to "the King James Psalms" on occasion, but without referring to what the King James version is translating). But this perspective, in which the extraordinary variety of the world's prosodic systems comes to occupy one pole of an antithesis with free verse, becomes available only after the modernist revolution has "denaturalized" the whole of previous English metrics. It's anything but clear that, before this occurrence, readers had any concept of "traditional" or "conventional" form to which all poetry in English belonged. Steele remarks that "when Dryden and Wordsworth objected to overly-poetical mannerisms, they did not include conventional metric among the qualities they wished to remove from verse; they continued to write in the traditional measures of English poetry" (7). This statement, however, reflects the modernist notion that the "subject and manner" of a poem are entirely separate matters from its prosody, a notion that leads one to posit that the contemporary reader of "Tintern Abbey" would have found its form entirely unremarkable, "conventional blank verse" (55). But this simply isn't how readers in the past thought about prosody; although English never developed the highly articulated and consistent generic system of the classical languages, particular formal choices nevertheless did entail specific presumptions about "subject and manner" (55). Wordsworth's writing a sort of stropheless ode in blank verse would have struck many of his readers as bizarre, not least because of the form he chose; this use of blank verse was anything but "conventional." Many of the more heated controversies in the history of English poetry become inexplicable if we suppose that for hundreds of years poets simply used forms that they took to be conventional and traditional. Citing T. S. Eliot's disparagement of Kipling for having unreflectively used existing forms rather than "searching for form," Steele remarks, "One feels that Eliot's remark about searching for form would entail a devaluation of virtually every fine poet from the eighth century B.C. forward. Shakespeare, for instance, wrote thirty-seven five-act plays in iambic pentameter and approximately 150 sonnets in the same line" (164). Putting aside the question of whether Shakespeare was aware that he was writing five-act plays, to take the fact that lines in both *Henry VI, Part 1*, and *Coriolanus* generally contain five feet of an unstressed followed by a stressed syllable to mean that Shakespeare was using an identical form in both is to be prosodically deaf; the difference between Shakespeare's blank verse, early and late, goes far beyond the natural variations in rhythm that distinguish any particular line from the abstract metrical pattern. An extremely general prosodic description could, of course, be devised that would cover most of the lines in both plays. To suppose, however, that the existence of that general description means that Shakespeare was not innovating formally is absurd. George Wright, the closest student of Shakespeare's metrical practice, remarks:

> Shakespeare appears, within a few years, to have made the verse, too, as problematic as these other elements [linguistic, imagistic, thematic, and ethical patterns]—not to be grasped at once but heard or only half-heard from one passage to another. . . . Shakespeare himself, throughout his career, is unmistakably examining new possibilities of arrangement in which short lines, extra syllables, heavy syncopation of medial syllables, prose, lines that pause in several places, or sentences that run from midline past the endline barrier are given key roles in the development of a new verse art. [282–83]

Between his early and late plays Shakespeare's handling of verse undergoes an enormous transformation, and little good is likely to come of defining that transformation, which well deserves to be called a search for form, out of existence.

Steele's, then, is an entirely ahistorical understanding of meter, in which one pentameter is as good as (and the same as) any other. It's clear, though, why this must be the case; for Steele to admit that prosody evolves would reinstate free verse within the general history of English metrical development, in which one might see the colloquial freedoms taken by Browning, the dissolution of accent in Tennyson, and Hardy's movement toward what even Steele refers to as a "rhymed accentual verse" as stages toward the eventual step of more radical "free" prosodies. The problem is of more than historical interest, I think, and is symptomatic of a difficulty that emerges in New Formalist poetry as well. The reduction of traditional form to the bare outlines of metrical schema, divorced from the historical dynamic of their evolution, leads to an impoverished understanding of metrics, an impoverished understanding that underlies, I think, much of the effect of metrical monotony that a sensitive critic like Alan Shapiro finds in New Formalist verse ("The New Formalism" 205).[5]

I'll instance a passage from Gjertrud Schnackenberg's "Supernatural Love," a poem that appeared in her highly praised volume *The Lamplit Answer* and which Robert Richman reprints in his tendentious anthology of contemporary poetry in traditional forms, *The Direction of Poetry*. The poem presents, in the present tense, a recollection of a scene that occurred when the speaker was four. The speaker and her father are absorbed in their respective occupations—stitching a sampler and looking up words in a dictionary—until the moment of drama that arrives at the poem's close. I quote the final four stanzas (83):

> I twist my threads like stems into a knot
> And smooth "Beloved," but my needle caught
> Within the threads, *Thy blood so dearly bought,*
>
> The needle strikes my finger to the bone.
> I lift my hand, it is myself I've sewn,
> The flesh laid bare, the threads of blood my own,
>
> I lift my hand in startled agony
> And call upon his name, "Daddy daddy"—
> My father's hand touches the injury
>
> As lightly as he touched the page before,
> Where incarnation bloomed from roots that bore
> The flowers I called Christ's when I was four.

One might at first suppose that the rhythmic monotony of the poem arises from an attempt at imitative form, in which the naïveté of the speaker's four-year-old self is represented by a deliberately unsophisticated prosody. But the formal strategies of this poem are similar to those of other poems in the same volume, and in any event iambic pentameter would be a curious choice of meter for such a strategy, given its extensive history of intensely sophisticated and self-conscious application. The absolute construction of "my needle caught" is, too, a sophisticated (and rather hard to follow) piece of syntax, inappropriate if an effect of naïveté is intended.

What produces the effect of monotony in this passage? One might at first suppose that the lack of rhythmic variation is the source of the problem. Almost all of the lines are perfect pentameters, variations are largely unadventurous, and accent within lines falls within a fairly narrow range; in "I twist my threads like stems into a knot" and "The needle strikes my finger to the bone," for instance, the four accented syllables in the line are very close to one another in stress. But I think the problem lies, rather, in the prevalence of monosyllables and in the placement of caesura. While ten low words creep in only one of the lines in this passage, monosyllables predominate, which means that the boundaries of words and the boundaries of metrical feet almost always coincide, a sure producer of prosodic monotony. The treatment of caesura is even more problematic. All caesuras in the passage occur after the fourth, fifth, or sixth syllable of the line. This is technically unadventurous but not in itself a problem; the difficulty occurs, rather, in the poet's penchant for repeating line structures. In six of the first seven, and seven of the first nine lines in the passage, caesura occurs after the fourth syllable; the last three lines all break after the sixth. It's this repetitious line structure that is the chief culprit, I think, in the impression of stiffness and monotony in the handling of meter.

Good metrical writing involves a great deal more than filling out a pattern of accented and unaccented syllables with occasional variation. It requires an understanding of many other elements of poetic form, an understanding that only an awareness of the historical development of prosody can provide. The ahistorical notions of form embodied in Steele's argument and prevalent among the New Formalists obscure that awareness and so make a problematic guide to practice. Persuasive use of "traditional" forms demands not simply an adherence to a body of prosodic rules but an effort to master and extend the technical resources available to poetry.

A number of New Formalist partisans, Steele among them, make the curious argument that writing formal verse will return to poetry the broad audience it has lost and enable poetry once again to "fulfill an important role in our culture" (Steele 293). For Dana Gioia, "revivals of traditional technique . . . both reject the specialization and intellectualization of the arts in the academy over the past forty years and affirm the need for a broader popular audience" ("Notes" 403). Robert McPhillips remarks of the New Formalists that "they seem interested in reestablishing an audience of common readers" (WNANF 207). While the New Formalists, like the Language poets, have generally operated outside or on the fringes of the academy, it hardly appears that they have created a broad popular audience, and it's far from clear how conventional meter, in and of itself, could possibly produce such an audience, much less restore poetry's lost cultural importance. One might remind these partisans that the most genuinely "popular" poet in postwar America (excepting, of course, "inspirational" writers like Rod McKuen and Hugh Prather, and celebrities like Suzanne Somers and Leonard Nimoy), the one with the broadest and most diverse readership, has been Ginsberg, who is practically the devil himself in New Formalist demonology. New Formalist partisans often accuse free versers of being obscure or inaccessible, but readers also turn away from triviality, and one may be trivial (as indeed one may be obscure or inaccessible) in measured as well as free verse.

Paul Lake tries to make a connection between formal verse and popularity: "Song lyrics, whether of Rock or Country or Pop music, still have meter and rhyme—and millions of listeners. Why then . . .

should a lyrical poetic art want . . . to remove the song-like rhythms and rhymes of formal verse?" (118). This is an analogy fairly often reached for in New Formalist polemic, but one that proves less than its makers suppose. It seems plausible to suggest that popular music now does a good deal of the cultural work that was once done by lyric poetry, but it does not follow that one could regain that territory by making poetry more like popular songs. A number of twentieth-century poets have written popular songs; the names Auden and Elizabeth Bishop come immediately to mind. But those songs were intended for the consumption of an elite audience, one that recognized the song conventions but was also aware of the relation of such works to the rest of the poet's oeuvre; neither Auden nor Bishop, surely, supposed that he or she would win a broad popular audience in this fashion. Both *Beowulf* and rap songs are written in a four-stress accentual line, but it seems unlikely that the epic could compete successfully with hip-hop for the attention of young people in south central Los Angeles, despite sharing with one strain of rap the themes of acquiring gold and inflicting violent death; for starters, you can't dance to it. Noting that formal poetry in the 1950s was associated with "academicism" and "elitism," Robert McPhillips contrasts the "new" formalism to the "old": "Characteristically, the diction of the New Formalist poem is colloquial rather than elevated. If the poem concerns cultural objects, they are likely to be from popular culture and to be indigenously American" (WNANF 200). Again, the connection between writing about popular culture and finding a broad audience may not be as direct as McPhillips assumes, and the connection between using conventional verse forms and these various populist impulses seems even more elusive. Poetry is not likely to regain its lost popularity, much less its lost cultural authority, by attempting to compete directly with popular culture, or by attempting to match the accessibility of popular cultural goods. And in a world where younger professors of literature, not to mention younger poets, often appear to be only hazily informed about the principles of versification, it's difficult to see how metrical composition will, by itself, engage the interest of a broad, nonspecialist public.

I've discussed at length the theoretical underpinnings of Language poetry and New Formalism because both propose, at least in principle, to reconfigure the relation between poet and audience. In theory, Language poetry, by actively seeking to be "unreadable," transforms the formerly passive reader into an active meaning maker (or at least meaning seeker), with the inevitable concomitant of political awakening. In practice, it appears that Language writing's best opportunity for broadening its audience beyond the coterie of practitioners to which it has been so far confined lies in evangelizing the professoriat, some members of which already seem well disposed to the movement on the basis of its consonance with their ideological and theoretical presuppositions. Indeed, in its mode of being far more intensely esoteric, intellectualized, and theoretical than the average professor of literature, Language writing illustrates a curious phenomenon of intellectual life in the last decade or so—the popularization of advanced theoretical discourses outside the academy. This dissemination of theory has been most evident, of course, in the art world, where every real estate developer turned collector can speak the lingo of the precession of simulacra (Crow 1), but Language writing shows that poetry has not gone untouched by this development. The taste for high theory outside the universities, however, is unlikely ever to be more than an epiphenomenon of academic intellectual work. Striking as has been its ability to persevere without academic support up to this point, Language writing clearly depends on the academy to produce the sophisticated, theoretically inclined readers it assumes; when the movement has run its course, I suspect it will have confirmed David Trotter's dictum that "it is now [1984] not so much the development of academic criticism as developments within academic criticism which create readerships"

(144). New Formalism seeks to reunite poetry with a broad popular audience through what it sees as the natural magic of conventional form, which retains undiminished all of its power as a fundamental convention joining poet and reader. In practice, the appeal of New Formalism seems closely linked to the humanist pieties that generally form the ultimate horizon of justification for its enthusiasts and practitioners (it's worth remarking in this regard a modest revival of Christian thematics among certain younger formalist poets, most notably Alfred Corn and Gjertrud Schnackenberg). Here, for instance, is Timothy Steele's strangely unself-conscious profession of humanist faith:

> What is most essential to human life and to its continuance remains a love of nature, an enthusiasm for justice, a readiness of good humor, a spontaneous susceptibility to beauty and joy, an interest in our past, a hope for our future, and above all, a desire that others should have the opportunity and encouragement to share these qualities. An art of measured speech nourishes these qualities in a way no other pursuit can. [294]

The likelihood of New Formalism's succeeding in regaining for poetry an audience of "common readers" seems connected to the (in my view highly unlikely) possibility that such pieties will suddenly regain the allegiance of thinking people, that the "disenchanting" effects of modernism (by which I refer to a whole social process rather than merely a literary movement) can abruptly, by fiat, be reversed.

Again, while not supposing that a single poem can stand for an entire movement, I'll discuss a poem by one of the most prominent of the New Formalists, Brad Leithauser. The poem is called "Angel."

> There between the riverbank
> and half-submerged tree trunk
> it's a kind of alleyway
> inviting loiterers—
>   in this case, water striders.
>
> Their legs, twice body-length, dent
> the surface, but why they don't
> sink is a transparent riddle:
> the springs of their trampoline
>   are nowhere to be seen.

Inches and yet far below, thin
as compass needles, almost, min-
nows flicker through the sun's
tattered netting, circling past
   each other as if lost.

Enter an angel, in
the form of a dragon-
fly, an apparition whose
coloring, were it not real,
   would scarcely be possible:

see him, like a sparkler,
tossing lights upon the water,
surplus greens, reds, milky
blues, and violets blended
   with ebony. Suspended

like a conductor's baton,
he hovers, then goes the one
way no minnow points: straight
up, into that vast solution
   of which he's a concentrate.
[*Hundreds of Fireflies* 68–69]

The poem seems at first very much in the Richard Wilbur vein of
artful celebrations of the things of this world, but with diction and
syntax tempered, according to New Formalist precept, to a more
colloquial register. There's an occasional piece of ostentatious verbal
cleverness, as in "transparent riddle," a bit of whimsy in "trampo-
line," and a subdued wit in the play with the technical meanings of
the terms "solution" and "concentrate," but the poem largely oper-
ates in a slightly heightened conversational idiom, whose most delib-
erately self-conscious moments are the two instances of enjambing
a word across a line break.

   "Angel" is reprinted in Robert Richman's anthology *The Direc-
tion of Poetry*. In the introduction to that volume, Richman de-
scribes the poems gathered there as "appealing and accessible," a
description Leithauser's poem certainly fits. He goes on to state that
the poets in the anthology "are united in their use of metered lan-
guage" (xv), by which he distinguishes them from the writers of
"hybrid" verse, "in which the pretense of a traditional form is used

without employing any of its technical attributes" (xiv). This sort of verse he sees as a symptom that "the entire conception of form has been corrupted" in our poetic culture (xv). Against this corruption, Richman promises that "the consistent use of a metrical foot . . . unites the poets in this anthology" (xvi).

A glance at the prosody of "Angel," however, shows that a fairly latitudinarian view of consistency would be required to bring it within Richman's announced principles. At first one might suppose that these lines, which certainly give the impression of being precisely measured, are in syllabics, as might be expected from a poet who has professed an affinity with Marianne Moore, but some counting quickly proves the hunch false. Scanning the poem as iambic, the first stanza seems to work out tolerably, tetrameter alternating with trimeter, with a final couplet, though the acephalous tetrameters of the first and third lines fall outside the list of variations that Richman, following George Saintsbury, is willing to accept (xvi), and the rhyming of a stressed with an unstressed syllable (*loiterers*/*striders*) strikes any sensitive ear as a barbarism, even in a poem that makes free use of slant rhyme.

Problems arise with an iambic scansion in the subsequent stanza, however, and grow more serious as the poem proceeds. The opening line of the second stanza, "Their legs, twice body-length, dent," can be resolved into iambic tetrameter only by allowing a substitution, against all traditional practice, of a single stressed syllable for the final iamb. By the fourth stanza, any prosodic consistency has completely collapsed: "Enter an angel, in / the form of a dragon- / fly." The first line might be scanned as iambic, with a trochaic first foot substitution (though Leithauser ought to be aware that the shorter the line, the less it can sustain substituted feet), but it surely is only a trimeter, in a position where tetrameters have been the rule. The second line, similarly, can have no more than two stressed syllables and seems much more like an acephalous anapestic dimeter with a feminine ending than like any kind of iambic line;[6] here the rhyming of stressed with unstressed syllable is even more obtrusive and infelicitous than in the previous instance. The opening lines of the fifth stanza fall into a perfectly regular trochaic cadence, trimeter followed by tetrameter: "see him, like a sparkler, / tossing lights upon the water." The opening line of the final stanza, on the other hand, seems to scan most plausibly as a brachycatalectic dactylic trimeter: "like a conductor's baton."[7] If Leithauser's ambition were to include every one of the standard metrical feet in a single poem, he has perhaps succeeded, but the poem's prosodic chaos seems radically out of alignment with the program put forward in Richman's introduction. It's easy to understand the forces that produced this muddle; Leithauser wants to avoid any wrenching of syntax to meet the demands of meter so that he can preserve the colloquial ease of the poem's "voice." But when that ease is purchased at such a high cost in metrical rigor, the whole project of a "new formalism" is thrown into question.

"Angel" is based on the kind of metaphor that might have made for an extended neometaphysical conceit in the hands of a 1950s formalist, but which Leithauser refrains from pressing too hard; his dragonfly is a figure for an angel only in that both are winged and ethereal. The poem seems to equivocate between immanent and transcendental points of view, between celebrating the beauty of the natural world for its own sake and seeing that beauty as a mere figure of a transcendental realm. In this way Leithauser tries to satisfy both the secular, skeptical perspective, which knows that angels do not exist, and the idealizing urge that sees in the beauty of the created world an assurance that some larger order superintends it. So the dragonfly, though it at first seems as if it will organize the chaotic motions of the minnows, "like a conductor's baton," instead returns "straight / up" into its own element, "that vast solution" being either air or light. This is the relation, the poem seems to imply, that a real angel would stand in with regard to our world, which might well seem heavy, dark, and chaotic to a creature compounded of light. Leithauser's equivocation is artful, but ultimately, I think, unsatisfying; the poet seems to want to invoke the beauty and comfort of transcendental beliefs without taking responsibility for them. And there's a jarring evasion of responsibility of another kind in the poem, in the opening lines of the third stanza, where the minnows are described as "thin / as compass needles," a phrase that, to any reader of contemporary poetry, immediately brings to mind Robert Lowell's description of Colonel Shaw on his monument, "lean / as a compass-needle" (*For the Union Dead* 71). The language itself would probably have brought the Lowell passage to mind for most readers, but Leithauser's wrapping the phrase around a line end as Lowell does makes the echo particularly obtrusive. And yet, what can Leithauser mean by it? Lowell's poem is one of somber magnificence, its subject of the utmost gravity; by comparison, "Angel" is trivial in subject and slack in style. Perhaps Leithauser, with the ring of Lowell's passage in his ear, simply forgot its context, a context that would render the echo entirely inappropriate. This sort of sloppiness undermines the claims of a movement that defines itself through its relation to poetic tradition and is of a piece with the equivocations of other aspects of the poem. Ultimately, Leithauser's kind of writing, like Charles Bernstein's, makes things rather too easy on the poet.

Barely tolerated, living on
   the margin
In our technological society, we were always having
   to be rescued
On the brink of destruction, like heroines in *Orlando
   Furioso*
Before it was time to start all over again.
—John Ashbery, "Soonest Mended"

Many "we"s are addressed by this passage from John Ashbery's "Soonest Mended"; surely one of them is we poets, or we who care about poetry. Ashbery acknowledges that poetry has been pushed to the edges of our society, but at the same time he gently mocks the pose of heroic alienation with which the modernist poets typically confronted their isolation. We are on the margin "in" technological society, in it and not of it, perhaps, and yet it is our society (our belonging to it somehow makes it belong to us); the margins themselves are inside the society we inhabit. As against the role of heroic rescuer so often assumed by the modern artist, Ashbery likens "us" to "heroines" of a heroic poem already heavily shaded with irony. No longer able to rescue ourselves, our only recourse, as Ashbery later remarks, is "forgetting the whole thing." Throughout, his language suggests a sense that this drama of danger and salvation has been played out so many times that it is no longer possible to believe in either alternative—destruction or rescue. And yet Ashbery seems somehow confident that we, we poets and we readers of poetry, will muddle through.

If poetry seemed marginal to Ashbery in 1970, some observers in our own day wonder whether it has ceased to exist at all. The conservative critic Joseph Epstein a few years ago opened up a still ongoing debate with an article in *Commentary* titled "Who Killed Poetry?" That debate has perhaps generated more heat than light; even so, what Dana Gioia refers to as its "extravagantly acrimonious" character ("Can Poetry Matter?" 96) is itself testimony to the extent to which Epstein's charges hit home, to which they raised fears and anxieties among the community of poets that had lain dormant but powerfully alive before Epstein articulated them. I agree that the situation of poetry is dire, but I think we're well advised, when imagining how poetry might be rescued, to keep in mind Ashbery's suggestions that such a project demands both a sense of irony and a thorough awareness of the society poetry must inhabit. If poetry is on the margin, it exists nevertheless within "technological society," a society "disenchanted" in Max Weber's sense, and any hopes of a cure for poetry must take that context into account.

Epstein's article raises the question of the death of poetry without, alas, shedding much light on it; those concerned with poetry can only look with envy at the extensive, thoughtful, and philosophically sophisticated debate regarding the "death of painting" that, while ongoing throughout the twentieth century, seems to have taken on a particular urgency in recent years. But envying another medium its discourse of demise is perhaps too macabre, and a recent discussant of the death of painting begins by cautioning that each of the various rhetorics of ending which we have grown so used to hearing—the end of ideology, the end of history, the end of the real, the death of the author, the death of man—has its specific trajectory, its particular tone,[1] and there is unfortunately little in the debate on the condition and possibility of painting that can be directly applied to the state of poetry. Certainly photography, the mechanical, instrumental, dehumanized other of painting, is far more radically alien to the substance of that medium than prose is to poetry, and so photography's threat to painting has been formulated in sharper and more coherent terms, by both artists and critics, than the challenge posed to poetry by prose. Photography appears in the history of painting as an intervention from the realm of technology. The way in which the expansion of the domain of prose embodies a long trajectory of development in the technology of writing is less obvious, which permits Epstein to treat the increasing encroachment of prose upon territory once held by poetry as owing to the deficiencies of poets, and thus to ignore the larger historical dynamics at stake.[2]

Epstein entertains various hypotheses in answer to the question asked in his title: that creative writing programs are "lowering the high standard of work which is poetry's only serious claim on anyone's attention" (17), that science has undermined poetry's authority to speak on important issues, that poetry's decline is merely part of a more general decay of language. But Epstein professes himself unconvinced by any of these explanations and falls back on an archetypically conservative view that rejects historical and social determinations for a focus on individuals: "No doubt romanticism, modernism, and other literary movements have all had their effect in landing poetry in the position it finds itself in. . . . Institutional, linguistic, historical factors have also doubtless exerted their influence in pushing poetry into the dark corner it now inhabits. Yet nearly every explanation of the situation of poetry in our time . . . seems to let the poets themselves off the hook" (17). If poetry is no longer cared about and taken seriously by thinking people, Epstein implies, it's the fault of poets, who have simply failed to produce poetry that readers find compelling.

Most of the responses to Epstein's article were in kind. If Epstein asserted that poets weren't writing poems that mattered, poets asserted that they were; if Epstein wrote that poetry had lost its audience, his respondents insisted that the audience was bigger than ever. Donald Hall's is typical of the replies to Epstein both in the defensiveness evident from his very title, "Death to the Death of Poetry," and in his effort to deflect the blame for poetry's condition back from his own cohort, the poets, and onto Epstein's, the critics: "Our trouble is not with poetry, but with the public perception of poetry" (74). Yet when Hall elaborates on this statement, he ends up sounding a great deal like Epstein. He acknowledges that journals for the intelligent general reader, such as the *New York Times Book Review*, *Atlantic*, the *New York Review of Books*, and *Harper's* (in which

Hall's piece appeared), have largely ceased to pay much attention to contemporary American poetry, and he goes on to remark about this situation that "it is poetry's loss, and the poetry reader's—for we need a cadre of reviewers to sift through the great volume of material" (74). Epstein remarks that "contemporary poetry . . . has been . . . released from the burden of undergoing tough criticism" (19). Hall is calling for more reviews, Epstein for more bad reviews, but both believe that the situation of poetry would be improved if readers had more and better guidance through the enormous out-pouring of current verse.

Hall and Epstein agree as well that poems are being published and purchased in America now in far greater numbers than in the 1930s or the 1950s, periods that for Epstein fall into a happier moment when poetry held a place of importance in general literary culture. For Hall this is sign of health, for Epstein a symptom of poetry's retreat into a specialist subculture: "The entire enterprise of poetic creation seems threatened by having been taken out of the world, chilled in the classroom, and vastly overproduced by men and women who are licensed to write it by degree if not necessarily by talent or spirit" (20). Dana Gioia, in an intelligent and deeply pondered contribution to the debate, extends Epstein's line of argument into a comprehensive account of contemporary American poetry as a subculture, inbred and marginalized, and increasingly isolated from general readers and most of "the intellectual community" ("Can Poetry Matter?" 105). Hall, focusing on mere numbers, cites a good many statistics to buttress his contention that poetry is enjoying a period of enormous popularity; Gioia looks not merely at the number but also at the kinds of readers poetry has, and makes a persuasive case that the expansion in the number of poetry's readers has accompanied a decline in its cultural importance.

Though Gioia is himself a New Formalist, he's sufficiently disinterested that his prescriptions for delivering poetry from its sub-cultural imprisonment have nothing to do with returning to traditional forms; they fall, rather, into the domain of what one might call marketing. When poets give public readings, they should read the work of other poets as well as their own; poetry readings should be mixed with performances of other arts; poets should write prose about poetry more often, and when they do should avoid mere log-rolling; teachers of poetry should stress performance over analysis; poets and arts administrators should use radio to expand poetry's audience; such are Gioia's suggestions for restoring poetry to a position of cultural importance ("Can Poetry Matter?" 106). The program is sensible in every particular, and yet strangely beside the point. Gioia's aim is to return poetry to the general reader, and if the general reader still existed, Gioia's program would stand every chance of success. But as Gioia himself states, "Poetry is not alone among the arts in its marginal position. If the audience for poetry has declined into a subculture of specialists, so too have the audiences for most contemporary art forms" (105). He goes on to refer to "the unprecedented fragmentation of American high culture during the past half century" (105). That all of the arts (with the exception, as Gioia notes, of the visual arts) have been subject to a similar marginalization and atomization probably indicates that a powerful set of cultural forces are at work, and that it will take more than better marketing to put poetry back together again.

The program proposed in Jonathan Holden's recent book *The Fate of American Poetry* seems to found itself on similarly dubious premises. Holden imagines a series of reclamations, proposing that poetry can retake ground formerly ceded to prose; in successive chapters he suggests ways in which poetry might "reclaim some of its neglected didactic potential. . . . might reclaim some of the storytelling functions that seem to have become virtually the exclusive province of the novel and the short story. . . . might reclaim some of the discursive subject matter currently regarded as belonging in the province of nonfiction prose" (109). Holden's project to some extent, then, parallels that of Robert Pinsky's *The Situation of Poetry* (1976), which argued, against what one might describe as the preciosity of the image-based poetics prevalent in the 1970s, for the return of the prose virtues to poetry. For Pinsky, this is a matter of a quality he calls "discursiveness," a combination of "personal utterance [and] plain rhetoric" with "abstract definition and vocabulary" (161–62). Pinsky tries to imagine a way in which the intellect can appear in poetry without seeming mandarin or self-consciously clever. For Holden, the reclamation he imagines is more a thematic than a stylistic concern: "It is in its subject matter, its 'content,' that American poetry, accomplished as it already is, can further enlarge its capability" (137). Holden's vision of American poetry's future turns on the unlikely proposition that readers will want to get from poetry what they can more expeditiously and easily get from prose. Like Gioia, he supposes that poetry's most urgent task is to make contact with general readers, but unlike Gioia, he sees the academic institutionalization of poetry as the development that ensures poetry a broad audience: "The basis of the 'broader popular audience' which Gioia dreams of . . . *is* the university" (14). By the trick of identifying poetry's subcultural status with its health as an art, Holden is able to grant many of Gioia's observations about the situation of poetry at the same time that he shares with Hall a sense that the art is fundamentally robust and flourishing.

As I made clear in my opening chapter, I'm unable to share Holden's enthusiasm for the current state of poetry, or for the notion that poetry should base its appeal to readers on "the types of subject matter we find in novels, sermons, and essays" (14). Poetry, for the most part locked into a self-justifying culture of lyricism in creative writing departments, has suffered an enormous loss of intellectual respectability;[3] the kind of people, both inside and outside the academy, who have an appetite for challenging reading are no longer much attracted to poetry. Rosalind Krauss's 1981 remarks are even more true now, given that those she refers to as "students" have graduated into teachers and critics themselves: "[Graduate] students, having experienced the collapse of modernist literature, have turned to the literary products of postmodernism, among the most powerful examples of which are the paraliterary works of Barthes and Derrida. . . . what is clear is that Barthes and Derrida are the *writers*, not the critics, that students now read" (295). The specifics of Krauss's remarks now seem dated—Derrida's star is very much on the wane, and an enthusiasm for Barthes "places" one generationally—but if the names have changed (we might for the moment substitute Foucault and Baudrillard for Barthes and Derrida), the point remains; what might broadly be termed "theory" now occupies the place in intellectual life that contemporary literature once held. This is reflected in the way contemporary literature has increasingly become an academic subspecialty. It used to be assumed that most people concerned with literature would be interested in the literary productions of their own day; now, each literature department has a specialist who "does" contemporary, and when he or she wishes to speak to colleagues, literary theory is likely to provide the common ground of shared texts and issues.

Some members of the writing program culture have applauded its isolation from the university literature department, seeing in poetry's marginalization its chance for avoiding the contaminations of theory. In a recent issue of the *AWP* (Associated Writing Programs) *Chronicle*, D. W. Fenza, a confessed reformed deconstructionist, celebrated the writing program as a haven from the heartless world of literary theory: "In the past decade especially, creative writing programs have provided a refuge . . . from the babble of literary specialists. Writing workshops and seminars have been places where one could talk about books in a public tongue, and talk about them as if they were extensions of one's life . . . [as] talismans or friendly accomplices . . . rather than as texts with endless indeterminacies" (20). But however problematic the skepticisms that now dominate academic literary study, if poetry simply withdraws into the writing programs, shielded from the general intellectual culture of hermeneutic suspicion, impoverishment will surely result. If poets refuse to confront any uncomfortable challenge to their presuppositions, they will remain marginalized and will have no hope of winning the attention of the readers poets should most wish to attract, readers who are not afraid of difficulty and who seek in reading complex and thoughtful representations of experience.

Reconnecting poetry with the intellectual reader is an urgent matter not merely for the health of poetry but also for the health of the intellect. While the notion of a peculiarly "poetic" form of language defined as a disruption or negation of language's ordinary state of denotation and communication has in our moment understandably been an object of considerable theoretical suspicion, imaginative writing, and especially poetry, might still be seen as fulfilling a set of functions that other forms of writing cannot. A program of skepticism invites its own form of complacency, an inclination to take the abstractions in which skepticism necessarily deals as a wholly adequate representation of its objects of scrutiny; resisting too quick a translation of object into concept is a role poetry has long been credited with playing, and one that remains valuable. Any skepticism must be tested against experience, to see how far it illuminates experience and whether it can, in fact, be "lived"; whether, that is, its insights are able to clarify in useful ways our experience of the world. I've tried to suggest some ways in which the three poets at the center of this book do that, and in particular the ways in which they represent the experience of inhabiting the kinds of skepticism in which the contemporary mind makes its home. I hope that recognizing and describing this aspect of their work may help to point toward fruitful avenues for poetry to explore.

I've focused on particular aspects of the achievement of three poets —Bishop's skeptical uses of metaphor, Merrill's strategies of self-doubt and hesitation, and Ashbery's experiments with syntax and poetic structure—because it seems to me that the reception of these three poets, particularly in terms of their influence on other poets, has often mistaken what is central and vital in their work. The crux of Bishop's work has too often been taken to be a combination of modesty and direct observation, with the result that much of the poetry that shows her influence also shows a disturbing deficiency of intellectual challenge. The gorgeous furniture of Merrill's imagined worlds has distracted quite a number of his followers into adopting the erudite cosmopolitanism of his persona without its consuming and often self-directed irony. Ashbery's innovations in syntax and poetic structure, and the enormous range of tone and diction in his work, have been less in evidence in the work of most of his followers than a kind of surrealist whimsy ostensibly derived from his practice. Poets of a younger generation would do well to reflect more carefully on the resources these poets have made available and on the lessons their work embodies.

But Bishop, Merrill, and Ashbery came of age, as poets, in a situation shaped by a very different set of pressures than those operating on poetry today. The strongest and most productive elements of their influence are likely to be found not among those poets who are most closely identified as their followers but among others who have assimilated that influence more fully and who have shaped their work less on particular aspects of the style of one of these poets than on the principles that informed that style. I turn my attention here to some poetic work of the last two decades that suggests promising possibilities for American poetry, relating that work to some of the issues I raised in previous chapters.

While I'm by no means certain that Elizabeth Bishop's work has exerted a significant influence on Robert Hass, his poems manifest a combination of virtues similar to hers: a highly precise vocabulary of observation with a richly nuanced sense of the way that conceptual categories shape perception. "Heroic Simile" explicitly takes metaphor as its subject, mounting an extended reflection on the tension between "direct treatment of the 'thing,'" in Pound's phrase (*Literary Essays* 3), and the symbolist creation of imagined worlds—a tension that has done much to shape American poetry since modernism. Hass's title announces that poetry will itself be, in some measure, the subject of the poem, but it also embodies a fundamental irony that informs the poem throughout. The heroic simile is a standard part of the furniture of epic, but Hass's poem belongs unmistakably to the genre of lyric, in its brevity and, more crucially, in its imagining "I" that comes to occupy the center of the poem's action, as opposed to the distanced narrator of epic. The poem's real subject, in fact, becomes the gulf between epic and lyric, between heroic and commonplace, between shared understandings and "separate fidelities." Here is the poem:

> When the swordsman fell in Kurosawa's *Seven Samurai*
> in the gray rain,
> in Cinemascope and the Tokugawa dynasty,
> he fell straight as a pine, he fell
> As Ajax fell in Homer
> in chanted dactyls and the tree was so huge
> the woodsman returned for two days
> to that lucky place before he was done with the sawing
> and on the third day he brought his uncle.
>
> They stacked logs in the resinous air,
> hacking the small limbs off,
> tying those bundles separately.
> The slabs near the root
> were quartered and still they were awkwardly large;
> the logs from midtree they halved:
> ten bundles and four great piles of fragrant wood,
> moons and quarter moons and half moons
> ridged by the saw's tooth.
>
> The woodsman and the old man his uncle
> are standing in midforest
> on a floor of pine silt and spring mud.
> They have stopped working
> because they are tired and because
> I have imagined no pack animal
> or primitive wagon. They are too canny
> to call in neighbors and come home
> with a few logs after three days' work.
> They are waiting for me to do something
> or for the overseer of the Great Lord
> to come and arrest them.
>
> How patient they are!
> The old man smokes a pipe and spits.
> The young man is thinking he would be rich

if he were already rich and had a mule.
Ten days of hauling
and on the seventh day they'll probably
be caught, go home empty-handed
or worse. I don't know
whether they're Japanese or Mycenaean
and there's nothing I can do.
The path from here to that village
is not translated. A hero, dying,
gives off stillness to the air.
A man and a woman walk from the movies
to the house in the silence of separate fidelities.
There are limits to imagination.
[*Praise* 2–3]

The opening stanza posits a kind of effortless translation across cultural boundaries of the idea of heroism. Ironies abound, most prominently in the repeated references to the material technologies that enable the transmission of heroic images, Cinemascope and dactylic hexameter, with a further irony in the juxtaposition of the ancient epic meter with the modern process of mechanical reproduction. And yet the analogy between Kurosawa's swordsman and Homer's warriors is meant to persuade us, and part of the persuasion is the perfect, and recognizably Homeric, form of Hass's simile. The reader's sense of an easy commerce across cultural boundaries is perhaps enhanced by an awareness that Kurosawa's samurai films are powerfully influenced by Hollywood westerns, and that *Seven Samurai* was in turn remade as a Hollywood western (*The Magnificent Seven*). And this sense of the fluidity of boundaries is reinforced in the extravagant leap that, in a fashion one might call cinematic or even cartoonish, turns the pine from the rather perfunctory vehicle of a metaphor into a representation that forms the basis of a narrative of its own; it's as if, in a film, the depicted scene within a painting had come to life and expanded to fill the entire screen.

In the second section the poet elaborates on the cutting up of this once metaphorical pine, employing a richly sensual vocabulary of physical detail, as if trying to make us forget that the tree has been conjured, as it were, out of thin language. In the third section, however, planes of representation again shift, not with the audacious assurance of the first stanza but tentatively, as if admitting that this magisterial illusion cannot be sustained. The poet enters the poem with an admission of his own negligence or inadequacy: "I have imagined no pack animal / or primitive wagon." If the literalizing of the simile in the first stanza is the act of a supremely confident and powerful, one might even say heroic, imagination, the entry of the poet at this point in the poem likens him and his art rather to the woodsman and his uncle, commonplace figures far removed from the heroic altitudes of the characters of epic.

And yet, the poet is also a kind of "overseer," one whose failures of foresight have indeed "arrested" the woodsman and his uncle. Leaving behind the world of epic to focus on a scene of ordinary labor, the poet acknowledges his distance from the heroic myths that sustained the epic attitude, just as his insertion of himself into the poem transforms the distant, impersonal recording of the second stanza, a style we associate with "naïve" creations like the Homeric epics (and modern movements like imagism that attempt to re-create premodern modes of apprehension), into a postmodern revelation of the artifice behind the artifact. But the poet finds himself equally far from the figures of patience and endurance with whom he is at first tempted to identify. If he inhabits an age in which the grand myths of epic are no longer viable, neither can his art sustain an analogy to the anonymous craft of these peasant figures, and the poet's ability to imagine them becomes increasingly uncertain: "I don't know / whether they're Japanese or Mycenaean." The poem, then, witnesses the breakdown of a whole set of assumptions and models for poetry, most particularly the image of the poet as self-effacing craftsman that played, and plays, so large a part in mainstream poetics. The permeability of boundaries posited in the opening sections grows more and more distant as the poem proceeds, until the poet is forced, finally, to abandon his imagination of these figures and narrow the audacious imaginative reach of the poem's opening.

The poem ends with a return from the poet's mental voyaging that successively backs out of the various frames constructed by the poem. Where the poem's opening implies shared understandings across vast reaches of space and time, the final lines of the poem invoke the "separate fidelities" of a couple, fidelities to one another and to the experience they have just had; the poem opens with a series of extravagant leaps, but closes in a condition of separation and limitation. The final line acknowledges a series of "limits to imagination": the poet's inability to inhabit a heroic mode, his inability to sustain the fiction of poetry as craft, the reassertion of the boundaries that prevent a complete imagination of another's life and feelings. The final line is perhaps rueful, but not resentful; the poet admits his distance from the heroic imaginings of modernism as much as from the world of Homeric epic. The limits of imagination the poet inhabits are those of postmodernity, in which the arbitrary nature of all imaginings haunts the artist's sense of the artistic endeavor. So the rich physicality of the description of labor here, so similar to many passages in Hass's first volume, *Field Guide*, is emptied by the poet's acknowledgment of the constructed nature of the scene. The poet, finally, is unable to lose himself in his creation, unable to silence the voice of skeptical irony that returns to haunt the poem. The dynamics of the poem, then, are similar to those of a poem like Bishop's "The Monument," in which an imagined construct is described in rich and precise detail; but where Bishop's poem is a celebration, however skeptical, of imagining, Hass's poem is touched with a chastening sense of the fragility of the poet's powers of imagination and sympathy.

I'll look at another poem in which the movies play a significant role, by a poet of an earlier generation than Hass, to try to point to some ways in which what the New Formalists like to call "traditional form" might be employed more effectively than any New Formalist has yet managed. David Ferry's "Dives" shows that iambic pentameter, so inert in the hands of poets who lack a rich sense of its evolution, can still produce a compelling range of effects:

> The dogheaded wild man sleeps in the back alley,
> behind the fence with bittersweet adorned,
> in the corner of the garden over near
> where the viburnum flowers or fails to flower,
> depending on whether or not we water it.
> Many times over again it has survived.
> The leaves are homely, crudely rough-cut, with
> a texture like sandpaper; an unluscious green,
> virtuous in look, not really attractive;
> like Kent in *Lear* plainspoken, a truth-teller,
> impatient with comparison as with deceit.
> [*Dwelling Places* 4]

The poem begins quietly, the meter roughened by frequent anapests; we know it is pentameter as much by the look of the lines as by their sound. Just as the meter of the poem seems distracted, wandering away from the iambic, so the poet's attention seems to wander away from the "wild man" who is his subject.

In the middle of the second stanza, however, the language of the poem suddenly becomes heightened, and the meter becomes more regular and more powerfully marked:

> The wild man sleeps in the maple-shaded valley
> hidden behind the garden fence behind
> the wooden garden seat weathering gray
> in the corner of the garden over near
> where the Orson Welles movie theater used to be,
> from which in former days you faintly heard
> the voices of the great dead stars still vying
> in rich complaint, or else in exaltation
> of meeting or farewell, in rituals
> of wit o'ermastered, or in ecstasy
> of woe beyond the experience of saints.
> [4]

The speech of "the great dead stars" is not heard directly but is rather represented through the artificially poetic language used to describe it. The disappearance of the theater seems to stand for the disappearance of the intensely artificial machinery of glamour that operated in the star system, and the representation of that language as an intonation robbed of content parallels the language of the wild man himself, as if the vanished voices of the film stars had been reincarnated in the voices the deranged man hears, which can only be guessed at. And both become identified with poetic language, the language that was fashioned to fit the traditional pentameter. The poet thus identifies the pentameter with the vanished glamour of the "great dead stars," which seems as out of place in the contemporary world as the atavistic wild man in the environment he inhabits.

In the final stanza the wild man becomes a kind of man on the dump, as Ferry's poem swerves from Stevens's by restoring the social and economic contexts that Stevens veils:

> In the alley between the yard and the old theater
> the wild man is, covered with leaves or clad
> in the bark of our indigenous flourishing trees,
> elaborately enscrolled and decorated

the philosophy section where she dreamed
of a possible love. Is that what she means

by "empathicalism"? Imagining
we can bypass the film that divides us
from former selves as from each other
by a poorly marked private detour
stumbled on, repeatedly, in the dark?
"How long has this been going on?" she sings,
her timbre unfixed in spite of lessons.

The story of the poem emerges only obliquely, partly because the
poem seems highly personal, such that the poet has no need to ex-
plain the narrative situation to herself, and partly because the poem's
disjunctive style is meant, I think, to reflect the necessarily frag-
mented and incomplete path of any self-knowledge. The poet, seeing
the film *Funny Face*, is reminded of her first viewing of the film, as
a child, projected on a wall because her mother had forgotten to
rent a screen (the "casual fault"), and the memory sets off a reflec-
tion on the way movies embody a set of cultural narratives that have
powerfully shaped the poet's sense of herself.

The poem assumes a good deal of knowledge, for the most part a
sort of knowledge that women are substantially more likely to have
than men. *Funny Face*, the key intertext, does not quite belong to the
canon of classic cinema; it's instead something of a "woman's pic-
ture." It enhances our understanding of the poem to know that the
"New Look," the fashion revolution imposed by Dior and Givenchy
in the late 1940s, was a refeminization of styles after the masculin-
ized fashions of the war period. The specifically "feminine" range of
experience the poet invokes is meant, I think, to suggest how much
of the knowledge taken for granted in literature is, in fact, male
knowledge; allusion here becomes a way for the poem to define the
kind of reader it addresses. In *Funny Face*, Audrey Hepburn plays
a young bookstore clerk who is a devotee of the French philosophi-
cal movement "empathicalism," obviously a sidewise reference to
existentialism. Photographer Fred Astaire "discovers" her and turns
her into a model, but only after she has encountered, in Paris, the
founder of empathicalism and found out firsthand that he is a fraud.
The film poses, then, a fundamental dilemma in the growing up
of many middle-class women—should I cultivate my looks or my
mind?—and answers firmly for looks.

The poem is about pedagogy; it assumes, in Simone de Beauvoir's words, that one is not born a woman but becomes one; but it is also about the complex patterns of shaping and resistance involved in the process of acculturation. Watching the film, the poet overlays onto the present image her memories of her first viewing of it, projected on buckling paneling. The moment in *Funny Face* where Fred Astaire shows Audrey Hepburn the first photograph he has made of her is very much a scene of instruction; he is showing her how he sees her but also teaching her to see herself this way. The paneling's "rephrasing it slightly," introducing a flaw into the perfect image the Astaire character, and the film, have produced, is an emblem of the way memory reshapes experience to yield a "lesson" somewhat different from the intention. The poet suggests at once the indelible effect of her encounter with the film and the unforeseeable nature of its effect on her; the image speaks both of the shaping power of early experience and of the ways in which we inevitably inflect and transform mass cultural goods in our consumption of them.

In the film, Audrey Hepburn learns both "to renounce" and "to love"; the placement of the two terms at successive line ends reinforces the sense of a necessary relation between those two actions. In the poem's account, accepting the photographer's image as a definition of herself means not merely removing herself from the book in which she was "buried," but also acquiescing in her own objectification; the poem describes the photographer as discovering "it" (her face) rather than "her." The poet resists, though, the education the model accepts, finding that she "can't detach her from the scene / of her earliest associations," a scene that formulates "a possible love" different from her "love" for "bearing the standard of the New Look." And yet the poet's attitude is a murky blend of resistance and identification; the poet herself seems unable to measure precisely the ratio between the two: "Imagining / we can bypass the film that divides us / from former selves as from each other / by a poorly marked private detour / stumbled on, repeatedly, in the dark?" The punning wit of the last line quoted, in which the cliché "in the dark" is revitalized by its reminding us of the material scene of movie viewing, should not obscure the urgency of the question. The poet, now grown to skeptical adulthood, finds herself distanced from the unreflective involvement in this Cinderella myth that characterized her childhood response, but she is also divided from the person she might have become in a world less saturated by myths of this sort. The film's only answer to the poet's repeated question is another question, which in the film refers to Audrey Hepburn's discovery of her feelings for Fred Astaire, but which the poem's context rephrases to mean something substantially different. How long, the poet seems to ask, have the culture's myths been at work, shaping her sense of herself and of what her desires and destiny should be? This sort of lesson, the poet implies, is what goes on "in the dark," in the innumerable scenes of instruction staged continually by the culture we inhabit, which shapes us without our realizing it. And yet the poem's final line holds out a space of potential resistance; Audrey Hepburn's singing (despite the lessons she received in the course of production) remains "unfixed." If her image has been frozen in "fixative," her voice, the poem suggests, cannot be so easily controlled, as the poem's own appropriation of her words demonstrates.

The story I've been telling about the poem involves a critique—a rich and subtle one, I think—of the film and the many mass cultural works similarly built around this fundamental narrative, in which a knowing man tells a young woman who she should be, and she in turn is delighted to recognize the image he creates as her true, and most truly desirable, self. The poet acknowledges the attractions of that myth at the same time that she explores the space of resistance any cultural narrative such as this one must, however unwittingly, open. If the film instructs women that it is better to leave behind books and accept men's definitions of you, the very need for such a lesson suggests the possibility that women might not want, on their own accord, to do so. The poem is clearly informed by contemporary feminist thought on the role of mass culture in the production of gender, and by theoretical work on popular culture that seeks to chart spaces of resistance within hegemonic narratives. The power of the poem, however, is in the way those concerns emerge through an account of experience, the way the abstractions of theoretical discourse are made concrete by a subjectivity that reflects on its own constitution. The assurance with which various abstract discourses have been assimilated is most manifest in the poem's freely varied diction, which mixes into its offhand slanginess ("half-baked") one of the signature verbal tics of poststructuralist writing, the phrase "always already." The poet's rephrasing of this by now empty verbal gesture gains an added irony from our awareness of *Funny Face*'s parodic treatment of the fashionable French philosophy of its day; but the joke has its serious side as well, reminding the reader of the gulf between the portentous abstractions of philosophy and the mundane realities, the casual faults, of experience. Informed by a body of skeptical contemporary thought, the poem nevertheless recognizes that skepticism can freeze into a reflex itself.

These three poems explore the limits of imagination, crafting formal strategies that trouble the illusion of voice and question the place and viability of lyric subjectivity. At the same time, that questioning maintains, in each poem, a firm hold on the particulars of experience as a stay against the formulaic quality that gestures of unmasking or deflation, in our culture of suspicion, can too easily acquire. Hass's sudden shifts of metaphoric register, Ferry's studied artificiality, and Levy's fragmented and oblique narration make reading difficult by demanding continual readjustments on the reader's part. In discussing these poems I've focused on formal devices that embody the combination of lyrical and skeptical attributes that seems to me most urgently needed in our poetry. I now turn my attention to some poems that, while perhaps not as formally adventurous, indicate areas of subject matter particularly rich in opportunities for the representation of contemporary experience.

Thylias Moss's "Almost an Ode to the West Indian Manatee" is a reflection on the extinction of species, sparked, as a note tells the reader, by a series of photographs in *National Geographic*. Ultimately, though, its central concern is the broader theme of the disappearance of the "natural" as a realm of otherness and resistance to human ends;[5] "almost an ode," the poem becomes instead a kind of elegy. The poet formulates a range of possible relations between human and natural in the course of the poem but, in the strange concluding image, figures the photographs that have inspired the poem as a kind of tombstone for the difference that the natural once represented. The poem closes with a kind of apocalypse, but it is an apocalypse of domestication and sameness.

> Once James Balog had said *her snout was soft as deerskin*
> *but the rest of her hide had the rough tautness of a football*
> *made of sandpaper* that was ode enough.
>
> In the facing photo, the hamadryas baboon snubs me, her
> nose's uptilt such that the nostrils are mosques
> dark with shed sins and the doom that opposes pilgrimage.
> She is in love.
>
> I'll buy that; what can't happen at a Florida circus
> with twin monkey girls (their hair like pipeworks follows

the spines beneath their costumes exiting mid-rump slits like
prehensile tails neglected into dredlock rip off) and a resident
hawker whose chest hair grows in question marks. Also

Guernsey cow with six stomachs each separately fed by the
angle of head at grazing, the particulars of the lowing, variety
of the moo, the sweetness of the quackgrass and clover
and all the different mood-matched milks on country tables
in pitchers with pouring lips wide as a pelvic bone.

The rhino's horn hollowed out is cornucopian. I never
think of this when it would do some good. Already
the manatee and baboon are starting to taste extinction,
welcoming it as a resolution of a forgotten craving deep in
the proliferation of Guernsey cream white as a light-emitting
lake that makes manatee and baboon glow when they catch
    sight
of themselves during their dive at the moment in which
the dive becomes inevitable, the cream displacing
into a crown as they enter, then settling
as if they never existed.
[*Rainbow Remnants* 26]

The photographer's description of the manatee's texture is a piece
of found poetry, quoted directly from the caption in *National Geo-
graphic*. The poet defers to the photographer because of the simple
eloquence of his words, but also because he has actually touched this
soon to disappear animal, which the poet most likely never will. The
subsequent two stanzas further reflect on the ironies of our relation
to the natural; the baboon is credited with the human feelings of
disdain and love at the same time that it becomes an emblem of "the
doom that opposes pilgrimage," an otherness that discourages em-
pathy. The "monkey girls" are paired with the cow; on the one hand
a wholly factitious fantasy of blurring between human and animal,
on the other an image of the natural converted almost entirely into
the cultural, nature as productive mechanism. As against the insis-
tence on particularity and individuality in Balog's encounters with
the endangered animals, the Guernsey cow is multiple and generic,
one of millions. Moss communicates the contrast, however, by treat-
ing the cow as if it and its products could be minutely particularized;
the poet's irony is deepest where her tone is most matter-of-fact.
    The final stanza elaborates a deliberately bizarre extended image,

which embodies in highly compressed form a complex set of meanings. The poet posits a death drive at the root of the mechanisms that are leading to extinctions, an urge toward sameness and inertia that she ironically ascribes to the disappearing species themselves. The cow's milk mentioned in the previous stanza swells phantasmagorically into a "lake," parodic reminder of the "oceanic" goal of the death drive, at the same time that it is identified with the white background against which Balog has photographed the animals. Extinction is figured as a plunge into this lake of cream, a lake that figures both the generalized blankness and homogeneity of a world in which the "natural" seems to have disappeared for good, and also one of the chief contingent causes of extinctions—the encroachment of human operations on wildlife habitats. The poem's protest against destruction is embodied in the absurdity of its imagery, a protest made all the more powerful by the oblique and ironic means used to communicate it. The poem finally implicates the poet as well; its attraction to things-in-their-farewell is a stock in trade of romantic poetics, but this taste comes to seem decidedly ambiguous and double-edged as it savors the "glow," which might be defined as the aura that gathers around what is soon to disappear. The poet's skepticism extends even to her own celebration of these doomed creatures as she acknowledges that their doom is a good part of what makes them available as aesthetic objects for both photographer and poet.

In Douglas Crase's "The Revisionist," the poet's metaphor for his relation to history is "thrashing," his nearest approach to a self-portrait being his description of the brown thrashers in Prospect Park who "forage . . . Among the leaves by poking into them bill first / And whipping their heads from side to side." While history, a specifically American history, is the matrix of Crase's poem, it's far from Pound's notion of epic as "a poem including history." The history invoked in Crase's poems cannot be enclosed or contained; it overflows unpredictably, constantly subject to the process of revision that gives the poem its title. That title alludes, of course, to the revisionist historians who in the 1960s and 1970s transformed received accounts of American history. Like them, but in a different key, the poet stages a revision of the American past that points to a vision of the American future. The poem, in its wide-ranging reference, presumes a wide range of knowledge, but the kind of knowledge acquired in high school civics, social studies, and history classes and most often forgotten shortly after the exam. Crase's revisiting of the past is also a redemption of that shared education in civic life and citizenship that in the fragmented and alienated public sphere we inhabit has ceased to be a living part of our culture.

Crase's strategy for revitalizing the dusty particulars of history involves investing them with the emotional intensity each of us feels about his or her private past and future. He does this through the peculiar device of addressing America in the way one would a lover, adapting the language of the quintessentially private genre of love lyric to the historical subject matter associated with epic. The tactic might at first seem bizarre, but Crase's deft handling makes the conceit seem entirely natural; anyone, the reader is likely to imagine, whose concerns range as widely and whose knowledge is so minute must actually feel about citizenship the kind of intimacy and urgency most of us feel only in love:

> In every district where there is
> Restitution owing, where your riches inspired plunder
> Instead of care, my outrage gathers on your interests
> To give them form. Out of the asphalt in Kansas City
> I will accomplish the resurrection of the Board of Trade,
> Out of the parking lots of Buffalo I will recover
> The Larkin Building's uncompromising piers . . .
> Like a vengeful Johnny Appleseed I'll girdle each
> Male ailanthus tree and like a Know-Nothing I'll close
> The ports to chestnut blight and the Dutch elm disease. . . .
> Immediate, I will break
> The 1811 grid that imprisoned New York, I will reopen
> *McCulloch* v. *Maryland* to honor the offended states,
> I will expose the payoff that humbled Tilden
> And reduced the Union victory via President Hayes.
> Remote or present, I have seen you traded through public
> And private hands until every account against you
> Excites me to personal revenge. (I will expel the five-
> Million-dollar Velasquez and bring the Jackson Pollock
> Home.)
> [*The Revisionist* 5–6]

The extravagant impossibilities the poet promises belong to the Petrarchan tradition of romantic hyperbole, while the steady accumulation of detail brings to mind political oratory as much as poetic tradition. The politics of this outburst are clearly utopian and fantastical, and the poet shades his outrage with a good deal of irony, and yet the catalog of losses he presents, more effectively than the pitch of his rhetoric, communicates a genuine sense of sorrow and dismay over the damage we have wrought upon what we should have cared for.

The poet's mention of the Know-Nothings, the nineteenth-century nativist political movement opposed to immigration, prepares the shift in the next section of the poem toward a more complex understanding of damage and restoration. The poet acknowledges that his fantasies of restitution are impossible, not merely for contingent reasons but also because origins always recede unrecoverably the more they are sought:

> What I am after to remember is not what was,
> And what I am anxious to save is not the same
> For in the moment I saw you, you were changed.
> In the most intimate of fields you may
> Never have been known, and in the most natural
> Of flowers it's possible to read the account
> Of my interferences instead. Together,
> I thought we were having an honest childhood
> Of daisies, dandelions and Queen Anne's lace
> Only to discover these come wrapped tightly
> In the same colonial history as my own. Together
> I thought we were fragrant of spearmint, chicory
> And the multiflora rose only to find these
> Were fugitive as the others who came to give you
> The recognizable smell of home. . . .
>   Loosestrife, the purple filler
> At the low end of the field, came vagabonding
> In the wool of distant English sheep and docked
> At a Hudson River factory and now the Japanese
> Lady's thumb, having arrived as a stowaway
> With the china, packed in straw, is deftly
> Fulfilling its version of manifest destiny. . . .
>   The moment I saw you my natural
> Love began, twisting and turning, to love you
> The more the way you were and as I complicated you.
> [6–7]

Where the previous section imagines restoring some rightful and original state of affairs, this movement of the poem acknowledges that no such unspoiled and authentic moment is available to be retrieved. Again the poet deftly balances general statement with the patient accumulation of particulars, as he seems to scour the continent with the eye of a naturalist who finds culture rather than nature waiting for him at every turn. At the end of this section of the poem the poet declares his "natural / Love," separating adjective and noun across the line ending in a most unnatural way to reinforce the realization that caring, which had seemed a conservative impulse toward the static, is itself an agent of change. Again, it's not entirely clear whether citizenship is a metaphor for love or vice versa; what is clear is that the facts the poet adduces here transform our understanding of the previous section's heated rhetoric in a way that expands our understanding of both.

Alan Shapiro's "The Sweepers" invokes a very different kind of history, at once more remote in time and more immediate in its almost physical impingement upon the reader. The poem responds to recent developments in our understanding of the past, the rise of social history with its shift in focus from the actions of powerful elites to ordinary lives, and the increased skepticism toward the heroic and martial values once routinely celebrated in historical writing. Struck by a passage in a history book, the poet attempts to imagine the feelings of these nameless, long-dead "sweepers," an endeavor that takes the form of a series of questions that remain unanswered by both the poet and the "writer" of the history:

> Who were they? The writer just calls them "sweepers," clear-
> ing
> the streets, leveling a path for the army through the smolder-
> ing
> debris of ancient houses torched and toppled all about them. . . .
> their fingers blistering as they plied crowbar and boat hook,
> dowel and axe, the pain a punishment for the dumb animal
> persistence that so easily and thoroughly turned friend and
> relation,
> the whole rich tapestry of customary feeling, law, memory
> and lore
> into mere fill for gullies?—Did they resent the half-dead
> for their clumsy fit, their ineffectual resistances,
> the ones stuffed head down, legs above the surface
> writhing pathetically to get away, like giant insects,

or the ones feet first, their heads above the surface
unable even to flinch as the horses trampled over face and
    skull?
    [*Covenant* 3]

The poet seems less interested in answering the question that opens the poem than in imagining the quality of the experience these sweepers undergo, an experience that brings together the exceptional carnage and horror of war with the everyday pain of labor. Without ever invoking the language of ethics, the poem becomes a meditation on the costs of the "dumb animal persistence" that provides the continuity in human history across moments of even the most cataclysmic upheavals.

In the second section of the poem the poet draws away from engagement and sympathy with these anonymous figures, neither victims nor victors, to underline the disproportion between the "few lines" they merit in history and the "six days and nights" spanned by their labors:

> The writer doesn't say. For a few lines in my Roman history,
> for six days and nights, nameless, stateless, ever diligent
> they clear the streets, they make the way smooth for Scipio,
> who, it is said, was weeping, sunk in thought, as he looked on,
> weeping at the fortunes of cities, peoples, empires:
> the Assyrians had fallen, and the Medes, and the Persians
> after them had fallen, and so too, latest of all,
> latest and most brilliant, the Macedonians blotted out,
> destroyed, as Ilion had been destroyed, and Priam,
> and the people of Priam of the strong ash spear . . .
>
> Here one turns the page, and goes on reading.
>   [4]

Scipio is the elite man of culture who looks at the destruction before him and responds with a recognition of tragedy informed by historical and poetic knowledge at the same time that this fatalistic recognition comports with his role as destroyer of Carthage; culture and barbarism are, as Walter Benjamin reminds us, near allied. The poet is perhaps tempted to a similar indulgence in pathos but instead turns the page, implicitly aligning himself with the sweepers, whoever they are, who bury the dead and living just like the poet who turns the page on them. The pathos and heroism of the *Iliad* are invoked, only to be quickly shunted aside; the poet's engagement is neither with the conquerors nor with the brilliant doomed victims, but with those who doggedly and blindly persist. And yet, even those figures are finally beyond the range of the poet's identification; his response, finally, is to turn the page. The prevalence of dramatic monologue in the modernist era and after rested on the assumption of a universal availability of sympathy, of the poet's ability to enter the experience of others, no matter how remote their situation. In their different ways Hass and Shapiro both subject this assumption to a decidedly skeptical evaluation.

The poets I've discussed here by no means exhaust the ranks of the contemporaries I admire; I regret particularly that I do not have room to treat the works of Frank Bidart and John Peck. Nor do the strategies and subjects I've examined in these poems exhaust the possibilities I think poetry might profitably explore. In particular, the impact of contemporary scientific revolutions, with their ongoing redefinitions of some of the most fundamental terms of our self-understandings, is a theme little explored by poets, an omission all the more striking when one of our most powerful contemporary novelists, Thomas Pynchon, has made the languages and structures of scientific inquiry a central focus of his work. But I've already been sufficiently presumptuous on enough occasions in this study, and I won't presume to prescribe the kinds of subjects poetry ought to treat. Whatever its subject matter, though, any poetry that can satisfy the demands of the time will certainly need to find ways of bringing together the energies of intellectual abstraction with whatever remains viable of the lyric impulse.

In doing so, poets will need to make things difficult, not merely for their readers but for themselves. Neither of the current aspirants to the role of poetry's rescuer, Language poetry and the New Formalism, promises to do that to a sufficient extent. The New Formalists for the most part seem to imagine that poetry can stand aside from the general tide of culture and restore an earlier form of community by resurrecting earlier poetic forms. The Language poets, it seems to me, attempt to embody too directly the skepticisms they subscribe to; their poems are demonstrations of certain tenets of thought, but we learn from them almost nothing about what it *feels* like to inhabit those thoughts, to believe those beliefs. I'm well aware that any notion that poetry needs to provide some sort of experiential grounding may easily be "interrogated," to use the dreadful current idiom, as a reactionary mythification. At the risk of seeming more tenderhearted than tough-minded, I propose rather that what we need in poetry (and what we need poetry for) is a way to reconcile or bring together the authority of skeptical reflection with that of experience. Neither is adequate by itself.

Poetry is dead. With that judgment I have no interest in arguing, if what it means is that poetry is unlikely in any foreseeable future to regain an audience like the one enjoyed by Tennyson, or even by Frost. But it seems to me that poetry still has an enormous job of work to do, posthumously, as it were. If nothing else, poetry's death should haunt the rest of culture; there seems something monstrous about the notion that the form of expression which through most of the history of human culture was considered the highest, most powerful, and most prestigious should have now become a sort of leisure sector of mental life, avoided by those who seek to wield genuine cultural power. And marginalized as poetry may be, the very fact of its apparent diminishment and anachronism may give it a peculiar vantage and a point of leverage. Adorno, in one of the maxims of the *Minima Moralia*, remarks on the role of the "defeated" in history:

> If Benjamin said that history had hitherto been written from the standpoint of the victor, and needed to be written from that of the vanquished, we might add that knowledge must indeed present the fatally rectilinear succession of victory and defeat, but should also address itself to those things which were not embraced by this dynamic, which fell by the wayside—what might be called the waste products and blind spots that have escaped the dialectic. It is in the nature of the defeated to appear, in their impotence, irrelevant, eccentric, derisory. What transcends the ruling society is not only the potentiality it develops but also all that which did not fit properly into the laws of historical movement. [98]

Poetry now seems to many observers "irrelevant, eccentric, derisory." This, perhaps, is its opportunity—having been repressed, to return to trouble the culture that has exiled it to the margins, both as a reminder of what has been lost in the process that has diminished poetry's status and as a carrier of values that resist incorporation into the degraded language of public discourse or into the idioms of the dominant intellectual skepticisms.

It's just this kind of resistant individuality I've tried to trace in the work of the three poets at the center of this volume. Each combines a fundamentally lyric apprehension of experience with an intense, and intensely self-aware, skepticism about his or her poetic enterprise. It is this self-awareness, this irony toward the claims implicit in their own work, that distinguishes these poets from the contemporary aspirants to poetic renewal. Poetry is not going to attract the attention of thinking people unless it acknowledges its own diminished situation in some forthright and tough-minded way. The poets who inhabit what Gioia refers to as the poetry "subculture" do this only by a limitation of claims and a narrowing of the intellectual scope of poetry that for the most part ends up indistinguishable from complacency. Neither the avant-gardist fantasies of the Language poets nor the populist fantasies of the New Formalists hold much promise in this regard. Both of these recent movements make things too easy for themselves insofar as they place their faith in a body of techniques that, rigorously followed, will yield a renewed relation to the audience as a natural consequence; they demand assent to their premises as the price of admission to the writing. But if poets are going to regain some of the stature they have lost, they will have to show a willingness to reflect on and question their own assumptions to a far greater extent than either movement has yet done.

Poetry ought, then, to present its readers with exempla of the kind of mind that continually guards against passing fictions upon itself, that reflects on the operations of its own language and weighs them against a tough standard. Poetry can offer us images of the activity of making language authentic, whether that involves rejecting a phrase that "first enhances, then debases," or mining clichés for the core of vitality that remains in them. But poetry can also warn us against the temptation to imagine that we have arrived at an absolute and unassailable lucidity. Poetry, because it has the potential to be the most difficult kind of writing, can most effectively pose the demands of experience, as they are sedimented and embodied in the language we use, against their reduction in the formulas of skepticism that now come so naturally to our minds and lips. It has become easy for us to identify the categories and habits of thought produced by the skeptical intellect with truth, even when we have dissolved the notion of truth back into a language game or an effect of power. Poetry, by bringing us to a greater awareness of the languages by which we understand our experience, should help us resist the reduction of experience to formulas, whether those are the formulas of lyricism or of lucidity. But to do so it will have to be difficult.

NOTES

Introduction: Difficulty and the Postwar Poet

1. William Chafe plausibly and concretely argues that difficulty (what I am here calling obscurity) is produced in written language by departures from the practices of spoken language.

2. John Hollander's chapter "Romantic Verse Form and the Metrical Contract" (in *Vision and Resonance* 187–211) contains a penetrating reflection on this metaphor of contract.

3. I adopt this term from Pierre Bourdieu, who has exhaustively, if reductively, examined the role of intangible goods in the establishment and reproduction of societies; see his *Distinction*.

4. The best description of the culture and assumptions prevailing in writing programs is Alan Shapiro's "Horace and the Reformation of Creative Writing" 7–8.

5. I discuss the *Morrow Anthology* and what it indicates about the state of American poetry more fully in my review of the volume; see "The Place of Poetry" 434–35.

6. The term is Robert Pinsky's; see his *Situation of Poetry*.

7. Robert von Hallberg discusses, rather unsympathetically, the "camp" aspect of Merrill's sensibility (109–13).

8. David Kaufmann discusses these two movements in relation to the problem of subjectivity in his "Subjectivity and Disappointment in Contemporary American Poetry."

9. Timothy Steele is at great pains to deny any connection between meter and diction in his *Missing Measures*; see especially pp. 32–45.

10. Mutlu Konuk Blasing discusses the way that, for the Language poets, "the literary past . . . becomes largely irrelevant" (300).

11. Robert Pinsky's *Situation of Poetry* argues for the reintroduction of the prose virtues into poetry.

Elizabeth Bishop's Silences

1. Octavio Paz subtitled his brief discussion of Bishop "The Power of Reticence."

2. The "neighborly" Frost is on display even in the titles of George Elliott's "The Neighborliness of Robert Frost" and P. L. Benjamin's "Robert Frost, a Poet of Neighborliness"; David Bromwich's "Some Uses of Biography" discusses the relationship between estimates of Frost's character and his poetry (238–39).

3. See "The Geography of Gender."

4. Bonnie Costello refers to Bishop's "symbolist and surrealist rhetoric" (15) and to the "symbolist aesthetic" at work in poems such as "The Weed" (59); Travisano characterizes the early Bishop as "a reluctant master of the symbolist's private world" (7).

5. Travisano discusses this transformation extensively in the third chapter of his monograph (55–97).

6. Wyatt Prunty briefly considers Bishop's use of similitude (240–49). His argument that "contemporary poets appear to have favored, in place of symbol and allegory, simile-like tropes" (19) is generally relevant here. See as well Robert Pinsky's review of Bishop's *Complete Poems*, which discusses the poet's penchant for simile over metaphor in terms of her "metaphysical doubt" ("Geographer of the Self" 24–25).

7. David Kalstone discusses Bishop's influence on Lowell (*Becoming a Poet* 173–88).

8. Willard Spiegelman's brief article "Heirs and Heirlooms" makes a good start toward characterizing Bishop's influence on the succeeding generation of poets.

9. David Bromwich contrasts this aspect of Moore's practice with Bishop's ("That Weapon, Self-Protectiveness" 67–72).

10. Bromwich links the poem to a tradition of reflections on art's power to outlast time that include Shakespeare's sonnet "Not marble, nor the gilded monuments" (EBDH 78).

11. We're past the point, one hopes, where a split infinitive is thought of as incorrect, and split infinitives are normal in the speech of even the most educated speakers. But the splitting in this phrase is probably one that would be avoided by careful writers.

12. Jeredith Merrin argues this view of Bishop with particular attention to the poet's relation to Wordsworth (81–106).

13. This is a term Bishop used about her own work (Goldensohn 58–59).

Public and Private in James Merrill's Work

1. "The Book of Ephraim" initially appeared in 1976 in the volume *Divine Comedies*. *Mirabell: Books of Number* was published in 1978, *Scripts for the Pageant* in 1980. These three sections were collected, with a coda, in *The Changing Light at Sandover* in 1982.
2. This inversion resonates with the poet's remark, later in the poem, that he obeys his parents "inversely"; his inversion of their values is reflected in his inversion of their language.
3. Paul Breslin's article "American Poetry and/or Surrealism" cogently discusses these developments.

John Ashbery's Difficulty

1. The song is Peaches and Herb's "Reunited" (Tranter 101–2).
2. Mutlu Konuk Blasing's article on James Merrill contains a penetrating discussion of the literary-historical assumptions held by the heirs of the Projectivist tradition (299–302).

The Return of the Repressed: Language Poetry and New Formalism

1. Alan Shapiro's is probably the most astute description of the culture and values that prevail in the writing programs; see "Horace and the Reformation of Creative Writing" 7–8.
2. John Hollander thoughtfully discusses this celebrated instance of radical enjambment, from the Cary-Morison ode, in *Vision and Resonance* (142–43); see as well Paul Fry's remarks on these lines (25).
3. Most readers will be reminded of e. e. cummings by a good many of Language poetry's practices; it's telling that the Language poets and their boosters maintain an absolute silence about cummings, despite his having been favorably mentioned by the great progenitor of the Language movement, Charles Olson ("Projective Verse" 154). The reason for this silence is readily apparent; cummings employed many of the techniques currently used in language writing but was romantic in temperament and reactionary in his politics. cummings's work puts into jeopardy, then, the connection the Language writers wish to draw between those poetic techniques and political radicalism.
4. While it may seem petty to point out that neither "free verse" nor "the iambic line" can properly be termed a genre, the error in terminology indicates the power, for many of the New Formalists, of the fantasy of a real system of genres, as in ancient Greek or Latin poetry, in which subject matter and poetic form are bound tightly together by a body of traditions and conventions.
5. I should note that Shapiro specifically exempts Steele's poetry from his remarks.
6. The line might be scanned as an iambic dimeter with an anapestic substitution in the second foot, but on the principle of economy, it seems to call for less metrical gymnastics to take it as anapestic.
7. Of course, the line could be scanned as an iambic trimeter with a trochaic substitution in the first foot and an anapestic substitution in the third. Given that

it scans perfectly in dactyls and requires a rather odd bundle of substitutions to fit into iambics, the line strikes this ear, at least, as much more "naturally" dactylic.

Directions for Poetry

1. I refer to Yve-Alain Bois, "Painting: The Task of Mourning"; Bois's essay succinctly lays out the issues in and sketches the history of the "death of painting" debate.
2. By "technology" here I mean not only such things as the development of printing presses, cheap paper, markets, and distribution networks, but also developments within prose itself—extensions of its flexibility, accuracy, and range of representation. Ezra Pound was fond of pointing out that Chaucer was capable of narrating and describing with perfect clarity in verse, while his treatise on the astrolabe is unintelligible. What now seems like prose's natural ability to present a subject simply and precisely is in fact a capacity it acquired only through a long and arduous process of refinement and extension.
3. I discuss the situation more fully in "The Place of Poetry" (430).
4. "Wire" should, I trust, be pronounced as a disyllable, as is common in American speech.
5. Fredric Jameson posits this disappearance of the natural as one of the central postmodernist themes; see his *Postmodernism* (ix–x).

WORKS CITED

Adams, Hazard. "The Difficulty of Difficulty." In *The Idea of Difficulty in Literature*, ed. Alan Purves, 23–50. Albany: State U of New York P, 1991.

Adorno, T. W. *Aesthetic Theory.* Trans. C. Lenhardt. London and New York: Routledge and Kegan Paul, 1984.

———. *Minima Moralia.* Trans. E. F. N. Jephcott. London: Verso, 1974.

Allen, Dick. "Transcending the Self." *Crosscurrents* 8.2 (January 1989): 5–10.

Altieri, Charles. *Self and Sensibility in Contemporary Poetry.* Cambridge: Cambridge UP, 1984.

Alvarez, A. "Imagism and Poetesses." *Kenyon Review* 19.2 (Spring 1957): 321–29.

Andrews, Bruce. "Constitution/Writing, Politics, Language, the Body." $L=A=N=$-$G=U=A=G=E$ 4, ed. Bruce Andrews and Charles Bernstein. Published in *Open Letter* 5.1 (Winter 1982): 154–65.

———. "Text and Context." In *The $L=A=N=G=U=A=G=E$ Book*, ed. Bruce Andrews and Charles Bernstein, 31–38. Carbondale and Edwardsville: Southern Illinois UP, 1984.

Ashbery, John. *As We Know.* New York: Viking P, 1979.

———. "Craft Interview with John Ashbery." *New York Quarterly* 9 (Winter 1972): 10–33.

———. *The Double Dream of Spring.* 1970. Reprint. New York: Ecco P, 1976.

———. "Frank O'Hara's Question." *Book Week* 4.3 (25 September 1966): 6.

———. *Houseboat Days.* New York: Viking P, 1977.

———. "The Invisible Avant-Garde." In *Reported Sightings*, 389–95. New York: Knopf, 1989. Originally published in *Art News Annual* 34 (October 1968): 124–33.

———. *Rivers and Mountains*. New York: Ecco P, 1977.

———. *Self-Portrait in a Convex Mirror*. New York: Viking P, 1975.

———. *The Tennis Court Oath*. Middletown, Conn.: Wesleyan UP, 1962.

———. *A Wave*. New York: Viking P, 1984.

Bartlett, Lee. "What Is 'Language Poetry'?" *Critical Inquiry* 12.4 (Summer 1986): 741–52.

Benjamin, P. L. "Robert Frost, a Poet of Neighborliness." *Survey* 45 (27 November 1920): 318–19.

Benjamin, Walter. *Charles Baudelaire: A Lyric Poet in the Era of High Capitalism*. Trans. Harry Zohn. London: Verso, 1983.

Berg, Stephen, and Robert Mezey, eds. *Naked Poetry*. Indianapolis and New York: Bobbs-Merrill, 1969.

Bernstein, Charles. "The Kiwi Bird in the Kiwi Tree." *Rethinking MARXISM* 1.4 (Winter 1988): 84.

Bernstein, Charles, ed. *The Politics of Poetic Form: Poetry and Public Policy*. New York: Roof Books, 1990.

Bishop, Elizabeth. *Collected Prose*. New York: Farrar, Straus, Giroux, 1984.

———. *Complete Poems: 1927–1979*. New York: Farrar, Straus, Giroux, 1983.

Blackmur, R. P. *Language as Gesture*. New York: Harcourt, Brace, 1952.

Blasing, Mutlu Konuk. "Rethinking Models of Literary Change: The Case of James Merrill." *American Literary History* 2.2 (Summer 1990): 299–317.

Bly, Robert. "A Wrong Turning in American Poetry" (1963). In *Claims for Poetry*, ed. Donald Hall, 17–37. Ann Arbor: U of Michigan P, 1982.

Bois, Yve-Alain. "Painting: The Task of Mourning." In *Painting as Model*, 229–44. Cambridge, Mass., and London: MIT P, 1990.

Boland, Eavan. "An Un-Romantic American." *Parnassus: Poetry in Review* 14.2 (1988): 73–92.

Boone, Bruce. "Writing's Current Impasse and the Possibilities for Renewal." $L=A=N=G=U=A=G=E$ 4, ed. Bruce Andrews and Charles Bernstein. Published in *Open Letter* 5.1 (Winter 1982): 121–28.

Bourdieu, Pierre. *Distinction: A Social Critique of the Judgement of Taste*. Trans. Richard Nice. Cambridge, Mass.: Harvard UP, 1984.

Breslin, James. *From Modern to Contemporary: American Poetry, 1945–1965*. Chicago and London: U of Chicago P, 1984.

Breslin, Paul. "American Poetry and/or Surrealism." *American Scholar* 47 (1978): 357–76.

———. *The Psycho-Political Muse: American Poetry since the Fifties*. Chicago and London: U of Chicago P, 1987.

Bromwich, David. "Elizabeth Bishop's Dream Houses." *Raritan* 4.1 (Summer 1984): 77–94.

———. "Poetic Invention and the Self-Unseeing." *Grand Street* 7.1 (Autumn 1987): 115–29.

———. "Some Uses of Biography." In *A Choice of Inheritance: Self and Community from Edmund Burke to Robert Frost*, 232–46. Cambridge, Mass., and London: Harvard UP, 1989.

———. " 'That Weapon, Self-Protectiveness.' " In *Marianne Moore: The Art of a Modernist*, ed. Joseph Parisi, 67–80. Ann Arbor and London: U of Michigan Research P, 1990.

Brooke-Rose, Christine. *A Grammar of Metaphor*. London: Secker and Warburg, 1958.

Brooks, Cleanth, and Robert Penn Warren. *Understanding Poetry: An Anthology for College Students*. New York: Henry Holt, 1938.

Chafe, William. "Sources of Difficulty in the Processing of Written Language." In *The Idea of Difficulty in Literature*, ed. Alan Purves, 7–22. Albany: SUNY P, 1991.

Cohen, Ted. "Metaphor and the Cultivation of Intimacy." *Critical Inquiry* 5.1 (Autumn 1978): 3–12.

Costello, Bonnie. *Elizabeth Bishop: Questions of Mastery*. Cambridge, Mass., and London: Harvard UP, 1991.

Crase, Douglas. *The Revisionist*. Boston: Little, Brown, 1981.

Crow, Thomas. "These Collectors, They Talk about Baudrillard Now." *Discussions in Contemporary Culture*, no. 1, ed. Hal Foster, 1–8. Seattle: Bay P, 1987.

Cucullu, Lois. "Trompe l'Oeil: Elizabeth Bishop's Radical 'I'." *Texas Studies in Language and Literature* 30.2 (Summer 1988): 246–71.

Curtius, Ernst Robert. "T. S. Eliot." In *Essays on European Literature*, 355–71. Trans. Michael Kowal. Princeton: Princeton UP, 1973. Essay originally published 1927.

Davie, Donald. *Purity of Diction in English Verse*. New York: Oxford UP, 1953.

de Man, Paul. *The Rhetoric of Romanticism*. New York: Columbia UP, 1984.

Edelman, Lee. "The Geography of Gender: Elizabeth Bishop's 'In the Waiting Room.'" *Contemporary Literature* 26.2 (Summer 1985): 179–96.

Eliot, T. S. "The Metaphysical Poets." In *Selected Essays*, 241–50. Originally published 1921.

———. *Selected Essays: 1917–1932*. New York: Harcourt, Brace, 1932.

———. "Tradition and the Individual Talent." In *Selected Essays*, 3–11.

———. "The Waste Land." In *Collected Poems 1909–1962*. New York: Harcourt, Brace and World, 1963.

Elliott, George R. "The Neighborliness of Robert Frost." *Nation* 109 (6 December 1919): 713–15.

Empson, William. *Seven Types of Ambiguity*. Third edition. Norfolk, Conn.: New Directions, 1953.

Epstein, Joseph. "Who Killed Poetry?" *Commentary* 86.2 (August 1988): 13–20.

Fenza, D. W. "Tradition & the Institutionalized Talent." *AWP Chronicle* 24.4 (February 1992): 11, 14–20.

Ferry, David. *Dwelling Places*. Chicago and London: U of Chicago P, 1993.

Friedlander, Marc. "Poetry and the Common Store." *The American Scholar* 14.3 (Summer 1945): 362–65.

Frost, Robert. *Complete Poems*. New York: Holt, Rinehart and Winston, 1949.

———. *Selected Letters*. Ed. Lawrance Thompson. New York: Holt, Rinehart and Winston, 1964.

Fry, Paul. *The Poet's Calling in the English Ode*. New Haven: Yale UP, 1980.

Fuhrmann, Manfred. "Obscuritas: Das Problem der Dunkelheit in der Rhetorischen und Literarästhetischen Theorie der Antike." In *Immanente Ästhetik, Ästhetische Reflexion: Lyrik als Paradigma der Moderne*, ed. Wolfgang Iser, 47–72. Munich: Wilhelm Fink Verlag, 1966.

Gangel, Sue. "John Ashbery." In *American Poetry Observed*, ed. Joe David Bellamy, 9–20. Urbana and Chicago: U of Illinois P, 1984.

Gioia, Dana. "Can Poetry Matter?" *Atlantic* 267.5 (May 1991): 94–106.

———. "Notes on the New Formalism." *Hudson Review* 40.3 (Autumn 1987): 395–408.

Goldensohn, Lorrie. *Elizabeth Bishop: The Biography of a Poetry*. New York: Columbia UP, 1992.

Hall, Donald. "Death to the Death of Poetry." *Harper's* 279 (September 1992): 72–76.

Harmon, William. "The Lightweight Contenders' New Clothes." *Parnassus: Poetry in Review* 15.1 (Spring 1989): 99–124.

Hass, Robert. *Praise*. New York: Ecco P, 1979.

Holden, Jonathan. *The Fate of American Poetry*. Athens, Ga., and London: U of Georgia P, 1991.

Hollander, John. *Vision and Resonance: Two Senses of Poetic Form*. New York: Oxford UP, 1975.

Hough, Graham. *Image and Experience: Studies in a Literary Revolution*. London: Duckworth, 1960.

Jameson, Fredric. *The Political Unconscious: Narrative as a Socially Symbolic Act*. Ithaca: Cornell UP, 1981.

———. *Postmodernism, or, The Cultural Logic of Late Capitalism*. Durham, NC: Duke UP, 1991.

Jonson, Ben. *Discoveries and Conversations with William Drummond of Hawthornden*. London: Bodley Head, 1923.

Kalstone, David. *Becoming a Poet: Elizabeth Bishop with Marianne Moore and Robert Lowell*. New York: Farrar, Straus, Giroux, 1989.

———. *Five Temperaments*. New York: Oxford UP, 1977.

Kaufmann, David. "Subjectivity and Disappointment in Contemporary American Poetry." *Ploughshares* 17.4 (Winter 1991–92): 231–49.

Keats, John. *The Letters of John Keats*. 2 vols. Ed. Hyder Rollins. Cambridge, Mass.: Harvard UP, 1958.

Koethe, John. "An Interview with John Ashbery." *SubStance* 37–38 (1983): 178–86.

Krauss, Rosalind. "Poststructuralism and the Paraliterary." In *The Originality of the Avant-Garde and Other Modernist Myths*, 291–95. Cambridge, Mass., and London: MIT P, 1985. Originally published in *October* 13 (Summer 1980).

Kristeva, Julia. *Revolution in Poetic Language*. Trans. Margaret Waller. New York: Columbia UP, 1984.

Lake, Paul. "Toward a Liberal Poetics." In *Expansive Poetry: Essays on the New Narrative and the New Formalism*, ed. Frederick Feirstein, 113–23. Santa Cruz: Story Line P, 1989.

Lazer, Hank. "The Politics of Form and Poetry's Other Subjects: Reading Contemporary American Poetry." *American Literary History* 2.3 (Fall 1990): 503–27.

———. *What Is a Poet?* Tuscaloosa and London: U of Alabama P, 1987.

Leavis, F. R. *Revaluation: Tradition & Development in English Poetry*. New York: George W. Stewart, 1947.

Leithauser, Brad. "The Confinement of Free Verse." *New Criterion* 5.9 (May 1987): 4–14.

———. *Hundreds of Fireflies*. New York: Knopf, 1982.

Levy, Ellen. "Rec Room." *New York Review of Books* 33.20 (9 October 1986): 20.

Lewis, C. Day. *A Hope for Poetry*. Oxford: Blackwell, 1934.

Lowell, Robert. *For the Union Dead*. New York: Farrar, Straus, Giroux, 1964.

———. "An Interview with Frederick Seidel." In *Collected Prose*, 235–66. New York: Farrar, Straus, Giroux, 1987.

McClatchy, J.D. "On *Water Street*." In *James Merrill: Essays in Criticism*, ed. David Lehman and Charles Berger, 61–96. Ithaca and London: Cornell UP, 1983.

McGann, Jerome. "Contemporary Poetry, Alternate Routes." *Critical Inquiry* 13.3 (Spring 1987): 624–47.

—— [Anne Mack and J.J. Rome, pseud.]. "Marxism, Romanticism, and Postmodernism: An American Case History." *South Atlantic Quarterly* 88.3 (Summer 1989): 605–32.

——. "Postmodern Poetries." *Verse* 7.1 (Spring 1990): 6–8.

—— [Anne Mack, J.J. Rome, and Georg Mannejc, pseud.]. "Private Enigmas and Critical Functions, with Particular Reference to the Writing of Charles Bernstein." *New Literary History* 22.2 (Spring 1991): 441–64.

Mac Low, Jackson. " 'Language-Centered.' " *L=A=N=G=U=A=G=E* 4, ed. Bruce Andrews and Charles Bernstein. Published in *Open Letter* 5.1 (Winter 1982): 23–26.

McPhillips, Robert. "Reading the New Formalism." *Sewanee Review* 97.4 (October–December 1989): 73–96.

——. "What's New About the New Formalism?" In *Expansive Poetry: Essays on the New Narrative and the New Formalism*, ed. Frederick Feirstein, 195–298. Santa Cruz: Story Line P, 1989.

Mazzocco, Robert. "A Poet of Landscape." *New York Review of Books* 9 (12 October 1967): 4–6.

Merrill, James. *Braving the Elements*. New York: Atheneum, 1972.

——. *The Changing Light at Sandover*. New York: Atheneum, 1982.

——. *Divine Comedies*. New York: Atheneum, 1985.

——. *Nights and Days*. New York: Atheneum, 1966.

——. "November Ode." *New York Review of Books* 35.16 (27 October 1988): 14.

——. *Recitative*. San Francisco: North Point P, 1986.

——. *Water Street*. New York: Atheneum, 1962.

Merrin, Jeredith. *An Enabling Humility: Marianne Moore, Elizabeth Bishop, and the Uses of Tradition*. New Brunswick and London: Rutgers UP, 1990.

Moffett, Judith. "Sound Without Sense: Willful Obscurity in Poetry." *New England Review* 3.2 (Winter 1980): 294–312.

Moore, Marianne. *The Complete Poems*. New York: Macmillan, 1967.

Moss, Thylias. *Rainbow Remnants in Rock Bottom Ghetto Sky*. New York: Persea, 1991.

Olds, Sharon. *The Dead and the Living*. New York: Knopf, 1984.

Olson, Charles. "Projective Verse." In *The Poetics of the New American Poetry*, ed. Donald Allen and Warren Tallman, 147–58. New York: Grove P, 1973.

Orgel, Stephen. "Affecting the Metaphysics." In *Twentieth Century Literature in Retrospect*, ed. Reuben Brower, 225–45. Cambridge, Mass.: Harvard UP, 1971.

Parker, Robert Dale. *The Unbeliever: The Poetry of Elizabeth Bishop*. Urbana and Chicago: U of Illinois P, 1988.

Paz, Octavio. "Elizabeth Bishop, or the Power of Reticence." *World Literature Today* 51.1 (Winter 1977): 15–16.

Perloff, Marjorie. "Mysteries of Construction: The Dream Songs of John Ashbery." In *The Poetics of Indeterminacy: Rimbaud to Cage*, 249–87. Princeton: Princeton UP, 1981.

Pinsky, Robert. "Geographer of the Self." *New Republic* 188.13 (4 April 1983): 24–28.

——. *The Situation of Poetry*. Princeton: Princeton UP, 1976.

Poirier, Richard. *The Renewal of Literature: Emersonian Reflections*. New York: Random House, 1987.

Pound, Ezra. *Literary Essays of Ezra Pound*. Ed. T. S. Eliot. New York: New Directions, 1968.

————. *Personae*. New York: New Directions, 1971.

Prunty, Wyatt. *"Fallen from the Symboled World": Precedents for the New Formalism*. New York and Oxford: Oxford UP, 1990.

Ravo, Nick. "Poetic Injustice? A Grocer Sees Insults in an Ode." *New York Times*, 25 November 1988.

Rawson, Claude. "Bards, Boardrooms, and Blackboards." In *On Modern Poetry: Essays Presented to Donald Davie*, ed. Vereen Bell and Laurence Lerner, 181–91. Nashville: Vanderbilt UP, 1988.

Remnick, David. "An Interview with John Ashbery." *Nassau Lit* (Spring 1980): 54–64.

Rich, Adrienne. "The Eye of the Outsider: The Poetry of Elizabeth Bishop." *Boston Review* 8.3 (April 1983): 15–17.

Richman, Robert, ed. *The Direction of Poetry*. Boston: Houghton Mifflin, 1988.

————. "Our 'Most Important' Living Poet." *Commentary* 74.1 (July 1982): 62–68.

————. "Poetry and the Return to Seriousness." *New Criterion* (Summer 1985): 39–48.

Ross, Andrew. "The New Sentence and the Commodity Form: Recent American Writing." In *Marxism and the Interpretation of Culture*, ed. Cary Nelson and Lawrence Grossberg, 361–80. Bloomington: U of Indiana P, 1988.

Ryan, Michael. " 'Difficulty' and Contemporary Poetry." *AWP Newsletter* (November–December 1987): 1, 14–15.

Sáez, Richard. "James Merrill's Oedipal Fire." *Parnassus* 3.1 (Fall–Winter 1974): 159–84.

Schnackenberg, Gjertrud. *The Lamplit Answer*. New York: Farrar, Straus, Giroux, 1985.

Schwartz, Delmore. "The Isolation of Modern Poetry." In *Selected Essays*. Chicago: U of Chicago P, 1970. Essay originally published in 1941.

Shapiro, Alan. *Covenant*. Chicago and London: U of Chicago P, 1991.

————. "Horace and the Reformation of Creative Writing." *American Poetry Review* 21.2 (March–April 1992): 7–13.

————. "The New Formalism." *Critical Inquiry* 14.1 (Autumn 1987): 200–213.

Shetley, Vernon. "The Place of Poetry." *Yale Review* 75.3 (Spring 1986): 429–37.

Shoptaw, John. "Investigating the *Tennis Court Oath*." *Verse* 8.1 (Spring 1991): 61–72.

Silliman, Ron. "Canons and Institutions: New Hope for the Disappeared." In *The Politics of Poetic Form*, ed. Charles Bernstein, 149–74. New York: Roof Books, 1990.

————. *The New Sentence*. New York: Roof Books, 1987.

Simmel, Georg. *On Individuality and Social Forms*. Chicago: U of Chicago P, 1971.

Simpson, Louis. "The Character of the Poet." In *What Is a Poet?* ed. Hank Lazer, 13–29. Tuscaloosa and London: U of Alabama P, 1987.

Smith, Dave, and David Bottoms, eds. *The Morrow Anthology of Younger American Poets*. New York: Morrow, 1985.

Snodgrass, W. D. *In Radical Pursuit*. New York: Harper and Row, 1975.

Sommer, Piotr. "An Interview in Warsaw." In *Code of Signals*, ed. Michael Palmer, 294–314. Berkeley: North Atlantic, 1983.

Spiegelman, Willard. "Heirs and Heirlooms: The Legacy of Elizabeth Bishop and James Merrill." *Kenyon Review*, n.s., 13.2 (Spring 1991): 154–59.

Starbuck, George. " 'The Work!': A Conversation with Elizabeth Bishop." In *Elizabeth Bishop and Her Art*, ed. Lloyd Schwartz and Sybil P. Estess, 312–30. Ann Arbor: U of Michigan P, 1983.

Steele, Timothy. *Missing Measures: Modern Poetry and the Revolt Against Meter*. Fayetteville and London: U of Arkansas P, 1990.

Works Cited

Steiner, George. "On Difficulty." In *On Difficulty and Other Essays*, 18–47. New York and Oxford: Oxford UP, 1978.

Stevens, Wallace. *The Collected Poems*. New York: Knopf, 1954.

Stevenson, Anne. *Elizabeth Bishop*. New York: Twayne, 1966.

Tate, Allen. *On the Limits of Poetry*. New York: Swallow Press and William Morrow, 1948.

Tindall, W. Y. "Exiles: Rimbaud to Joyce." *American Scholar* 14.3 (Summer 1945): 351–55.

Tomlinson, Charles. "Elizabeth Bishop's New Book." *Shenandoah* 17.2 (Winter 1966): 88–91.

Tranter, John. "An Interview with John Ashbery." *Scripsi* 4.1 (July 1986): 92–102.

Travisano, Thomas. *Elizabeth Bishop: Her Artistic Development*. Charlottesville: UP of Virginia, 1988.

Trotter, David. *The Making of the Reader: Language and Subjectivity in Modern American, English and Irish Poetry*. New York: St. Martin's, 1984.

Turner, Frederick, and Ernst Pöppel. "The Neural Lyre: Poetic Meter, the Brain, and Time." In *Expansive Poetry: Essays on the New Narrative and the New Formalism*, ed. Frederick Feirstein, 209–54. Santa Cruz: Story Line P, 1989. Originally published in *Poetry* (August 1983).

Unterecker, John. "Elizabeth Bishop." In *American Writers: A Collection of Literary Biographies*, ed. Leonard Unger, Supplement 1, Part 1, 72–97. New York: Scribner's, 1978.

Vendler, Helen. "Domesticity, Domestication, and the Otherworldly." In *Part of Nature, Part of Us*, 97–110. Cambridge, Mass., and London: Harvard UP, 1981. Originally published in *World Literature Today* 51.1 (Winter 1977).

———. *The Music of What Happens: Poems, Poets, Critics*. Cambridge, Mass.: Harvard UP, 1988.

von Hallberg, Robert. *American Poetry and Culture, 1945–1980*. Cambridge, Mass.: Harvard UP, 1985.

Weiner, Hannah. Untitled contribution to "Forum." In *The Politics of Poetic Form: Poetry and Public Policy*, ed. Charles Bernstein, 226. New York: Roof Books, 1990.

Wilbur, Richard. *Things of This World*. New York: Harcourt, Brace, 1956.

Wilson, Edmund. "Is Verse a Dying Technique?" In *The Triple Thinkers*. New York: Oxford UP, 1948.

Wordsworth, William. *Poetical Works of William Wordsworth*. 5 vols. Ed. Ernest de Selincourt and Helen Darbishire. Oxford: Oxford UP, 1947.

———. Preface to *Lyrical Ballads*. In William Wordsworth and Samuel Taylor Coleridge, *Lyrical Ballads*, ed. R. L. Brett and A. R. Jones. London and New York: Methuen, 1968.

Wormser, Baron. *Good Trembling*. Boston: Houghton Mifflin, 1985.

Wright, George. *Shakespeare's Metrical Art*. Berkeley and London: U of California P, 1988.

Yeats, William Butler. *Plays and Controversies*. New York: Macmillan, 1924.

Yenser, Stephen. *The Consuming Myth: The Work of James Merrill*. Cambridge, Mass., and London: Harvard UP, 1987.

209

Vernon Shetley is Associate Professor of English at
Wellesley College.

Library of Congress Cataloging-in-Publication Data

Shetley, Vernon Lionel.

After the death of poetry : poet and audience in contemporary
America / Vernon Shetley.

Includes bibliographical references and index.

ISBN 0-8223-1325-1. — ISBN 0-8223-1342-1 (pbk.)

1. American poetry—20th century—History and criticism.

2. Authors and readers—United States—History—20th century.

3. Bishop, Elizabeth, 1911–1979—Appreciation—United States.

4. Merrill, James Ingram—Appreciation—United States.   5. Ashbery,
John—Appreciation—United States.   6. Reader-response criticism.

I. Title.

PS323.5.S53 1993

811'.5409—dc20   92-35603 CIP